THE SCARIFF MARTYRS

War, Murder and Memory in East Clare

GW00646491

The following letters underline powerfully, the profound tragedy and sadness at the heart of the Scariff Martyrs' story. The first letter was written by Alphie Rodgers when he was a fourteen-year-old boy in Mungret College, Limerick. The second was written just days after his murder in November 1920. Both illuminate the essentially human experience buried in the history.

Mungret College, Limerick – 23 January 1912

Dear Mother,

Hope you are well. I received your parcel the other morning. The cake was grand and also the nuts and sweets. I am getting on grand here now and am as 'fat' as a little puppy dog. We had high mass here on last Thursday. Every morning at mass, I do say the five rounds of the beads for yourself and pop and then another round for myself and the children and sometimes I offer up my communion for ye. I know you will be glad to hear that. I am very fond of praying since I came here and all the lads call me a saint but I don't pay any heed to them as I think I am doing good ... I am enclosing a letter in this envelope for Gertie. Don't forget to give it to her. Them were grand beads she sent me.

P.S. Don't forget to tell Antie [sic] that I sent my best love to her.
Love to all from Alphie x

St Louis' Convent, Kiltimagh, Mayo–19 November 1920

He is now D.V. [God Willing] enjoying peace after all his trials of the last few months. Another martyr, in the long list of those who have given their all in the cause of our country. We little thought, when we saw him in April, with his splendid life opening up before him, what a terrible tragedy was coming ... we were talking today of the wild Alphie of long ago, with the little black and red skull cap, who used to tear around on the bicycle and of the splendid boy who was up here only three years ago. He was such a good proud boy in spite of all his pranks and that time he produced his beads for us and told us he was Our Lady's Pet, as he was born on her feast day. No doubt she has been guarding him all the time and now she has him safe at last, where no worries can trouble him again.

Your loving cousin,
Baby McDermott*

---

* Rodgers Collection, Alphie Rodgers to Mrs Nora Rodgers, 22 February 1912; Baby McDermott to Mrs Norah Rodgers, 19 November 1920. 11 February is the Feast day of Our Lady of Lourdes in the Catholic calendar. Alphie was born on 11 February 1893. 'Gertie' referred to in Alphie's letter was his younger sister, who was ten at the time.

THE SCARIFF MARTYRS

War, Murder and Memory in East Clare

TOMÁS MAC CONMARA

MERCIER PRESS

Tomás Mac Conmara is an oral historian and author from Tuamgraney, County Clare. He was awarded a PhD at the University of Limerick in 2015, for his study into the memory of the Irish revolutionary period. He began recording older people in his townland of Ballymalone as a teenager and is now recognised as one of the leading oral historians in Ireland. He has written several books including *Days of Hunger, The Clare Volunteers and the Mountjoy Hunger Strike of 1917, The Ministry of Healing, Cork's Orthopaedic Hospital* and the best-selling, *The Time of the Tans.*

DEDICATION

To Dan McNamara (1932–2019), my father.

MERCIER PRESS

Cork

www.mercierpress.ie

© Tomás Mac Conmara, 2021

ISBN: 978 1 78117 725 9

A CIP record for this title is available from the British Library.

Printed and bound in the EU.

Contents

Acknowledgements

Before I knew the history of the Scariff Martyrs, I knew the feeling of it. It was there, embedded in the way people spoke. Writing in 2021, after many years immersed in the story, I feel I have drawn closer to an understanding of that experience. My own philosophy of history does not simply surround the accumulation of knowledge about the past, but the cultivation of understanding. To this end, I have listened. To make such a pilgrimage to the innermost districts of our past, one must attend to the role of place, people, and memory in our historical consciousness. With this, I believe, comes a greater knowing; one that can illuminate the hidden contours of our historical experience and enable us, in our time, to inhabit a much richer landscape. For all this, I owe gratitude to many – firstly, to Mary Feehan at Mercier Press. Special thanks to the Rodgers family, in particular Mike and the late Paddy Rodgers, for their support over many years. Also, to the relations of Martin Gildea, especially his niece Kathleen Mitchell and of Michael 'Brud' McMahon and Michael Egan, my thanks for allowing me into your family memory. To the interviewees who contributed memories and tradition, I owe heartfelt appreciation. A singular thanks to my friend, Cllr Pat Hayes as well as May Ryan, Shane Walsh, and the late Dermot Moran of the East Clare Memorial Committee. Thank you to Prof. Bernadette Whelan (UL), Comdt Daniel Ayiotis, Noelle Grothier and Cecile Gordon (Military Archives of Ireland), Helen Walsh and Peter Beirne (Clare Library), Dr Críostóir Mac Cárthaigh in UCD and Dr Cliona O'Carroll, UCC. To the wonderful historian Tom Toomey for his valued guidance and to fellow historians, Liz Gillis, Lar Joye, Colum Cronin, David Grant, Ernest McCall, Paul Minihan, Daniel McCarthy, Dr David Fleming, Meda Ryan, Prof. Eunan O'Halpin, Jackie McCarthy Elger, Dr Pádraig Óg Ó Ruairc, Dr Eve Morrison and John S. Kelly, my respect. My gratitude to historian Ger Browne for his incredible work and generosity with RIC records in Clare and to Kevin Welch in New Zealand for restoring photos. My friendship to Frances

Madigan, Jack McCormack, Moira Talty, Comdt Stephan Mac Eoin, Ciarán and Joanne Maynes, Danny Morrison, John Moroney, Colm Scullion, Tomás Madigan, Carol Gleeson, Gerry O'Grady, Peter and Brian Flannery, Clive Kelleher, Kieran Brennan, PJ Kelleher, Seán McNamara, Matt Kelly and Marian Malone, Harry Duggan, Noeleen Moran, Paula Carroll, Shane O'Doherty, Brendan McMahon, Kevin Cullinan, Laura O'Brien, Michael and Marian Conroy, Teasie McCormack, Gordon Daly, Helen and Christy Venner, Derek and Elaine Venner King, Siobhán Reddy, Joe Fitzgerald and Darren Higgins. To Michael O'Gorman, Frank Mason, Patricia Sheehan, Gerry and Brian Quinn, Sarah Geraghty, Fintan McMahon, John Fahey, Carol McNamara, Una Kierse, Margaret O'Meara, John Joe Conwell, Joe Duane and the late Maeve Hayes for support and access to collections. A special word of thanks to my great friend Jimmy Walsh from over the fields in Caherhurley and to Tommy Holland, Whitegate, who have both given me constant support for many years and have remained loyal to the Scariff Martyrs since first they heard their story against the open hearths of their homes.

Thank you to my mother Annamae McNamara, whose uncle sang about the Scariff Martyrs and to my sisters Myra and Bríd and my brother Dónal. To Dara for her insightful and wise counsel on the book's more subtle expressions and for being the reassuring dawn of every day. Finally, to Dallán Camilo and Seód Nell Áine; clamber again and again, into that whirlwind.

Tomás Mac Conmara – May 2021

'I Cried after Them'

Prologue

A gentle, almost subconscious nudge of the turf led to a clash of fire that burst an intense moment of warmth. Forty-three-year-old Bridget Minogue quietly watched the embers of her old open hearth as she had done a thousand times before, locked in the ancient conversation between mankind and fire. The scent of turf smoke that escaped the chimney's draw wafted gently around the farmhouse as it had done for decades. Tradition and continuity were at home. Bridget was taking a brief moment of rest from the long, duty filled day of a rural housewife and mother.

The winter of 1920 had taken a firm hold of the east Clare landscape and the Minogues of Poulagower in Scariff were ready for the long dark nights ahead. It was November and cold. Although early in the evening, the light had already given way to the dark. Just feet away, her daughter, Margaret, allowed the warmth of the turf-fuelled glow to reach her cheek, before shaking away her distraction and returning to her duties. As Bridget pushed her hands against her knees to make her body rise, her mind drifted to the many faces that were warmed by the flames in the past. She recalled the old men who came 'on cuaird' (visit). She remembered the men quietly sitting, deferential to a storyteller, a craftsman weaving his tale for attentive listeners. Such scenes were rare of late. A strange vulnerability had ripped the community of its comfort and left a tension weighing heavily on its people.

Bridget had just stood and was slowly moving from the hearth when she was jolted by a loud bang on the door of her home. Sixteen-year-old Margaret's eyes widened as she drew a sudden intake of breath. After casting a momentary glance at each other, Bridget moved cautiously towards the door. The lack of a second knock or shouts from outside was somewhat reassuring. Nevertheless, the latch was lifted with trepidation. The opening door revealed a young man who stood casting a countenance lost somewhere between panic and fear. Margaret stood closer to the open hearth, her eyes fixed on the young man she did not know. She saw her mother's hand move to her mouth as the man spoke. She could make out the words 'Killaloe', 'murdered' 'all dead'. Instinctively moving closer, she heard names she knew, 'Alphie Rodgers, 'Brud' McMahon and 'Gildea who worked in Sparlings.' Another name was mentioned but by then her mind had rejected all noise and was focused internally: 'Not Alphie,' she thought, 'Not Brud'.

In November 2008, I sat with a 105-year-old woman at a nursing home in Newmarket-on-Fergus, Co. Clare. While gently moving through her memories, I asked a question that had been impatiently waiting on my mind: 'Do you remember the time the four lads were killed on the Bridge of Killaloe?' I knew Margaret Hoey was a native of Scariff and hoped she had some sense of the event, perhaps even remembered it.

Almost immediately, Margaret's countenance changed to one of outward sadness, her old shoulders dropping as if some heaviness had taken hold of both her mind and limbs. Before responding, Margaret's eyes already betrayed some long-held distillation of understanding. She began to take me back to 17 November 1920, when she was sixteen-year-old Margaret Minogue and when the story of the four men's brutal death was revealed to the community. Margaret had left her native place over eighty years before I recorded her memories, yet it quickly became apparent that her native place had never left her.

There are occasions when a disclosure of memory can be so powerful, so wrought with emotion, that for a brief moment you find yourself transported on a journey of recollection. So it was in Carrigoran Nursing Home when Margaret Hoey, born five years and a century earlier in 1904, revealed to me a moment marked indelibly on her memory. For a time, I felt as if I was there standing near the open-hearth fire of her home when her mother opened the door to a frantic IRA Volunteer. Four young local men had been killed. Margaret knew three of them. Within the fold of her memory, I walked and then ran with Margaret as she quickened her pace up the avenue adjacent to her home. She had been dispatched there to warn other IRA Volunteers who were 'on the run' and sheltered in a local safe house. Back then in 1920, she had cried as she ran. As I listened eighty-eight years later, she cried as she spoke.

I stood beside her as she knocked shyly on the door. I was there when the man of the house shouted at her, frustrated at her failure to speak words through her tears. It was the anxiety of a man who wanted to know but feared the knowledge. I saw his face change as those devastating words broke through Margaret's quivering voice:

> I was of course, I was crying like a child. Anyone would be upset. 'Twas a terrible thing. To say they were brought out and shot on the bridge in Killaloe, between Tipperary and Clare, between Ballina and Killaloe. Oh, 'twas a terrible thing! I did, I cried after them … the lads were all joined the Volunteers. There was a safe house, along an avenue in from us. One Volunteer, I didn't know who he was, came to the house and he said to my mother, 'could anybody give a message?' in the way there was lads 'on the run' in a house in the avenue. 'Oh', she said, 'Margaret can do that easily' and I was dispatched off in the avenue. And shur naturally, I was crying for I knew 'em. And when I went into the house where there was a couple of [IRA] lads asleep. I was crying and the man in the house let a shout at me, 'what's wrong with you?' And ah, [begins to cry] I told 'em. 'Twas bad news.[1]

With this simple but profoundly emotional disclosure, I became intensely aware of how forcefully the memories of the four men, who later became known as the Scariff Martyrs, had been imprinted on local memory.

Margaret Hoey died just weeks after that interview. The

emotion of Margaret's disclosure is a clue to the impact of the incident on the local community and can only begin to indicate the deep trauma suffered by the families affected. The story of the Scariff Martyrs is one of both history and memory. Why such a brutal and traumatic event became an enduringly remembered landmark in local history, and how so much pride and reverence has been embedded in the historical consciousness for the four victims, helps illuminate the Irish historical experience and the role of memory. From its foundation, there was duality of experience. On one hand, there was martyrdom and the pride of a community connected to such a site and moment of memory; on the other hand, there was the deep and enduring pain caused to the families involved. The families of Alphie Rodgers, Michael 'Brud' McMahon, Martin Gildea and Michael Egan did not want martyrs. All of the families regretted hugely the incident and likely lamented their sons' involvement with the IRA. This does not equate to a rejection of the cause for which they fought, nor does it betray a lack of pride in the story. It simply points to the primarily human impact of the story on those affected.

For the Egans, the blow struck deeper, perhaps, as the incident saw their son pulled into a vortex of violence that he had no role in creating. The story presents a remarkable confluence of dimensions: the young rebels committed to a cause, their betrayal by a spy, the virtue of Egan, their torture, their evident refusal to betray their comrades, the loneliness of their end, the liminal nature of their site of death on a bridge, the withholding of their dead bodies and their collective burial. All these dimensions, when combined, bequeath a moment of memory, which carries an enduring quality that has reverberated across the generations and continues to strike a deep chord within the local landscape of memory in east Clare and beyond.

INTRODUCTION

Sometime between 11.30 p.m. and 12.30 a.m. on the night of 16 November 1920, on the bridge connecting Killaloe in south-east Clare to Ballina in north Tipperary, four young men were shot dead by British crown forces, having been arrested earlier that day in the north-east Clare parish of Whitegate.[1] Three of the men, Martin Gildea, Michael 'Brud' McMahon and Alphie Rodgers, had been active members of the Scariff Company in the 4th Battalion of the East Clare IRA.[2] The fourth, Michael Egan, was a civilian who was the caretaker of Williamstown House in Whitegate, where the other three had been sheltering while 'on the run'.[3] British authorities reported that the men had been shot while attempting to escape. That was immediately countered by local claims that the men had been murdered in cold blood.

In social memory, the victims are referred to interchangeably as 'The Scariff Martyrs', 'The Killaloe Martyrs' and 'The Four Who Fell', depending largely on where the reference is made. The story endures as a landmark on the historical landscape and consciousness of east Clare with multiple commemorations, sites of memory and songs. Because of the way the story unfolded, three areas of east Clare inherited an enduring relationship with the incident: Whitegate, where the men were captured; Killaloe, where they met their deaths, and Scariff, where three of the men worked and where they were collectively buried on Saturday, 20 November 1920.

Until the Glenwood ambush in January 1921, where six members of a Royal Irish Constabulary (RIC)/Black and Tan patrol were killed by the East Clare IRA, the incident in Killaloe had been the most significant event of the Irish War of Independence within the brigade area.[4] It represented the single biggest military blow to the Clare IRA during the entire war, with three of its active members killed at one time.

13

The incident took place during arguably one of the most crucial months of the entire War of Independence. The president of Dáil Éireann, Éamon de Valera was close to the end of an intensive tour of America, where he was attempting to secure recognition of the Irish republic. Three weeks earlier, on 26 October 1920, Lord Mayor of Cork Terence MacSwiney died after seventy-four days on hunger strike in Brixton prison in England.[5] Ten days after the Killaloe bridge incident, members of D Company of the Auxiliaries, highly trained ex-officers sent in to further bolster the RIC and Black and Tans, murdered republicans Harry and Pat Loughnane with astonishing brutality in Galway.[6] Two days later, seventeen Auxiliaries attached to their colleagues in C Company in Macroom, were killed in the Kilmichael ambush on 28 November, led by Tom Barry of the 3rd West Cork IRA Brigade.[7] That four-week period included the hanging of eighteen-year-old Kevin Barry, the elimination of the 'Cairo Gang', a British intelligence network by Michael Collins' 'squad' and Bloody Sunday.[8] In the same month a twenty-four-year-old-pregnant woman, Eileen Quinn, was shot through the stomach by British forces as she sat outside her home in Kiltartan, Co. Galway and died eight hours later, by which time a cover up had already begun.[9] In just seven days from 20 to 27 November 1920, British forces in Ireland killed at least thirty Irish men, women and children, including four under the age of fourteen.[10] In the same month, fifty-seven members of the British forces were killed by republicans, including British army, intelligence servicemen and members of the RIC.[11] With a whirlwind of violence sweeping the country, the story of the Scariff Martyrs began to fade from the national discourse and was perhaps from that moment the preserve of the local.

During the revolutionary period, the four young men, forever bound together in history, lived in the same area. Rodgers, McMahon and Gildea worked in the same small town, where they were employed in the principle stores in Scariff, two of whom (McMahon and Rodgers) were the sons of those business owners.[12] Michael Egan had lived in Tuamgraney for a period and was a frequent visitor to Scariff town where he worked as a part-time postman.

Egan was born in Rinskea in Co. Galway on 26 October 1897 (the townland became a part of Clare a year later) to farm labourer and herdsman, Daniel Egan and his wife, Mary.[13] At the time of his death, he had only recently turned twenty-three and was the youngest of the four men. He was the oldest son of the Egan family and was one of ten siblings, with only his sister Bridget being two years his senior. Decades after his death, his neighbour Mary Joe Holland cried when describing to her daughters how Egan was 'as innocent as the flowers of May and was a really lovely innocent young man and fierce gentle and nice, always smiling and always had a kind word'.[14] In the autumn of 1920 at a house dance held in Drewsborough, Tuamgraney, nineteen year old Mary Hill from the townland of Ballymalone, my grandmother, danced with Michael, telling her son many years later about the shy and gentle countenance of the young man she was one of the last to dance with before his death.[15] Even the press at the time characterised Michael as a 'most inoffensive young man'.[16] Egan was not a member of the IRA. He was tragically pulled into the story by his decision to allow Rodgers, McMahon and Gildea to stay in the house where he was caretaker and his attempts to divert crown forces when they came to Williamstown looking for the men.

Michael 'Brud' McMahon was born on 12 April 1893, to Thomas and Bridget McMahon. He was the second eldest of four sons born to the couple who ran a hardware and grocery business in the town of Scariff. Having attended Scariff National School, Michael was sent with his brothers to Cork City for secondary education. At the age of eighteen, he was living in Cork City, while attending school with his brother, Patrick. His older brother, Denis, was working at Robert Scott and Co. Ltd, a large Hardware Merchants on St Patrick's Quay.[17] The three brothers lodged with Margaret Carbery in Sheare's Street. Margaret previously lived in Scariff, where her husband, RIC Constable John Carbery was based and where he died of pleurisy in 1898.[18] Evidently, a relationship was maintained between the McMahons and the RIC man's widow, a union of gentler times. In the revolutionary period, Michael seems to have taken a leading role in the cultural revival and was recognised as 'a member of the Fáinne' (Irish-speaking) and 'one of the principle people involved in the attempt to revive the Irish language in east Clare'.[19] He was also well known in Carrigaholt and Ring Irish colleges and frequently contributed articles to the press, advocating the promotion of Irish.[20] Described as 'very sincere', 'Brud' was a senior figure in the Scariff IRA Company at the time of his death.

In 2012, 100-year-old Matthew Birmingham told me that Mollie Behan, owner of the Burton Arms Hotel in Carrigaholt, had fallen for McMahon while he was staying there while attending the local Irish College. According to Birmingham, Behan, who in 1916 had sheltered local leaders during the Easter rebellion, never married because she 'had a particular standard' and 'could not find anyone to match McMahon and so would not settle for anyone else in her life'.[21] A family rumour indicated that McMahon was also romantically linked to Lillie Corbett, who in 1920 was a twenty-four year old from Scariff who shared McMahon's interest in the Irish language. Lillie later moved to France where she joined the French Sisters of Charity.[22]

Martin Gildea has been reported as being aged interchangeably as twenty-four and twenty-seven.[23] In fact, Gildea was born on 16 May, 1890 at Ashbrook, Woodlawn, in the parish of New Inn, Co. Galway, making him thirty years old at the time of his death, the oldest of the four and at a senior age for an IRA Volunteer.[24] Martin was born to Michael Gildea and Nora Kelly, who both worked at the estate of James Ryan, owner of Ashbrook House. After both her father and Ryan disapproved of her intention to marry Michael, Nora secretly followed Gildea to America, where they married and began a family.[25] Having returned years later due to Nora's ill health, Michael resumed his employment as a coachman for Ryan and moved his family into a house on Ashbrook estate.[26] There, Martin was born soon after their return. Tragically, Nora Gildea passed away in April 1899 at the young age of thirty-eight from phthisis, a progressive wasting disease, worsened by giving birth three months earlier.[27] Her register of death shows that her daughter and Martin's baby sister, Honoria, died just eleven days earlier. Martin was then only eight years of age.[28] As young man, he worked in Fahys Grocery Store in Loughrea, before later moving to Kilcullen in Co. Kildare, where he was employed as a shop assistant for businessman, Laurence Darby.[29] In approximately 1916, he moved to Scariff, where he began working for Denham Sparling, a merchant in the town and soon after that he joined the Irish Volunteers. Gildea had a strong interest in Irish dancing and taught it locally, which according to one interviewee endeared him to many in the community.[30] Like McMahon and Rodgers, Martin Gildea too left a young love at the time of his death. Twenty-one-year-old Sarah 'Lil' Fogarty from Lakyle in Whitegate was reportedly so distressed at the funeral that she had to be carried out of the church.[31] Lil never forgot her first love, choosing to remain unmarried for the rest of her life.[32]

Alphie Rodgers was the youngest of the three IRA men who died on Killaloe Bridge and was only Egan's senior by eight months, having been born on 11 February 1897. Alphie was the first child born to Edward and Norah Rodgers. He was remembered as 'happy go lucky', 'full of fun' and 'a bit of a devil' by those who knew him.[33] His oldest sister later underlined Alphie's generous nature, remembering; 'we thought he would give away all we had!'[34] Having attended Scariff National School for most of his youth, Alphie's father decided to remove him when it was established that the assistant teacher 'believed too much in the use of the birch'.[35] The Irish Jesuit Archives in Dublin, show that on 1 September 1911, Alphie was admitted to Mungret College, a Jesuit boarding school in Limerick where he remained until the summer of 1914, when his school career was recorded as 'very satisfactory'.[36] In a remarkable and tragic coincidence, Alphie and two of his classmates at Mungret, Timothy Madigan and Christopher Lucey, were shot dead within a month of each other. Lucey was killed fighting in the Ballingeary Ambush on the same day that Alphie was buried in Scariff.[37] Madigan was shot a month later, on 28 December, after he was captured by the RIC and Black and Tans in Shanagolden, Co. Tipperary.[38] Amongst obituaries to the above, *The Mungret Annual* of 1921 reflected on Alphie as a 'natural leader' with a 'compelling personality'.[39] For a short time in Mungret, Alphie also had as his schoolmate a young Tom Barry from Cork, later to become one of Ireland's most famous IRA leaders. According to one interviewee, before his time 'on the run', Alphie had been in a relationship with a twenty-three-year-old Irish speaker from Sixmilebridge called Lizzie Clandillon.[40] Senior brigade staff, in the East Clare IRA, later recorded in relation to his IRA service that Alphie Rodgers 'served under arms' and 'was never absent from duty up to the date he was shot dead'.[41]

His brother Gerald was included in the nominal list as a Volunteer in the East Clare IRA and his sisters Gertie and Kathleen were members of the local Cumann na mBan.[42] At the time of her brother's death, Kathleen (Keesha) was in a convent in Belgium as part of her training to become a nun with the La Sainte Union.[43] She later wrote that while there she 'received the terrible news that my brother Alphie was had been shot by the Black and Tans' and lamented 'this was a very heavy cross for me and my family'.[44] It was not the custom for postulants to leave the convent and so Kathleen did not attend her brother's funeral.[45] In the weeks after his death, Kathleen, then Sr Agnes, was given special permission to change her religious name to Sr Alphonse Columba, in memory of her brother.[46] On 27 November 1920, she wrote to her family in Scariff, poignantly expressing both her own grief and theirs:

> What can I say to you? Words are useless – God alone and the Mother of Sorrows can talk to the hearts broken by an overwhelming and too timely grief. He will console you and waft across the waters my unutterable sympathy. Yes, and the dear white soul now in his heavenly home will send down roses on you … For I feel that the sacrifice he has so willingly made of his young and so beautiful life has secured for him the goal of all good Christians … O Mamma dear! You will miss your white-haired darling boy – your eldest born, your dearest and your best … I even pray to him that we may all die as gloriously as he. Let us look forward to the day when he will cross the Heavenly courts to wish us a real 'Céad mile failte' into the mansion of eternal bliss … they [fellow sisters] say I should be proud to have a martyr in Heaven.[47]

The three IRA men had been well known in the town of Scariff. Their former comrade Tommy Bolton, fondly remembered the men's jovial nature when he was asked to describe them in a taped recording, made in 1989:

> Oh indeed I do and I knew 'em well. I knew 'em as well as my right hand. I remember buying the first razor, open blade razor from 'Brud' McMahon and poor Gildea came in the same day and he said 'Bolton, buy another of them, 'tis the time of the war they won't be ever got again.' Ah you know takin the lift of me you know![48]

When, in 2008, I asked 105-year-old Margaret Hoey to recall the men, she easily created an image of them:

> I knew Brud McMahon as well as I knew my brothers. Oh, Alphie Rodgers was as fine a fella as you every laid an eye on. Oh, a tall fine

lookin young fella … He was six foot, a fine young man … dark haired. Oh he was fine fella! But Brud McMahon, he was known as Brud, Michael was his name … was a fine fella too … Martin Gildea was a nice type of lad too. Gildea was a Galway man. Of course he was one of the boys [IRA]. He was shop hand at Sparlings. I knew him to see from going into the shop … I didn't know Egan.[49]

The importance of the Scariff Martyrs incident as a historical landmark is manifest in its reference in at least twelve local publications relating to east Clare.[50] While no publication has to date, exclusively addressed the incident, both 'A Salute to the Heroes of East Clare', written by Mary Moroney and Graney's 'East Clare's Calvary' offer two significant contributions. The latter, published in 1953 in *Vegilla Regis*, an annual journal from Maynooth College, contains interviews conducted with contemporaries to the event, including John Conway, one of the two Conway brothers who were arrested at Williamstown with the four men.[51] Conway testified to the beating of the four men and offered some crucial information which will be discussed later.[52] Importantly, a pamphlet written shortly after the incident by Romer C. Grey, a retired British civil servant, living in Killaloe and published by the 'Peace with Ireland Council', offers an essential account. Grey condemned the combined British forces in his booklet *The Auxiliary Police* and accused the Auxiliaries in Killaloe of 'murder'.[53] In *Ireland Forever*, Brigadier General F. P. Crozier also made some serious allegations against the Auxiliary Division, including those stationed in Killaloe.[54]

There are two predominant contested accounts about the event: an official explanation and a vernacular folk memory. The official version is encoded in reports from Dublin Castle, which ultimately stem from a military Court of Inquiry, held two days after the killings. There, the claim that the men were shot while trying to escape was asserted.[55] The vernacular memory offers a radically different version, which suggests the men were tortured and murdered by the British forces.[56]

A determined and public effort to remember was obvious from the first anniversary of the incident in November 1921. In fact, the Scariff Martyrs, with three connected monuments, six compositions and a consistent commemorative history, is one of the most memorialised, commemorated and remembered events of the period in Clare and across the country. The inclusion of the best-known song about the Scariff Martyrs, on a 1970s album by Christy Moore, drew national attention to the story.[57]

As always, however, the assessment of any memory is only fruitful if silence is attended to as a revealing dimension. A revelation of what is known and unknown, spoken and unspoken, privately remembered and publicly commemorated, assists a deeper understanding. For over seventeen years, I have researched the event, compiling multiple first-hand individual accounts, as well as the comprehensive collection and analysis of oral history and tradition associated with the affair.

Ultimately, I explore in this book how these four men were drawn together to form one of the most enduring stories in Clare's War of Independence. For a story so interchangeably dependent on history and memory, it is important for the book to commence by exploring the way in which the incident has been memorialised over the last century and to illuminate how that memory has effected both knowledge and emotion of the broader story.

1

'WE SHOULD TAKE OFF OUR HATS'

Remembering the Scariff Martyrs

On 17 November 1921, a large crowd gradually emerged from St Flannan's Roman Catholic church in Killaloe. The congregation, led by the clergy, slowly descended the steep hill leading towards the bridge of Killaloe. There, in deferential unison, a rosary was recited in Irish. After a hush fell on the assembled crowd, one man walked forward and with white paint made the sign of a cross on the north parapet of the bridge.[1] Exactly a year earlier, Michael Daly, a twenty-four-year-old railway worker from Canal Bank, had crossed the bridge and noticed at that spot a sight that never left his memory:

> I was going to work at 8.45 a.m. I could see blood from Danny Crowe's gate as far as the point where the monument was later erected. There was brain matter with the blood. There was so much blood on the bridge that at first I thought a cow had been killed … I swept in all the blood with a sop of grass or hay to the side of the wall and I found a cap beside the wall with Brud McMahon's name on it.[2]

In September 1922, Daly established a committee to raise funds for the erection of a monument at the site.[3] Largely as a result of Daly's efforts, the monument was erected just three years after the killings, making it one of the earliest republican monuments in the country.[4] Costing £72, in November 1923 the ornate monument made by Matt Nihil, a republican stone cutter from Hill Road outside Killaloe town, was integrated into the ashlar limestone on the north parapet of bridge.[5] As a small child, the late Jack Quigley from Killaloe was at the unveiling. At the age of ninety-two he told me:

> I can remember being there with my mother when they were

putting that monument on the bridge, 'Twas a big big do ... I was very young anyway. We couldn't get near it anyway. There was trains and all you know and a very big crowd and bands.[6]

Twelve months later, the county's newspaper commented that the new monument had become a 'centre of attraction' in the town and recorded that 'almost unceasingly visitors could be seen rapt in devout prayer' at the site.[7] Michael Daly emigrated to New York in August 1923 before its installation.[8] Having returned in the 1930s, he took responsibility to ensure that a commemorative wreath adorned the site each year.[9]

By 1938, the monument was clearly an established feature of remembrance and nineteen pupils from Tuamgraney National School recorded its presence and function as part of their contributions to the Irish Folklore Commission's School's Folklore Scheme. If the pupils in Tuamgraney needed any encouragement to write about the Scariff Martyrs, they would get it from their principal, Waterford native and Irish language revivalist, Pádraig Ó Cadhla. Ó Cadhla, who was appointed principal in Tuamgraney in 1919, had befriended Michael 'Brud' McMahon due to their shared interest in the Irish language. When his first child Brigid was born, he chose McMahon as her godfather. It was love of the Irish language that nurtured another friendship, which resulted in the choice of the godfather for his second daughter, Maura: Conor Clune. Sadly, both McMahon and Clune were murdered within days of each other in November 1920.[10]

In 1938, pupils wrote of the common practice and social expectation that when passing the monument on Killaloe Bridge, 'we should take off our hats and say a few prayers for those poor innocent boys'.[11] Thirteen-year-old Brigid MacMahon was assured that; 'in hundreds of years when we are dead and gone some child who will be passing will ask the story of that stone'.[12] Brigid was the niece of Michael

'Brud' McMahon. Twelve-year-old James G. Minogue also contributed to the scheme and similarly determined that 'children in hundreds of years' time will be inquiring about that stone'.[13] Minogue, who became a Roman Catholic priest, passed away in 2018. Seventy-six years after making the above determination, he told me in a recording in Limerick that the memory of the Scariff Martyrs had lost none of its potency.[14]

Whatever the exact occurrence on the bridge of Killaloe on that November night in 1920, from the moment news broke, the bridge took on a great significance for the people of Killaloe and of east Clare generally. A bridge with a practical and social function has since the night of the tragedy performed a third critical role: that of a landmark of memory, what the French historian, Pierre Norra, called a *Lieux de Memoire*.

Censoring Memory

While frequent commemorations were held at the bridge of Killaloe, evidence of a shift away from state involvement in republican commemorations emerged in a Dáil Éireann debate on 4 February 1942. Daniel McMenamin, a Fine Gael TD, asked Minister Frank Aiken 'if the Censor stopped the publication of a paragraph stating that a ceremony attended by members of the Local Defence force had been held about the 17th November last in memory of four men who had been shot on the bridge of Killaloe in 1920'.[15] The minister replied in the affirmative but did not elaborate on the reason. While official records indicate that permission had not been granted for participation, it is probable that the censorship related to the government's move against the IRA.[16] Over 1,000 IRA Volunteers were then interned in the Curragh Camp (known to republicans as Tintown), arrested under the Emergency Powers Act, which allowed for internment and executions.[17]

Despite the attempted censorship of the Killaloe commemoration in 1941, the *Clare Champion* carried a report on 22 November on a commemoration held on the bridge of Killaloe the previous week. The paper reveals that the commemoration, held to mark the twentieth anniversary of the Scariff Martyrs deaths, involved members of the Killaloe and Ballina Local Defence forces.[18]

The commemorations continued, regardless of censorship. On Easter Sunday 1949, a former IRA commandant of the East Clare Brigade stood on the bridge of Killaloe as he knew there was only one place to mark the occasion. Joe Clancy, a former British soldier and IRA commandant from Kilkishen was then living in Killaloe and although the large crowd around knew Clancy, their instinct was to move back as he fired three shots into the air. Clancy had just delivered an oration at the site of the monument on Killaloe bridge. Clancy had known the men and spoke to them in the days before their capture and deaths. On that day, the Irish Republic was declared.[19]

On the bridge that day was John Fahy, who recounted his memories to me in 2019:

> In 1949, the same year that the Republic of Ireland was declared, I was on the bridge when Joe Clancy held a commemoration to the four men. I remember him well pulling out a gun and we all scattered. He fired three shots into the air in memory of the Martyrs.[20]

From the early 1970s, following the death of Mike Daly, another Killaloe native continued the tradition of laying a wreath at the monument on Killaloe Bridge. Maeve Hayes accepted this responsibility from Nellie Grimes who like Mike Daly before her had laid the wreath for many years. Maeve told me how she was once approached by Nellie in the 1960s and asked to 'put a few flowers on the bridge on the 16th of November'. That request led to a fifty-year commitment that Maeve annually honoured, even arranging for a nail to be added to the monument in the 1980s to elevate the wreath from the ground, thereby ensuring it was more prominent and remained at the site for longer.[21]

'A Suitable Memorial' – Scariff Monument

In Scariff, where the men were buried, the emotional connection to the killing has remained very strong. On the first anniversary of the incident in Scariff in 1921, 'a great demonstration' was held attended by approximately 5,000 people, including 1,600 Volunteers.[22] Among the priests in attendance at Scariff was Fr Murray who acted as a chanter. Six weeks before their deaths, Rodgers, McMahon and Gildea had taken shelter with Fr Murray on their return from an IRA action in O'Brien's Bridge. Ironically, Fr John Greed, who while the men sheltered with Fr Murray, was on his way to attend to the men they had shot, was also in the choir at the service. At the conclusion of the mass, IRA members in attendance moved in unison and structure to the year-old gravesite. There, under the command of Michael Brennan, a volley was fired over the graves. There followed an address by Brennan, then O/C of the East Clare IRA Brigade.

The Black and Tans were gone by this point and yet Ireland's troubles were not over. The following year, the second anniversary was also marked when requiem mass was celebrated at Scariff church in November 1922. The divisions that had been emerging in 1921 were more pronounced twelve months later, as East Clare members of the Irish Free State Army led the congregation.[23]

In early 1945, the East Clare Memorial Committee was formed with the primary objective 'of erecting a suitable memorial' at the gravesite.[24] A meeting was held at 14 Parnell Square in Dublin in early March of that year and appeals for funds were made at a national and local level through the press.[25] Later that year, a monument was erected over the graves of the four men in Scariff.[26] Before its erection, four independent white crosses, carrying the names of the men, had marked the grave. There in Scariff in November 1945 was Martin Gildea's fourteen-year-old niece, Kathleen, who had travelled with her father from New Inn in Galway:

> My father brought myself and my sister to Scariff in 1945 for the twenty-fifth anniversary. I remember there was a big crowd there and we saw the grave … I don't think it meant as much as it does now. I was too young then. There were shots somewhere because I was frightened. I thought it was the Tans! I had been hearing it so long about the Tans![27]

On the monument erected in 1945, Rodgers, McMahon and Gildea are inscribed with the rank of captain, while Egan, who although not an IRA Volunteer, is described as a lieutenant.

In December of that year, the *Clare Champion* published the names and contributions of 827 people, including ten listed anonymously as 'friends', predominantly from within Co. Clare, who donated between two shillings and £5 towards the construction of the monument.[28] Amongst the subscribers were An Taoiseach, Éamon de Valera and Col George O'Callaghan Westropp, whose father had been at the centre of evicting tenants during the infamous Bodyke Evictions of 1887.[29]

Commemoration continued and in November 1947 the Scariff Memorial Committee held a fundraising dance, which was 'very well patronised'.[30] Four years later, in March 1951, the Tuamgraney Village committee declared their intention to honour the contribution made by men and women of east Clare.[31] The memorial, which features a Calvary scene, was given significant financial support from New York and was finally dedicated on 20 July 1952 and attended by a crowd of over 2,000 people.[32] Two years later, the park was formerly dedicated as the 'Republican Memorial Park'.[33]

In November 1970, it was revealed that a fiftieth anniversary commemoration would be held in Scariff where the four martyrs were to 'be honoured with all the dignity and pomp they deserve'.[34] The Tulla Pipe band, followed by surviving members of the East Clare IRA Brigade and Cumann na mBan, led the parade. A ceremony was held in Killaloe also.[35] Twenty-five years later, a large event was held to mark the seventy-fifth anniversary in Scariff chapel.[36]

From the 1970s onwards, the withdrawal of the state from overt commemorative displays, resulted in a reduction of commemorations in north East Clare. However, republican groupings, including Sinn Féin, continued to hold commemorations at the Killaloe site during the period of 'the Troubles'.[37] In 1972, following the murder by the British Army of thirteen civilians in Derry on Bloody Sunday, hundreds marched to the memorial on the bridge of Killaloe in solidarity with the victims.[38]

In 1983, the East Clare Memorial Committee was reformed. A member of that committee recalled how the group were frustrated in their efforts by the local Catholic parish priest who labelled them 'subversives'.[39] Since the 1980s, that committee has continued to annually commemorate the men, inviting people connected with the story to lay a wreath in their honour at the grave in Scariff each year, including from 2008 to 2012, when Paddy Gleeson and John Michael Tobin, the last two people then alive to have attended their funeral, laid wreaths. Of the over-100 identified commemorative sites associated with the war in Clare, monuments concerning the Scariff Martyrs have generated the most consistent commemorative activity in the county.[40] Despite the Covid-19 restrictions imposed in 2020, the centenary was marked by the East Clare Memorial Committee, in both Scariff and Killaloe, where latterly a ceremony was held exactly 100 years to the moment of their deaths on Killaloe bridge.[41]

'Rang from Shore to Shore' – Song and Story

The story of the Scariff Martyrs was not told alone within the embrace of the east Clare landscape but often travelled to distant parts of the world where people of that area voyaged. In the early hours of 28 January 1993 in the Lord Newry Public House in North Fitzroy, Melbourne Australia, the last singer of the night cleared his throat. He had sat respectfully as thirty previous compositions had been offered by musicians from all across Ireland who were then living in Australia.

Joe Fitzgerald from Corigano in east Clare was encouraged to add a thirty-first and final composition. The east Clare man did not have to think long for his selection and drew the lonesome lament of the Scariff Martyrs all the way from the mountains of east Clare to the shores of Australia. Helen O'Shea, later an Honorary Research Fellow at the University of Melbourne was present that night and was taken with the emotion in Fitzgerald's rendition, describing it as 'impassioned and dignified'.[42] As a teenager in the 1950s, Joe Fitzgerald had sung the song within his own community shortly before he and his entire family emigrated to Australia in the early 1960s, leaving their mountainside home to fade with time.[43] In October 2018, an open-hearth fire warmed that home once more, as Joe Fitzgerald spoke to me in the house he had restored, about his connection to the song:

> When I heard the song first, it was from a man called Joe Joe Guerin down in Baba McCormacks [Tuamgraney]. The song is about four famous men and four great men who fought for our freedom and died for our freedom and they gave us the freedom to roam these mountains, the mountains of Corigano and Caherhurley at our will, without anyone telling us what to do in our own land … When I heard the song, I thought, these men gave us freedom and why not sing about them … I love singing that song and I sang it in Australia and I sang it in England! Maybe there'd be a few that wouldn't like to hear it but I don't care about that so much. I'd sing it anyway![44]

'The Scariff Martyrs' was made nationally popular when it was sung by Irish singer/songwriter Christy Moore in the 1970s.[45] Moore first heard the ballad in Murphy's pub in Tulla in 1964 and also spoke to Teddy Murphy's mother, who had attended the funeral in 1920.[46] John Minogue, from Kealderra in Scariff, recalled being taught the song in Cooleen Bridge National School early in the 1930s by Bridget Cuneen, who was the sister of Margaret Hoey, mentioned earlier.[47] At the same time as Minogue was learning the song in an east Clare school, Rody O'Gorman, a twelve-year-old pupil from Derryoober, Woodford in Co. Galway, wrote the full song as his contribution to the 1938 School's Folklore Scheme.[48] The ballad was known well in that area and was sung later by both Harry Nevills and Michael Joe Tarpey.[49] Musician Cyril O'Donoghue included a musical version of the song in his 2003 album *Nothing but a Child* and described the way in which exposure to the song as a young boy led him to adopt it in his music much later:

> With regards to the song, I first heard it as a child sung by my father [Paddy O'Donoghue] in a pub in Broadford late one night and he told me the story of the killings and later heard it sung by another man in Bodyke who my father got it from. It always stuck in my mind.[50]

Several contributors recall hearing the song at social occasions, such as during 'the Cuaird', a nightly social visiting practice in rural Clare.[51] Anna Mae McNamara took me in the 1950s to the mountains above Tuamgraney:

> I remember as a child hearing my uncle Thomas Hill sing the Scariff Martyr's song in Ballyvannon at a house dance. That would have been the mid-1950s and I can still recall the respect people gave my uncle when he was singing the song. The 'Scariff Martyrs' seemed to mean the most to the people there.[52]

However, J.P. Guinnane and Paddy Clancy from Kilkishen

revealed that the song was not immune to opposition. J.P. explained how, on one occasion, a man called Mikey Quinn was singing the song in a public house in Oatfield when a former Black and Tan, who had stayed in the area, interjected and stopped him.[53]

Still, as explained by the daughter of one of the East Clare IRA's most active members, Martin 'The Neighbour' McNamara, if one wanted to find out about the Scariff Martyrs 'you'd get it all in the song'.[54] Tom Lynch, a native of O'Callaghan's Mills also recalled 'a Hussey girl from Bodyke' deliver the song in Lucas' pub in Whitegate and remembered how 'you could hear a pin drop'.[55]

While the song is well known and has since been covered by established artists, its origin is unclear.[56] The local contention is that Jamsie Fitzgibbon, a native of Ballyhurly in Ogonnelloe was the composer.[57] However, in a collection of papers, belonging the Rodgers family, the origin of the composition is contested. An original hand-written version of the song was sent to Mrs Rodgers on 8 March 1922. An associated letter claims that 'D.P. O'Farrell', who described himself as 'The Ogonnelloe Poet', was the songwriter. He also disclosed that he wrote the song on Christmas Eve 1920, less than two months after the incident, lamenting that 'a copy of some sort' had already been circulated locally. He explained that his reason for writing was that he wished for the family to have 'a correct version' of the song, before declaring that 'they never fail here or beyond who fall in a great cause'.[58]

The song has performed a critical role in terms of both knowledge and sentiment. The infusion of a deep lament into the lyrics and tone of the song resulted in a repeated invocation of sadness across the decades, summed up in its characterisation by McLaughlin's as 'a bitter lament that tugs hard at the emotions'.[59]

A number of later songs were also composed to commemorate the men and the incident. For example, Jack Noonan, a well-known poet from Killaloe, composed 'The Four Who Fell', which is written from the Killaloe context and was popularised by The Shannon Folk Four.[60] Interestingly, in an indication of the influence of songs on social memory, research finds that where interviewees from the north-east Clare area surrounding Scariff, refer to the men as 'the Scariff Martyrs', in Killaloe, they are referred to predominantly as 'The Four Who Fell'.[61] When Lena McGrath returned from Sheffield for her annual holiday, she would recite a poem she learned in the late 1920s in her native Gurtaderra, outside Scariff. Lena would deliver one particular verse with an appreciably greater intensity, referring to 'Alfred Rodgers' with 'a soul so pure and grand' proudly proclaiming each time that Alphie was her godfather.[62]

A confluence of song, monument, commemoration and story has generated a powerful memory which elevated the men to hero status within the local community. Other methods too were employed to preserve their story. Memorial cards have been an important method of preserving the memory of fallen republicans. In August 1921, the family sent a photograph of Alphie Rodgers to J. Stanley Photography Studio in Westmoreland Street in Dublin, where 200 mortuary cards were produced at a cost of £2.[63] When his nephew Fr Manus Rodgers was a teenager in St Flannan's College, he noticed a fellow pupil from Portroe in Tipperary with one of those cards in his prayer book.[64]

The admiration in local social memory for the Scariff Martyrs was potently reflected in interviews I carried out over from 2000 to 2020. Tom Lynch, born in 1929 recalled 'they'd talk with reverence and they'd nearly pray for them'.[65] For Michael O'Gorman 'There was great reverence like. If they could have canonised them they'd have done it'.[66]

Two emotions predominate in stories about the Scariff

Martyrs: pride and sadness. For those closest, the latter was overpowering. From the lowered head and perpetually sad countenance of Norah Rodgers to Mary Joe Holland's tears whenever their names were evoked, a tremendous heaviness about how their young lives ended was palpable. When asked to characterise Alphie Rodgers and Michael 'Brud' McMahon, who she remembered from her childhood, Kathleen Nash broke down in tears, only managing to say 'they were lovely, they were lovely'.[67]

Referring to the effect of hearing the story of the Scariff Martyrs, the late Seán Crowe told me against the same open hearth fire where he had heard the story first:

> The shivers would run down my back when I'd hear of what was done to 'em. I was young and I was almost living through it when I'd hear about it. I heard they were captured, or they were taken. They were put into the boat and they were beaten and that they were thrown out of the boat and pulled in again. They were taken down to Killaloe and they were pulled out of the boat, brought up to the bridge. Their eyes were gouged out. They were bayoneted. And the cries of the ah [pause] of the suffering and the shouting of them that was mutilating 'em, that the people were awake in their beds and terrified in Killaloe and Ballina. They were left riddled and they were unrecognisable. And ah [becomes emotional], I can't tell you any more about 'em.[68]

Flan O'Brien from Ballymalone also evoked the violent nature of their treatment and deaths:

> The craters they were wore out from going and they were asleep and didn't they come in on them from the Shannon in the boat, do you see. They were spied on do you see in the house … They didn't get a chance to fight do you see. Them four men, if they saw 'em comin' they'd shoot 'em, they'd shoot a few of 'em anyway … To think of it like, takin 'em out of their bed there, the craters and take 'em down on a boat and tie 'em up with chords. Sure Jazus there could be eight or nine of 'em in that gang [Auxiliaries], there was only our of them [Scariff Martyrs] in it but they caught 'em asleep, they could do nothing. Shot 'em off that bridge, the same

as you'd shoot four crows. I mean wouldn't it sicken you like when you'd think of it! … Jazus when you think of it Tomás do you know. What they done.[69]

The brutality of their deaths was a theme that echoed across the generations, in some cases overstated. When, in 1938, Josie Moloney from Clonlara National School was told the story, it was relayed how 'their eyes were pulled from their sockets and their nails twisted. This torture was carried out for two hours before they were finally shot. They were unrecognised by their parents'.[70] Others heard the men were dragged behind police lorries, with their heads banging off the ground, while others still heard the men were bayoneted both before and after death.[71] In the west Clare parish of Cranny, the story was discussed when old men came 'on cuaird'. Morgie O'Connell told the folklore collector Patricia Sheehan how the story was described in that parish:

> They got a very bad death and they were heard pleading for their lives across the river … roaring for mercy like you know … They were very active Volunteers … They found 'em there in a big aul house … They did torture them, made 'em suffer before they died … a lot of the killing that the British army did was 'shot trying to escape' but how could they escape? They were delighted when they got 'em and they'd make an example out of them … I heard it in my own house on the cuaird like you know … 'twas a bad day for Scariff and Killaloe.[72]

To explain the pathos that surrounds the story, it is necessary to now reach deep into the recesses of the men's collective and community history. The force of their story was not built alone on the events surrounding their deaths, but on deeper tensions, feelings and emotions.

2

'FOR GENERATIONS THERE HAD BEEN A DEMAND'

Background in East Clare

To better understand the story of the Scariff Martyrs, far more than an assessment of the War of Independence or revolutionary period, is required. To establish how three young men (Rodgers, McMahon and Gildea), found themselves committed to a violent and dangerous confrontation with British rule, we must reach into their history. To penetrate the sadness that surrounds their story and their position within the historical consciousness of east Clare, we must engage with the historical context, deeply embedded in the heritage of their place.

As young men, they did not have a War of Independence to reflect on. They did not have repeated tales of rampaging Black and Tans to stir feelings of ancient enmity. Stories of British injustice were many, however. Such feelings of injustice rested on a historical understanding broader than those which are defined simply as political, agrarian or economic. In local folk memory, past injustices are often conflated and rooted in the most obvious and sometimes justifiable basic foundation. In tales told around open hearth fires in the east Clare of Rodgers and McMahon and Martin Gildea's east Galway, there was only one root cause: British rule.

Famine, land war and evictions, all formed a backdrop to repeated lore.[1] For McMahon, Rodgers and Gildea, who were all born between 1890 and 1897, those stories were connected with events in the very recent experience of their community.

'Unswerving Fidelity'

A discernible Fenian tradition existed in the north-east Clare area with many families, connecting back to the 1860s through former activists of that generation. On Easter Monday 1916, Jimmy Slattery from Derrynaheila between Feakle and Bodyke was in Jacob's Biscuit factory in Dublin, declaring rebellion against British rule in Ireland.[2] In anticipation of the insurrection, Slattery must have reflected on his uncle, Michael, who in 1866 was arrested in Feakle for his role in what was called the 'Fenian conspiracy'. He may have even visited his uncle's gravesite in Feakle, where a large monument was erected 'by the Nationalists of the County of Clare as a tribute to his unswerving fidelity to the cause of the country'.[3] Two years after the failed rising of 1867, a large Fenian rally was held in Scariff to celebrate the victory of Jeremiah O'Donovan Rossa in the Tipperary by-election. A reported 500 people marched 'up and down the town' before lighting a torch outside the parish priest's house, where he was called out to defend his attempts to prohibit the demonstration.[4]

In both Tuamgraney and Scariff, Fenian led parades were also held on St Patrick's Day 1874, where busy Irish Constabulary, now with the 'Royal' prefix, noted the singing of 'disloyal songs' and the wearing of 'seditious emblems'.[5] Such occasions underlined an increasing political consciousness at a grass roots level, as well as a growing inclination to confront the political system.

In 1881, ten Scariff men were identified by British authorities as members of the Irish Republican Brotherhood.[6] In that year, in the nearby village of Bodyke, tensions had boiled over in a dispute between Col John O'Callaghan and his tenants. During a confrontation on 1 June, the RIC, who had been escorting process servers to execute writs on the tenants, charged those assembled under the order of the county inspector. During the violence, an RIC constable struck fifty-year old John Molony from the townland of Caherhurley with his rifle butt twice in the head and Molony died twelve hours later.[7] One correspondent from the *Cork*

Examiner, characterised the episode as 'warfare of the guerrilla kind'.[8] A monument over his grave declares it was 'Erected as a tribute of respect to the memory of John Molony of Caherhurley who was killed at Bodyke by the Constabulary whilst defending the homes of his countrymen against the rapacity of landlord avarice in 1881'.[9]

Thirty-six years later, a young Volunteer in John Molony's native townland was handed a dummy gun and shown how to drill. It was then 1917 and the effects of the Easter Rising were being felt in east Clare. Tommy Bolton and his fellow Volunteers in the Caherhurley Company were watched closely by a returned emigrant, who smiled inwardly. That man was the son of John Molony. The Volunteer showing Tommy how to drill was John Dillon, Molony's grandson, characterised later as 'the principal IRA man in Caherhurley'.[10] The Battle of Bodyke remained imprinted on their minds and their activity in 1917 was inextricably bound up in the memory of their family and parish's history. Tommy Bolton remembered vividly:

> I did drill. A dummy gun. Ya and I drilled in Dillon's house. There was an uncle of his [John Molony's son Denis] home from England and he was delighted to see us at it! We did it inside in the kitchen, slow forms and form polls [*sic*] and that kind of thing and we used to drill up in a backward field.[11]

When asked to reflect on how the local episodes in the 1880s related to his generation of activists, Tommy confirmed the potency of that connection:

> Ah there was of course, terrible talk. A neighbour of mine got killed in it. John Molony. His grand-son was [John] Dillon. He was a great IRA man! Oh he'd shoot the English soldier! ... Dillon would rise up in a fury over the grandfather being killed over in Bodyke at Minogue's corner ... he took it up seriously against the army of the English![12]

While Dillon and his men trained with dummy guns in Caherhurley, a solider in the Australian Imperial Force visited the area to see his cousins, the Garveys, while on furlough from the First World War. Thirty-seven-year-old republican Denis Garvey later convinced Michael Keane to return to his base in France without his government issue pistol.[13] Like Dillon, Garvey's political commitment was forged decades before. When he was thirteen, Denis and his brothers, armed with 'shovels, candlesticks, and other improvised weapons', fought off bailiffs at their home in Ballydonaghane. The incident was characterised by O'Donovan Rossa, as part of 'the best news he had received in America for a long time'.[14] In 1917 and over the years that followed, O'Donovan Rossa had become a symbol and the Australian pistol was put to frequent use by Garvey, then first lieutenant of the Caherhurley IRA Company.[15]

When John Molony was killed during the 'Battle of Bodyke', his neighbour Patrick Purcell, was arrested after he struck a police horse with a stick.[16] Purcell's nephew Charlie Turner was often told by his own mother Margaret, Purcell's sister, of injustice in 1881.[17] Charlie went on to become a leading figure in the Mountshannon IRA, within the same Battalion as John Dillon and Denis Garvey. Six years after John Molony's death, tensions had reached their apex between O'Callaghan and his tenants, leading to one of the most celebrated episodes of the Land War in Ireland. The events of June 1887 in the village of Bodyke echoed across the country and to parts of Britain and even France and carried across the generations.[18] As a result of the Bodyke Evictions, the east Clare populace of the early 1920s only had to reach back less than thirty years to a highpoint of tension between local people and British rule. The evictions were relevant to all local rural people and bequeathed a very open and diffuse community memory.

That an explicitly British force executed the evictions was clear. The evicting party included the acting sheriff, a large contingent of RIC, fourteen 'emergency men' and a company of the 2nd Royal Welsh Fusiliers. There followed a period of two weeks when the tenants of Bodyke resolutely opposed the forces of the crown acting at the behest of John O'Callaghan, perceived inextricably to be part of the British establishment. The Bodyke Evictions lasted for the first two weeks of June and in the end twenty-eight family were evicted. All had been part of the Plan of Campaign, an approach supported by the Land League which saw tenants offer a rent they deemed fair to the landlord and if refused, was pooled as a resource to address the consequences of protest. By providing strong and sometimes violent resistance, the tenants in Bodyke enabled press attention to focus on the evictions and on the seeming intransigence of landlordism. After the evictions, twenty-six tenants (including twenty-two females) were brought to court, some of whom were imprisoned for three months' hard labour. The stand at Bodyke became a *cause celebre* for the local people and a touchstone for British injustice, with many later republicans tracing their activism to the episode.

On the first Tuesday of the evictions, after crowbar men broke the wall of Francis McNamara's home in Lisbareen, 'emergency men' led by RIC head constable, George Dowler, rushed inside. They immediately began to beat Annie and Bridget McNamara, young sisters who had repelled the eviction with boiling gruel. Their older brother Francis was 'bludgeoned' before he was 'dragged out manacled, with his face bleeding'.[19] Inside also was Johanna Kennedy, the McNamara's cousin, who was struck with batons. In truth, Johanna's stand was against both present and past injustices. Described by the English journalist Henry Norman as an 'extremely plucky creature', she declared to those assembled that; 'my father and mother were evicted by [Col John] O'Callaghan's father thirty-five years ago ... and their house burned over their heads and now today, praise God, I've given a bit back for it.'[20] Johanna, Francis and his sisters were imprisoned. Seven years later, on Christmas eve 1894, Francis welcomed his first son Patrick, and would go on to welcome six more. All seven would later play a role in the independence struggle.[21] Over 133 years after the Bodyke Evictions, two heirlooms are retained within the McNamara family. The first, a gold pocket watch is inscribed to 'Francis McNamara for Defending the Homesteads of Bodyke, 1887'. The second, is an IRA Service Medal presented to his son, many decades later for his role in the struggle for independence.[22] The medals are kept together. Tuohys, Baltons, Husseys, Moloneys, Hamiltons and Hogans are among other families evicted, whose descendants were active republicans. The father of Mattie and Dinny McGrath, two Feakle Volunteers, was also arrested and jailed during the evictions.[23]

For Clonlara man Seán Clancy, later an IRA Volunteer and Free State officer, stories of the Bodyke Evictions were constant during his childhood. Clancy was born in 1901, just fourteen years after the famous episode and was raised less than fourteen miles from Bodyke, a distance travelled daily by his father in 1887, in solidarity with those confronting landlordism.[24] Eighteen miles was travelled on foot by the hurlers of Crusheen who abandoned a match with Kilnamona and instead marched with their brass band to Bodyke to support the besieged tenants.[25] Among those besieged were Michael Hussey and his family, who were finally evicted from their homes after a valiant battle. Their resistance included the use of a hive of bees as a weapon, a story that made its way through the decades to John Minogue in Scariff. Minogue's father had watched the Husseys defend their home from an outer ring of supporters. In 2011, some 124 years after that eviction, John Minogue recounted the episode, affirming that his father had often underlined how 'they put up a great fight at Husseys in Bodyke'.[26] 101-year-old Kathleen Nash, from the same parish as John Minogue, also spoke of her father's attendance at the evictions. Martin Minogue, a native of Derrymore in Scariff, was amongst the cheering crowds in Bodyke:

> Oh God he did. He was at it ... Ah shur they were all put out of the houses. They went over to help 'em and I think some of 'em threw hot gruel out the window on top of them, out the window ... My father was there looking at that.[27]

The narrative of a heroic resistance in Bodyke was part of the oral tradition inevitably inherited by Michael McMahon and Alphie Rodgers as they reached school age in the early 1900s. It is almost certain that they were made aware of the stand made by the Hussey family.

Time of course moved on and they became history themselves, spoken about in later generations. In the 1950s, quietness descended on a public house in Whitegate, when a young woman was called on to sing a song. She sang about the Scariff Martyrs, about Rodgers, McMahon, Gildea and Egan.[28] The woman's surname was Hussey. It was her grandparents that defended their home in Bodyke in 1887. Her singing illuminates the often circular and unbroken nature of local history and memory.

A Rising Generation

In the decades after the Land War and particularly in advance of the Easter Rising of 1916, the country had undergone a time of political mobilisation. It is true that the Irish Volunteer force, first mobilised under the banner of the Irish Parliamentary Party and Home Rule, saw significant recruitment. However, following John Redmond's Woodenbridge call to arms in support of the British War effort in September 1914, the seeming unanimity was broken as the Volunteer force split in two. Despite this, a hard-core element, who had long yearned for a fully independent Ireland, abandoned Home Rule for the unnecessary compromise they had feared it was and renewed their commitment to separatism.

In 1915, the Redmondite Volunteers (then called the National Volunteers) continued to assemble, with a large gathering hosted by Edward MacLysaght at his manor in Tuamgraney. MacLysaght had been county organiser and remained hopeful that unity could be returned. Within a year, the National Volunteers were moribund and the emerging separatist Irish Volunteers began to see a gradual increase in support and membership.[29] It is to the latter formation that McMahon, Rodgers and Gildea eventually aligned themselves.

The Easter Rising came as a shock to many people in east Clare, as it did across the country. Only in Feakle, O'Callaghan's Mills, Garranboy and Meelick, did mobilisations take place.[30] Quietly, there were others who welcomed the rebellion, but such declarations had to wait for more comfortable times to express them. Paddy McDonnell, a former Bodyke hurler from Kielta, situated between Bodyke and Tuamgraney, remembered his remote contribution to the rebellion:

> In 1916 the British put up proclamations that the Rising was suppressed, but we tore them down again in Bodyke and we cut the telegraph poles from Scariff to Killaloe while the Rising was on, and in Tuamgraney.[31]

While 1916 undoubtedly had an impact on the consciousness of young men like McMahon, Rodgers and Gildea, it was in the year 1917 that the call to mobilise truly fell on receptive ears. It was in that year that the young men took their first steps into revolution. In 1917, February saw the first opportunity for the National Movement, emerging from the fog of the

Easter Rising, to put its message to the test. Count George Noble Plunkett stood on a platform in North Roscommon, which clearly connected him to the separatist sentiment at the heart of the Easter Rising. The results were significant, with Plunkett claiming 3,022 of the 5,403 votes cast.[32]

In May, signs were unmistakable of a growing militarisation in east Clare when Michael and John Brady from Tuamgraney became the first men charged for drilling in Ireland. The press recorded 'The First Case in the United Kingdom' under the Defence of the Realms Act. The Bradys were among twenty young men who marched towards the local handball alley (which Volunteers had used for training) to the sound of an accordion player.[33]

Close to where the Bradys were arrested stands the O'Grady Castle, built in the early sixteenth century. The castle was bedecked in the same month with the Irish flag, at that time banned by the British government, leading to RIC constables having to scale the thick walls to remove it.[34]

There is no question that the most significant mobilising influence across 1917, and that which had a dramatic effect on McMahon, Rodgers and Gildea, was the by-election in July of that year in Clare. Occasioned by the death of the sitting MP Willie Redmond, the nomination of Éamon de Valera as the candidate to represent the Sinn Féin position, triggered a period of rarely seen activism and energy across east Clare.

When the then largely unknown political contender made his way to north-east Clare for the first time, he delivered a speech in Scariff. Among the large crowd, inevitably, stood McMahon, Rodgers and Gildea, now in their early twenties. All republicans from the broader area were also present:

> The presence in the constituency of most of the men who took a prominent part in the Rising and the victory of the Sinn Féin candidate in the election made a big impression on the young men in our district and when a new Company of Irish Volunteers was

started in Scariff in July or August 1917, upwards of fifty or sixty men joined up.[35]

An increasingly irritated police force sought to quell the rising republican sentiment. For singing 'the soldier's song' (later *Amhrán na bhFiann*) in his native Whitegate, Percy Lucas was arrested and taken to Duggan's Hotel in Scariff. There Capt. Rigby, commander of the local military unit, reprimanded the young teacher, who had also organised a large dance in Rineskea House to raise republican funds.[36] In an election of unprecedented significance, there were many outbreaks of violence across east Clare. So too there was energy, with many republicans commenting later on how the campaign drew hundreds into the fold of the republican movement, owing to the momentum and enthusiasm throughout. When news finally broke from the count in Ennis that de Valera and, more importantly, Sinn Féin had won by a margin of almost 3,000 votes, supporters were ecstatic, observers stunned and opponents troubled.[37]

Following the election of De Valera, William Scanlan and others established a Sinn Féin Cumann in Scariff. This was part of a broader proliferation of Sinn Féin clubs across the county that eventually led to an excess of sixty clubs in Clare. Following his death on hunger strike in 25 September, many clubs, including Scariff, Tuamgraney and Feakle named their cumann after Tomás Ashe.[38]

The death of Ashe, as a result of force feeding while on hunger strike in Mountjoy Prison, was felt keenly in Co. Clare, with sixteen of the hunger strikers from the county. Three days before Ashe's death, Scariff-born Martin Blake was killed in Menin Ridge where he was fighting with the British Army. In an indication of the changed focus of the community, his death did not seem register in the locality.

In the months that followed, many imprisoned Clare

republicans began hunger strikes and were released under the Cat and Mouse Act, in an open challenge to British authority. This included Scariff's Tommy Walle, who in November was a twenty-eight-year-old labourer and IRA Volunteer, released from Dundalk prison after he engaged in a hunger strike. Walle was welcomed back to Tuamgraney and Scariff where bonfires illuminated his way home.[39]

In the same month as Walle's celebrated return, Scariff and Tuamgraney Conradh na Gaeilge branches united to more effectively promote the Irish language. While the political and cultural came together in greater intensity during the revolutionary period, the promotion of the Irish language had already been significantly developed through the work of Edward MacLysaght, who had established a Nua Gaeltacht at his Raheen estate. Families from Gaeltacht communities like An Roinn in Waterford were invited to come and live in the area, in return for contributing to the development of the language. There Edward MacLysaght gave them homes, employment and electricity – in the latter instance, four decades before rural electrification.[40]

During this time of heightened activism, Rodgers and McMahon are recorded as having participated strongly in the promotion of Irish, while Gildea was noted for his encouragement of Irish dancing in the town of Scariff.[41] At the end of 1917, republicans in east Clare and across the country faced towards the next year on the Gregorian calendar with an unprecedented confidence. What would be next for the people of east Clare was uncertain. However, in places like Scariff, Tuamgraney, Broadford and O'Callaghan's Mills, the old issue of land and the perceived injustices represented by landlordism – manifest in the Bodyke Evictions decades before – were once again the topic of more-than-hushed con-versation.

'Ceased to Recognise the Law' – 1918

Against the silence of rural Clare in January 1918, the sounds of the countryside could be heard from a distance. A young boy walking between Bodyke and Tuamgraney was first jolted from his serene thoughts by the unmistakable sound of approaching cattle. Above the sound of cattle, he could hear animated tones of excited voices. The image then appeared before young Paddy Gleeson of at least thirty men driving over forty cattle. He stopped on the road before instinctively moving to one side.

In front of the striking spectacle, two men walked confidently forward, firmly holding straps which enfolded the head of the large bullock that calmly walked between them. As they drew nearer, Paddy could make out a white placard, which seemed to hang from the foremost bovine. As they passed, the men gave a friendly wave of their sticks to the young boy, who had just read the clear writing on the placard. In black paint the sign declared: 'The land for the people and the road for the bullock!'

A month later, young Paddy Gleeson sat beside his aunt in the gallery of Ennis courthouse, from where he could sense the excitement. The energy had been building ever since the assembled supporters had taken their seats in the gallery. More stood as they waited for the prisoners to appear. His eyes darted towards the peculiarly dressed judge, who seemed to Paddy Gleeson like a weakened principal, having lost control of the class. His eyes then moved quickly to the floor and he moved imperceptibly closer to his aunt beside him, when he heard the judge loudly declare, 'Boys under 14 should not be in the court!' He kept his eyes on the floor until he realised that the judge's attention was instead drawn to someone close by who wore the unmistakable peak cap of a young boy. A second order directed the 'boy' to remove his hat in the court.

Paddy watched as a police constable approached and then declared in an uneasy tone that it was no boy. The offender was a girl. Paddy's head lifted in confidence now as all around him shouted and jeered in unison at the judge's mistake. The court was about to convene and Paddy could already feel that the power lay on his side of the bench. It was Friday 15 February 1918 and a month of sensation in east Clare was about to culminate.

A group of prisoners from the east Clare parishes of Bodyke and O'Callaghan's Mills, predominantly farmers, were brought into the court to thunderous applause. The prisoners in the court had been arrested on the morning of Tuesday 5 February, in a swoop by the RIC, resulting in the incarceration of twenty-three men who had participated in the driving of cattle from landlord estates in the weeks previously.[42]

Among those arrested was my grandfather, Batty Mc-Namara, a thirty-five-year-old native of Claremount in O'Callaghan's Mills. Also arrested were well-known Clare hurlers John Shalloo, Ned Grace and Tom McGrath. Most men refused to give bail and were remanded to Limerick jail. The following day, it was reported that the prisoners had engaged in a hunger strike.[43] Nine days after their arrest, the men were placed on board the outbound train from Limerick and began their journey towards Ennis. In east Clare, ponies and traps, horses and bicycles, conveyed scores of people, mainly from the parishes of O'Callaghan's Mills and Bodyke, from where the majority of the prisoners came. In 2004, at his home in Kealderra, after I offered a gentle prompt towards the story of the famous court case in 1918, centenarian Paddy Gleeson sat forward:

Oh Jazus, how well you have it! How have you that story? ... Oh, Jazus will you stop. Mother of God, will I ever forget the day they broke out of the court. I was above in the gallery alongside 'em ... My aunt decided to go to the trial and we had a horse and trap

> … all Bodyke was in it and all the Mills was in it. When we went into the court after the prisoners been taken in, we went up in the gallery. The court had a clerk, you see … the bench was there up high and outside was a platform and he said 'the case is going to start'.[44]

The local press reported from the court the 'sensational scenes' they had witnessed.[45] Sitting in the gallery, the young Paddy Gleeson also witnessed the levels to which the century's long grip of British rule in Ireland was weakening:

> Out of that the cheerin' started. 'Clear the court,' says McElroy … Kelly was writing down all the evidence. Dan Minogue jumped up and said, 'we'll clear too,' says Dan. Out of that the peelers inside went to hold 'em and stop 'em … The place was full inside. Mick Brennan was in the front gallery, out in the front. He was in the front over at the door going out to the main hall. 'Twas the first time that I ever saw the main Volunteer's uniform and the hat turned up here. He slipped out and he said, 'case dismissed'. And the ones abroad fell for it! They all walked out. They broke out of the court![46]

That most of the men were later rearrested did not matter. A public and undeniable strike against the legitimacy and power of British justice had been landed. The men in Ennis court were there to answer for actions a month earlier. By mid-January, the farmers of east Clare, supported by local republicans, decided to take the war to the land.[47] On 17 January, coordinated actions saw cattle driven off the estates of Mrs Morris and Mr Frost at Sixmilebridge, as well as John Warren in Kilkishen, and in neighbouring Broadford at Doon, Kiladerry and Violet Hill.[48] In Broadford, a party of police attempted to intervene with a baton charge and were beaten by the cattle drivers with sticks.[49]

The men also marched towards Derrymore in O'Callaghan's Mills. There, James O'Regan, a contractor for the British war department, ran a saw mill, where timber was being cut to be used as trench reinforcement for the British army, then still in the midst of the First World War. The men ordered the workers at the sawmill to cease operations, and were obeyed.

The large crowd of mostly young farmers and Volunteers then moved towards the estate of Dr Francis Cornelius Sampson at Kilgorey in the parish of O'Callaghan's Mills. Forty-three head of cattle were driven off Sampson's land, from where they were walked all the way to the landlord's place of residence in the townland of Moynoe between Scariff and Mountshannon, almost ten miles away.[50] It had been during this cattle drive that young Paddy Gleeson was rooted to the ground by the spectacle he saw before him. When the cattle drivers reached Scariff, three policemen were overwhelmed by the cattle drivers and their weapons were taken.[51] Before long the same group became involved in a confrontation with police at Moynoe, where a hut had been posted to protect the landlord Sampson.[52]

On 9 February 1918, Paddy Brennan, then brigadier of the Clare Volunteers, informed his forces that the laws of the movement did not permit cattle driving.[53] Nevertheless, cattle driving continued, as did republican support. On Sunday 24 February, a major cattle drive occurred between Manus outside Clarecastle and Newmarket-on-Fergus, in which John Ryan from Crossagh was shot by police in the neck and died a number of days later.[54] Two days later, Clare was designated by an official British proclamation as the first Special Military Area in the country.[55] This led to an increased military presence and the effective cutting off of Clare from the rest of Ireland. Indicating the levels of disorder in east Clare, the following week, Brigadier-General Charles Burnett issued specific proclamations for Scariff, Bodyke and Tuamgraney, that closed licensed premises, banned assemblies and imposed a curfew, specific to one and a half miles from their respective post offices.[56] Fairs were also prohibited. Restricting the economic life of a mainly rural people deepened frustrations, with one journalist asserting from London that, 'news of the suppression of Scariff Fair shows the storm of disaffection blowing over the land'.[57] Several people were imprisoned for breaking the order, including Bodyke's Dominick Stewart, as well as Michael Hogan, Michael Brady and Joe Noonan from Tuamgraney, who all refused to recognise the court.[58]

Having observed the rapid growth of the republican movement the previous year, in January 1918 the inspector general of the RIC Joseph Byrne observed: 'Its activity is now being turned towards the land, and in this move they are heartily supported by all farmers' sons and most of the farmers'.[59] A month later, Byrne made the following admission:

> I beg to report the condition of the county at the present time is very bad. Lawlessness is rampant, cattle drives, illegal ploughing, raids for arms, and what in my opinion is significant of the utter demoralisation and contempt of the law, highway robbery have occurred with frequency.[60]

The increasing tensions on the ground was matched at the highest political levels. In early February, Tuamgraney's Edward MacLysaght resigned disillusioned from the Irish Convention, an assembly which sat in Dublin from the previous July, ostensibly to engineer a constitutional resolution for Ireland's future. The high profile resignation prompted an angry response from Bishop Michael Fogarty who equated the British proposition of a 'sham Home Rule', as akin to 'an Irish farmer in the past who could not get his daughter married without permission of his landlord'.[61]

At the same time, Volunteers in Bodyke and Whitegate were drilled and told that 'their duty would be to fight for Ireland when the time comes' and that 'rifles would be put in their hands and it was their duty to learn how to use them'.[62] It was a time when anger and energy drew from whatever well was closest. For some it was land. For others it was politics. For both, the obvious obstacle was British rule. The intersection of land and politics was explained by one IRA Volunteer, Joe Noonan, who was part of the famous cattle drive to Sampsons of Moynoe:

> For generations there had been a demand in the district for the division of a number of big ranches, owned by members of the Ascendancy class who detested everything that the Volunteers stood for. It was only natural that the Volunteers were only too anxious to back up the popular agitation and, with the approval of their own Brigade Officers, took the leading part in it.[63]

Noonan was a central player in later attacks on Moynoe. For his generation, stories told around open hearth fires formed the foundation of their understanding of Irish history. Stories where locals confronted an unjust system, were likely narrated with sufficient ferocity to endure many decades later.

Almost a century before Noonan and others marched to Moynoe House, serious confrontations had taken place in 1820 when Ribbonmen attacked landlord estates in both Moynoe and Tuamgraney. The landlords in question then were John Sampson, the grandfather of Dr Francis Sampson, and John Read, who owned estates in Mountshannon and Galway. A letter, included in the chief secretary's office papers written in 1820 records that at Glebe House in Tuamgraney and Moynoe House, there were reported 'incursions and plunder of the Ribbonmen'.[64]

Joe Noonan's comment that the ascendancy class 'detested everything that the Volunteers stood for' underlines the bridge between the rural and landlord classes. The characterisation of the rebels as 'deluded wretches' in a letter written in 1820 helps to typify the division between opposing forces at the time and perhaps across the generations.[65]

In Martin Gildea's east Galway, the year 1820 also had significance, with a local leader of the Whiteboy movement,

Anthony Daly, hanged on the Hill of Seefinn for attempted murder, a story often told in his locality.[66] In February 1914, a large grazing farm at Abbeygormican, close to Martin's home place, had its stock driven off by a group of cattle drivers, leading to the eventual arrest of twenty-five local men who were returned for trial.[67] Therefore, a century on from 1820, as local rebels marched towards Moynoe House outside Scariff town, it is entirely possible that they did so with the folktales of their grandfathers at the surface of their consciousness.

The RIC Inspector General's Report for the month of March 1918 reveals that in that month, a bomb was thrown into the yard of Mrs Moroney in Scariff, where Capt. Rigby, commander of the local military unit was staying, but no damage resulted.[68]

An increasing militarisation was paralleled by a deepening sense of cultural awareness. During the same month, a lecture was held in Scariff Town Hall, presented by Canon William O'Kennedy, who in the previous year had risen to prominence nationally within the Sinn Féin movement. The press reported that a very large crowd were in attendance to hear the president of St Flannan's College discuss Irish history. It underlined the effect that the lecture had on the crowd and how O'Kennedy managed to 'show us how to regard Irish history' and remarked how the lecture 'stirred our curiosity and woke in us a sense of self inquiry'.[69] Given the significance of the lecture, it is highly likely that young Volunteers including Rodgers, McMahon and Gildea were in attendance. For example, Capt. Tommy Walle, a senior member of their Scariff IRA Company, was recorded as having been in the audience and sang for the occasion with such intensity that he 'almost brought down the roof with applause'.[70] Within weeks, Walle was in prison, where he would spend three months for 'unlawful assembly' at Moynoe earlier that year.[71]

In April 1918, the Scariff Board of Guardians strongly

appealed against the continuing imposition of severe restrictions in the area, imposed under a military order. The Conscription Crisis, which took effect during that month, compounded the previous alienation and tension between many in east Clare and the forces of the crown. It is true that many young men from east Clare had enlisted in the British and other allied armies. For example, at the end of that month, Scariff-born Michael L. Tuohy was killed in action while fighting with the Irish Guards in France.[72] Nevertheless, the Irish people rejected the suggestion of conscription outright. By May, the president of Sinn Féin and the Irish Volunteers, Éamon de Valera was presenting on the same platform as John Dillon, leader of the IPP, when it came to decrying the possibility of enforced conscription.[73] The 'German Plot' later that month, which saw senior Sinn Féin figures arrested for an alleged conspiracy to support a German military expedition to Ireland, only added to the feelings of resentment and anger amongst republicans.

In early July, locals in east Clare were told the news that Sinn Féin, Cumann na mBan, the Irish Volunteers and even the Gaelic League were proscribed. The disruption to GAA competitions came at a bad time for Scariff, who had ascended to the top of Clare hurling, winning the county championship in 1917.[74]

Conditions seem to have somewhat settled in the county by July, leading to the lifting of some military restrictions.[75] The rest of 1918 saw a rapidly increasing confidence within the republican movement, crystallised in a decisive victory for Sinn Féin in the December general election of that year. A dramatically emboldened movement embraced the year 1919. The Irish people, including those of east Clare, had spoken. The response to that voice, and its consequences, was be grave and transformed the community experience for all in the years that followed.

3

'SUFFER, ENDURE AND FIGHT'

The Experience of War in East Clare

When the War of Independence began in early 1919, it led to a dramatic shift in the daily experience of the Irish people. The war had national and international significance. Nevertheless, for the people of east Clare and elsewhere, it happened primarily at a local level. Its impact was felt most powerfully, was understood most intimately and endured most profoundly at that local level. Before examining the way in which the war evolved from 1919 in east Clare, it is worthwhile exploring the varying perspectives on the independence struggle, in order to better appreciate the environment in which the story of the Scariff Martyrs incident took place. A better understanding of that experience for local men, women and children, of all backgrounds, passive or active, will enable a greater understanding of the incident on Killaloe Bridge and its significance in local history.

Michael Brennan, the former leader of the East Clare IRA Brigade, once reflected on the period after he was presented with a ceremonial sword by his fellow Irish army officers. He recalled with great intimacy the winter in which the Killaloe incident occurred:

> Through the mist of years, I see you again in the East Clare Flying Column. I see you facing bitter winter nights in 1920, cold, wet, shelterless, hungry, hunted. I see your loyalty to one another, your trust in one and another and the love of the people for you. You had to learn how to suffer, endure and fight. You never flinched. You went through the fire and emerged as tempered steel.[1]

Later, MacLysaght evoked images of 'hardy men of the mobile column … sixteen hours constantly on the move, surrounded on all sides by hostile troops without food and no less than forty miles covered in the time'.[2] Narrative accounts of rebel encounters with enemy forces are critical to any account of a guerrilla war. However, a war fought around the mountains of east Clare and elsewhere created an inevitable vortex of activity that pulled the broader community into the experience. Active supporters, passive observers and virulent opponents therefore deserve to be considered. MacLysaght's framing of the struggle as consisting of 'a small well directed and fearless body of IRA, operating with the co-operation of the whole civilian population' is partially true.[3] The suggestion that the 'whole civilian population' co-operated, however, deservers more consideration.

In 1920, sixty-year-old Robert Francis Hibbert, a Justice of the Peace from England and a staunch unionist, had a somewhat different perspective on the experience than Brennan or MacLysaght. Hibbert, who lived at Woodpark House, Mountshannon, bemoaned what he characterised as the total breakdown of law and order in the area, particularly following the departure from Scariff barracks of the RIC in September of that year, at which he stated 'as there are no police and no petty sessions, there is no redress'.[4] Hibbert reported several raids on his own house by armed and masked men, with shots exchanged on a number of occasions. During one raid, a lady's maid was wounded, and one raider, reportedly shot by Hibbert. He also suggested that because of intimidation, 'respectable people' were afraid to report it to the authorities.[5] Significantly, he claimed that 'each night gangs of armed men assemble in different houses, and walk the countryside terrorising the respectable inhabitants'.[6]

Hibbert was also a retired officer of the British Army with an extensive estate and domestic staff including a butler, lady's maid, upper and under house maids, kitchen maids and a personal footman. When he married Florence Reade in 1887, he inherited Woodpark House and its associated 3,000 acres in Mountshannon. It is fair to say that Robert Frances Hibbert represented a man who had profited considerably from the British system of governance and so, with the threat of radical transformation to that system, he had much to lose. Hibbert was, however, supported by the inspector general of the RIC, T. J. Smith, who claimed in relation to east Clare in late 1920, that 'terrorism was rife' and that there was 'no such thing as independence of opinion'. He also suggested that the 'IRA were active and a very large part of the youth of the county were in it through sympathy or fear'.[7] At a superficial level, the statement strengthens Hibbert's claims and also implies coercion at the heart of IRA membership. However, it is important to note that there is of course a tremendous contextual distance between 'sympathy' and 'fear'.

Patrick Buckland examined the activity around Scariff as part of his study into Irish Unionism. However, instead of drawing on Hibbert's claims and underlining them with greater evidence, he seems instead to employ Hibbert's experience to represent the broader reality.[8] That republicans sought to intimidate those who supported in any way the British side of the conflict is without question. That this activity constituted the type of roaming bands of menacing terrorists, as characterised by Hibbert and later by commentators like Buckland, however, is subjective and more difficult to substantiate.

Allegations of coercion like the above challenged the assertion of Michael Brennan that £1,500 was collected among the people of east Clare during this time, as a demonstration of support for the republican movement. The Meelick man did concede that as a result of their activism, 'the IRA had brought misery and terror on nearly every parish in east Clare' but insisted that even the IRA were surprised at the levels of support they got in the area.[9]

Thomas Francis Molony, who during the War of Independence was Lord Chief Justice of Ireland, presided at the Clare Spring Assizes in March 1921. Molony spoke despairingly at the broader state of Co. Clare and in a bitterly hostile assessment of its population, asserted they had 'allowed themselves to be cowed, intimidated and downtrodden by a comparatively small number of reckless and wicked men'. Rather insightfully, he accepted however that the Clare people 'dislike the crime but they dislike more assisting the police'.[10] Molony lamented that back in December 1919 he had appealed to the Clare public to 'put an end to the state of things'. He accepted a year later that it had been conveyed to him in 'unmistakable language that the people did not want my opinion and would not act on my advice'.[11]

In Washington DC, PJ Guilfoil testified to an American Commission in December 1920 about his experience in east Clare from May to October of that year. Guilfoil, who was born in Scariff in 1880, was a US citizen since 1906 and had returned to his native country during its most volatile period. He spoke about the shootings in Killaloe, revealing he was a relation of Alphie Rodgers. Guilfoil strongly rejected the suggestion that locals resented republicans for 'stirring up the British', instead relaying his sense that in east Clare the people felt they 'had a right to rise' and that 'the whole countryside was with them [IRA]'.[12] While there is no question, the period was challenging for all concerned, for much of the local population any feelings of frustration towards the republican movement, intimated by Hibbert and others, were mitigated by increasing feelings of animosity towards the British authorities and forces, based on everyday experiences:

> First of all, they were afraid of the Black and Tans, to start with. Second of all, the Black and Tans taught the people how to hate. It was their behaviour that made people take a gun up in their hand. That is what hardened anti-British attitudes.[13]

In east Clare during the War of Independence there were divisions of opinion. There were those who supported the British crown, both actively and passively, and there were those who offered similar support to the movement challenging that system of rule. In addition, there were those who just wanted to keep their head down and get on with life. However, for the IRA to function and execute a relatively long campaign of resistance against the British forces, widespread and committed support was required. That support, manifest in a multitude of different ways, was real and it was extensive. The voices of opposition, like Hibbert, while often sounding from positions of influence, were in the minority. Nevertheless, they were to be found and were remembered within the local community. At the age of 105, Margaret Hoey spoke to me about local people in Scariff who may have favoured British rule and who may have been in opposition to the freedom struggle. After becoming decidedly agitated and leaning forward in her seat in Carrigoran Nursing Home, she angrily declared:

> Oh, everyone wasn't in favour! They wanted England all the time in the place. Indeed, we owe England nothing! I'd like to see 'em trampled on! They were no bargain for Ireland![14]

1919 – War Begins

At a national level, January 1919 saw the dual origins of military and parliamentary declarations of independence, with shots fired in Soloheadbeg, Co. Tipperary paralleling political calls made in Dublin where Dáil Éireann sat for the first time.[15]

On Tuesday 20 January 1919, the day before the ambush at Soloheadbeg, at a meeting of the Scariff Board of Guardians, a resolution demanding the 'release of all political prisoners, imprisoned by the Military Government of England' was passed.[16] With the behaviour of the RIC becoming an increasing focus of resentment among the local community, the resolution further criticised 'British Tyranny' and Const. Michael Harrington of the Killaloe RIC in particular, for a recent raid 'just to show his authority'.[17] Within Harrington's station, the RIC were becoming intolerant of anyone remotely associated with the national movement. On 16 January, Const. Patrick Rice handed in his resignation. He had served for over thirty-six years with the RIC and was just ten weeks away from qualifying for a pension of £164, when he was left with no option but to leave the force. The reason for Rice's enforced retirement was that two weeks earlier, his young daughters, Mary and Nora, sang at a New Year's Eve concert organised by the local nuns and deemed by police to be a 'Sinn Féin Concert'.[18]

From the outset, it was apparent that the IRA adopted guerrilla war tactics against the superior military machine of the British forces. This was reflected in the training, structure and deployment of the Volunteers committed to the movement. In Clare, the existing IRA Brigade was reorganised into three brigades in Mid, West and East Clare, with attendant battalions and companies now reporting to a brigade staff. The East Clare IRA Brigade, led initially by Paddy Brennan, consisted of six battalions. No. 1 comprised the district around Newmarket-on-Fergus, from Clonmoney to Quin, while No. 2 stretched from Cratloe to Clonlara southwards to the River Shannon. The 3rd Battalion covered the area of Broadford to Ogonnelloe, with the townland of Caherhurley north-eastwards to Whitegate, including Scariff, assigned as the 4th Battalion. No. 5 represented Tulla, Kilkishen, Bodyke and Glendree, while the Fenian-rich area from Feakle northwards to the Galway border was under the command of the 6th Battalion.[19]

For the majority of the period from the formation of the

East Clare Brigade, to the end of the War of Independence, Michael Brennan acted as O/C, after his brother Paddy fell out with IRA Headquarters in Dublin.[20] As with other parts of the country, the IRA gradually took on more disciplined and militarily recognisable structures. While it was not possible for the movement to maintain the type of centralised discipline typical of a conventional army, the adherence to structures and discipline was noteworthy, in context. The development of a structure in early 1919 was helped when Joe Clancy, a returned British solider, joined the IRA and began instructing young republicans.[21]

In April, Dublin-born republican, Robert Byrne died in Meelick from wounds received when police shot him during a rescue attempt from Limerick Workhouse Hospital.[22] In late May, Seán Treacy, Dan Breen, Seamus Robinson and Seán Hogan – participants in the Soloheadbeg ambush – spent time in east Clare. The presence of such wanted rebels resulted in a necessary reduction in activity to give the seasoned republicans a chance to recover from wounds received during the rescue of Hogan at Knocklong earlier that month.[23]

Some activity did continue, however, with periodic actions planned in the area. In early summer 1919, republicans from the Mountshannon Company travelled to Woodford in Co. Galway, to disarm an RIC patrol which had regular movements in the area. Tom McNamara, Cathal Turner, Patrick McInerney, Paddy Muggivan, Eddie Killeen and Michael Cleary were among the participants.[24] In the end only one RIC man was found and his weapon taken from him, the broader contingent of police failing to show up.[25]

For a movement determined to confront British rule, the most obvious manifestation of that rule were the armed and uniformed members of the RIC. For decades, the Irish landscape had been studded with local RIC barracks, which made unnoticed travel through any part of the countryside almost impossible. Dublin IRA Volunteer Martin Walton once claimed that it was impossible to go 'a distance of about seven miles, without going into three RIC outposts'.[26]

Throughout 1919, the RIC began to abandon smaller barracks in remote areas as a result of increasing attacks from local IRA units.[27] In April, Cork's Michael Fitzgerald had led an attack on Araglen RIC barracks where the garrison were overpowered.[28] On 20 July at Inch, outside Ennis, an RIC hut was attacked with bombs, revolver and rifle fire for over three quarters of an hour.[29]

Two weeks later in the village of Broadford, at 1.45 a.m., republicans quietly moved into position on the grounds of the local Catholic church, under the command of Eddie Larkin, O/C of the IRA's 3rd Battalion.[30] According to one participant, the intention was to 'harass the enemy' and that the action followed an IRA directive, seeing similar barracks attacked elsewhere.[31] Inside, Constables Molloy and Hurley were among those embattled. Speaking at the Ennis Quarter Sessions three months later, Const. Dominick Molloy claimed for £12 towards his suit of clothes, which he showed the court was 'perforated with bullets' to such a state that he 'would not be buried in them'.[32] Two days after the attack in Broadford, republicans overtook the RIC barracks in Newmarket-on-Fergus, securing a significant haul of weaponry. Days later, the sergeant in charge William Porter, attempted to commit suicide by cutting his throat.[33]

The consequent retreat of the RIC to larger barracks resulted in less interaction with the public. This was compounded by a national boycott which had been called on by the republican leadership on 10 April.[34] In Co. Clare, this boycott had been informally in place since the intensification of the struggle across 1917. Relations soured considerably further following the escalation of republican activism in the county throughout that year in the lead up the aforementioned

Mountjoy hunger strike and the subsequent death of Tomás Ashe.[35]

In addition to attacks on Broadford and Newmarket barracks, the month of August 1919 provided evidence of the increasingly dangerous nature of the conflict, with the issuing of a proclamation by the East Clare IRA. The proclamation cautioned against spies, informers and 'anybody answering questions from the police'.[36] Strikingly, it concludes with the chilling assertion that 'anybody charged with infringing this Order will be tried by Court-martial and if found guilty will be shot at sight.'[37]

Two days after the notice was printed, on 7 August 1919, a police hut established near the estate of Dr Francis Sampson in Moynoe, close to the town of Scariff, was attacked. The hut, established for Sampson's protection, was fired on by a reported group of over thirty men.[38]

There is deep irony in the Moynoe attack. As a medical doctor, Francis Sampson was principally responsible for registering the births in the locality and likely signed the birth certs of many of the young men then attacking his estate. For example, Sampson is recorded as registrar for the births of Alphie Rodgers and Michael McMahon, as well as Michael Egan.[39] In September 1895, he signed the birth cert of Joe Noonan, who twenty-three years later led the above attack on his house in Moynoe.[40] At the same time as the Moynoe attack, the courthouse in Mountshannon, as well as the local RIC barracks in both Mountshannon and Whitegate, were burned down by the IRA.[41] The ripple effects of such actions were felt that night.

The flames from Whitegate's burning barracks could be seen across the River Shannon in the townland of Glenbower in Co. Tipperary. There, on that night, Julia Flannery was in the last stages of labour. Her husband Mike travelled by boat to the O'Mearas, Julia's family in Islandmore to send someone for the doctor. The slumber of Julia's brother Paddy was soon disturbed and he was dispatched. In March 1976, he remembered the night clearly:

> That's the night Denis Flannery was born – His father came into the Island – oh around one o clock at night and I was called out of bed to go out to Nenagh, to send out Dr [William] Courtney. I got up out of bed and got my bike and got into the boat … 'Twas a very calm night … Went to Nenagh and called Dr Courtney. I went with Dr Courtney in the car to Flannerys and were weren't there half an hour and the police were in after us. There was a raid in Scariff at Dr Sampson's and there was a couple wounded or shot in it. I suppose I was followed along as I was going to the Doctor. They came in to Flannerys and the auld Sergeant or whatever he was, Dr Courtney told him what was wrong and they wouldn't take his word. They had to go in to the room to see the baby and his mother. Them were hard times then![42]

With increasing IRA activity came the need for more arms. Soon a directive from the IRA leadership came to east Clare, encouraging the procurement of arms by force if necessary from the civilian population. The order came from the brigade O/C:

> Most of these were in Unionist houses and their collection involved widespread raids. Except for a few shots which hit nobody, they were carried out quietly and with success. This helped morale, as I anticipated.[43]

Despite such actions, weaponry, particularly beyond short arms and shotguns, was challenging to obtain. To strengthen the limited arsenal of the East Clare IRA, in the summer of 1919, Rodgers, McMahon and Gildea led a daring operation to secure five service rifles for the brigade and went by motor car to Ballinasloe in Galway with Annie O'Mara, captain of Flagmount Cumann na mBan. It had been arranged through Annie's cousin, a Catholic priest, to purchase the rifles from draper Timothy Nevin in Dunlo Street.[44] So as not to arouse suspicion, at the outskirts of Ballinasloe, Annie left the three Volunteers and continued into the town. Before long, the twenty-six year old returned with the guns, which were transported back to east Clare and distributed across the battalions. While it was the bravery of Annie O'Mara that ultimately secured the rifles, the leading role in an operation of such military significance for the IRA, demonstrates forcefully the status of the three Volunteers within the movement, as early as mid-1919.

In August, severe restrictions were again imposed on the people of east Clare, when Brig. Gen. C. J. Griffin, issued a proclamation against the holding of all meetings and assemblies.[45] Against the backdrop of a restrictive environment, training improved for IRA Volunteers who were becoming more proficient with the gradually increasing number of weapons put through their hands. Some were used when in late September, two constables were fired on north of Scariff town.[46] Meanwhile, the intersection of the national and local continued. In late December, Tom Keogh (Kehoe) and Jimmy Slattery, two of Michael Collins' 'Squad', an elite IRA unit in Dublin, spent time in Bodyke following their involvement in an ambush on Lord French at Ashtown in Dublin.[47] In Killaloe Joe McEvoy, later skipper of the boat that took the Scariff Martyrs to Killaloe, was told that his son John, driver of French's car at Ashtown, had survived the attack.[48]

If the IRA were intensifying, crown forces too were mobilising. The British authorities became increasingly aware that the existing RIC were not sufficient to quell the rising insurgency and already the brain of Winston Churchill had conjured up what he felt would be a final solution. Posters began to appear across British cities, seeking recruits to 'face a rough and dangerous task in Ireland'.[49] Those who responded became known as the Black and Tans. More dangerous and violent times were certain to lie ahead.

From the start of 1920, it was clear that the war was being fought on both military and political fronts. In January, Sinn Féin emerged with forty-one per cent of the votes in urban council elections.[50] In June, when county and rural district elections were held, the party gained control of 338 out of 393 local government bodies, county councils, boards of guardians and rural district councils across the country.[51] In Clare, Sinn Féin were unopposed at the county council elections, with Tom McGrath, Henry O'Meara and Tommy Walle returned in east Clare.[52]

Rural district council elections saw more competition and showed the ability for the republican movement to use all methods to ensure success. In Caherhurley, Ogonnelloe and Killaloe, for example, polling stations were raided, returning officers held up and ballots interfered with by armed Volunteers.[53] At the same time, the gradual appropriation of legal and judicial functions by the republican movement further alienated the police force and British authority generally. A response was always likely and soon came.

In February 1920, a number of republicans in east Clare were arrested, including Joe Clancy, Thomas Dillon, Martin McNamara from the Kilkishen area and Tommy Walle from Scariff.[54] This was part of a national strategy of arrest and internment of IRA and Sinn Féin personnel.

Life continued in so far as was possible for Clare Gaels. James Foran, a fisherman and footballer from Kilkee was captain of the Clare footballers during much of the revolutionary period. His personal recollections, which I was given unique access to, provide a powerful insight into the experience of a young Clareman at this time. In early March 1920, he captained Clare's footballers when they played an inter-county game in Cork. Foran recorded how after travelling by train to Cork city, his team witnessed a baton charge in Patrick's Street as they made their way to the Victoria Hotel. The following day, the

Lord Mayor of Cork, Tomás Mac Curtain and his wife, Eilís, escorted the team to the match. After the Cork Fifers Band led the teams onto the pitch, Mac Curtain threw in the match ball. In his handwritten memories of the match, James Foran recorded that 'Lord Mayor Mac Curtain was shot dead a week later'.[55]

With growing violence across the country, the likelihood of a peaceful settlement was increasingly distant. That prospect seemed to evaporate entirely when on, 25 March 1920, a force of strangely uniformed men placed their leather-covered military boots on Irish soil for the first time. The Black and Tans would go on to linger as a dark shadow over Ireland's memory and historical consciousness.

The war had already settled into a clear dichotomy. On one side, those determined to liberate Ireland and prepared to use physical force to do so. On the other, those who were equally prepared to use violence to suppress that effort and maintain British rule in Ireland. This dichotomy did not fall on an easily defined Irish and English dissection. For example, there were Irishmen in the Black and Tans and more in the RIC who remained committed to crushing the republican movement. The presentation of this dichotomy is important. It was not a case of Ireland versus Britain. Put more accurately, it was a war between Irish republicans and British rule.

Following the introduction of the Black and Tans, however, the conflict had taken on a different dynamic. Just weeks after the Black and Tans were introduced to the war, the RIC barracks at O'Callaghan's Mills and Bunratty were attacked and destroyed by the IRA.[56] On 3 April, Michael Moloney, the O/C of the 5th Battalion, led his men in demolishing the recently abandoned barracks in Bodyke.[57] Just a week later, on 10 April 1920, the *Clare Journal* carried a report that recorded how, in the previous week, all able-bodied men in Scariff were horsewhipped. Twenty-four-year-old butcher Jimmy O'Brien was one of those men and his son, James, explained to me in 2012:

> One night, all the suspects in Scariff that were thought to have any involvement [with the IRA] … were ordered out of their houses and they were lined up in the street from the Commercial Hotel to the Market house. He was telling me 'twas about four o'clock in the morning … They were stripped to the waist and the horse whips came out and they were horsewhipped. That came straight from the man who was there.[58]

The IRA were not to be cowed, however. In June, a significant assault on the Sixmilebridge RIC barracks was executed with a diversionary attack in Feakle also taking place.[59] On the same night, minor attacks took place on barracks in O'Brien's Bridge, Killaloe and Broadford.[60] Republicans in the first half of 1920 destroyed 400 barracks across Ireland, as the RIC continued to abandon outlying posts in dramatic numbers. The resultant intensification of raids in the north-east Clare area drove IRA volunteers 'on the run'.

'Don't Look Out; the Black and Tans are Outside' – Local Experience

According to the training officer for the East Clare IRA, Joe Clancy, each Volunteer by the end of 1920 understood the mechanisms, care and usage of rifles, as well as short arms and bombs.[61] While many of the salient details of the Brigade's more notable actions are recorded, the day-to-day reality, both for active Volunteers and passive observers, requires attention. Closer attention to that daily experience will draw us nearer to the way in which Rodgers, McMahon and Gildea, as well as civilians like Michael Egan, lived at this time.

Many people who experienced the war first-hand are never mentioned in publications about the period, leaving a dramatic gap in our collective knowledge of that experience. For republican leaders to communicate with each other across the country, an intricate network of support was required. Covering addresses were needed for IRA HQ in Dublin to break through British defences and communicate intelligence and strategy to outlying leaders. In Middleline, outside Scariff, the home of William Sammon, a farmer in his mid-fifties, was one such place where IRA messages were sent before being moved on to their eventual revolutionary recipient.[62] At his thatched workshop in Flagmount, Tom Brady, a fifty-year-old shoemaker used his skill with leather to make holsters for the East Clare Brigade, as well as offering his home as a meeting place for the IRA. [63] Another who played a central, if understated, role was Gerry O'Connell, a native of Cork, who acted as a quasi-liaison officer between the brigade O/C and the local IRA in Scariff. As the manager of McKeogh's general grocers in the town (later Supermacs), O'Connell was somewhat above suspicion. A man of low physical stature and older than the average Volunteer, he was able to use his inoffensive countenance to good effect:

> Gerry was small little tiny man. He was so small, they had a series of boxes inside the counter with planks that Gerry would climb on to bring him over the top of the counter. But he had a brilliant mind.[64]

On occasion, O'Connell would be sent communications to be passed on to relevant officers in the area.

Late in the winter of 1919, Gerry and other republican Volunteers took a break from war to play cards. Christmas was coming and as was the custom in rural Ireland, men assembled to compete across a deck of cards for a festive bird:

> Nora Hannon's house was a safe house. The boys would go in there and play cards ... for a couple of geese and that sort of thing. Michael Brennan had sent in documents with some fella ... he passed them onto Gerry O'Connell above in the house ... there was not only a curfew but there was a curfew on lights, you couldn't show light. They had to keep the curtains closed tight ... because it

was so late in the year, the weather was terrible cold you know. She used to have a little fire and she used to have a little tea pot with water to dampen down the fire. Didn't the boys put paraffin oil into the tea pot (laughs) … later on when it started to blaze up she got the tea pot and she poured a load of paraffin oil and there was a big blaze up and set the chimney on fire. As rotten luck would have it, [Captain] Rigby was coming up the Connaught Road with a patrol of soldiers and he saw the blaze.[65]

Having arrived on the scene, Rigby found 'all the boys inside' and soon the interrogation began, before the men were brought to the Market House in the town for more intense questioning. According to Michael O'Gorman, before departing Nora Hannon's house, he looked at the portly and diminutive O'Connell and declared; 'Ah, we'll leave Fr Christmas, he's harmless'. As O'Gorman explained, of all the men Rigby could have taken, the one with the most significance was left behind; 'Oh Lord, if he took him, Gerry had all the documents in his pocket. They'd have been all shot, Nora included!'[66]

Martin 'ha ha' Murray from Deraney in Whitegate appeared outwardly 'somewhat simple' but was 'no fool' according to his nephew, who revealed that Martin regularly carried IRA weapons. He nephew described one occasion that his uncle encountered the forces of the crown while 'on duty':

When carrying a bag with bullets and grenades he encountered the British forces. He saw them up ahead, but he knew that if he turned back they'd follow him so he had to keep going. They asked him 'hey Paddy what have you got in the bag?' Martin replied straight away 'Oh, ha ha, potato seeds, ha ha! The finest potato seeds you ever saw, ha ha! Here, do you want to see them, ha ha?' Yer man told him to 'fuck off. I don't want to see your seeds!'[67]

By the time the War of Independence reached east Clare, Jimmy O'Brien and his father Michael had been in the butcher trade in the town of Scariff for many decades. The

O'Brien's were trusted to supply meat many of the 'big houses' and before long, the IRA recognised the potential for Jimmy O'Brien to function as a dispatcher and not arouse suspicion. According to his son, Jimmy was more than willing to oblige:

> He'd be an ideal man to carry dispatches. 'Twas on the side car that the meat was delivered and the dispatches were inside under the meat or inside in the meat itself … he was going into Woodpark [landlord residence] one night and they [crown forces] thought to stop him and search him but the officer in charge said 'let that man pass, he's going into [Robert Frances] Hibbert with the meat.' A short distance away he dropped off the dispatch, at Nashs' in Middleline.[68]

In a recording undertaken in the 1980s, Scariff native, Mary Kate Mason was asked what effect the war had on school life. Mason was then a young teacher and was able to offer a potent example of how the broader civilian population in east Clare were at the whim of the war:

> I was going up towards the school I met two Peelers and they having guns on their shoulders and about ten Cappabane men, married men and young men and some of them only having their pants and braces on. They were being marched down and a retinue of Black and Tans behind them. I looked at them and one of them smiled at me but I kept walking past them and went up into the school and there was a big armoured car outside the school gate.[69]

Twenty-four-year-old, Mary Kate Mason hurriedly organised her classroom in the hope that the body of men would move on and enable the day to return to some sense of normality. It was a faint hope:

> I went in to school and told the pupils that were there that there was little that we could do but if there were shots fired they should lie on the floor because there were big windows. Then May Bugler, I remember, got up on a chair and I said 'don't look out the Black and Tans are outside'. I didn't know much more and a Peeler and a Black and Tan came in and they said, there was a pile of copy books

on the desk, and he said, 'What are you teaching here?' So I said reading, writing and arithmetic and geography. 'Could you show me some of your books', he said. So I showed them the books. They were reading a composition. They wanted to know if there was anything 'political' about it and there wasn't shur … So they went out, that was about an hour later. They collected all the Tans and got into the big car and fired a few shots in the air.[70]

By mid-1920, increasing numbers of IRA men were 'on the run', seeking support and shelter across the countryside. There is no doubt that the presence of large groups of young men moving around the east Clare countryside brought pressure and worry on local inhabitants, even for those supportive of the struggle. In St Cronan's graveyard in Tuamgraney, the headstone of Michael Griffin from Derrymore in Scariff records its erection 'by his friends for harbouring IRA men "on the run" during the Black and Tan period'.[71] The inscription, explicitly recognising the role of the safe house, is the only one of its kind in Co. Clare and may be unique in Ireland. John Minogue, born two years after the War of Independence ended outside the town of Scariff, grew up in the area close to Michael Griffin's home:

> There was a man there, 'Ferrick' Griffin they used to call him. Those that were 'on the run'. 'Ferrick' killed two pigs and they ate the two pigs there, those that were 'on the run'. There was a dugout there overhead Daltons, Croaghrum. They used to stay there in the night-time.[72]

In Mountshannon, at the home of Patrick Muggivan and his wife Bridget, two pigs were also killed and given to Volunteers 'on the run'. One of the Volunteers was their son Paddy, whose own son Tony outlined to me the experience of his family:

> His parents were supportive. His grandfather gave him the gun. His mother [Bridget], she brought the groceries to feed the men here and she worked like a slave to take care of the men that came in and the food was handed out that window there … there is a valley

at the back of the house so they could come down in the valley and they wouldn't be seen … They had a dugout over in Noonan's place … They killed two pigs here in the winter of 1920-21 to feed the IRA … Oh god shur with a few chickens you'd nearly get a year out of a good pig.[73]

Once when Patrick and Bridget's daughter went out with food to her brother and his comrades, she had a narrow escape:

My aunt went out with food. She used to go out with goods across the mountain … She had two bags with her going across the mountain and weren't the British above on the road … she nearly got caught and she laid down above in the heather in the mountain. She heard 'em talking and she couldn't move or she'd be slaughtered. They went off and she continued on her journey.[74]

Within many poor homes, willing sentiment to support the fight did nothing to increase the resources they could offer. The often-harsh experience for IRA men 'on the run' that resulted, should not be underestimated. Seán Moroney recounted how Volunteers in east Clare survived on very little, often in the open countryside with just occasional bread, butter and eggs to sustain them. Scarcity of food and shelter was exacerbated by the increasingly ubiquitous 'republican itch', that inflicted some in the rebel army across the country, including east Clare. The ailment, a severe form of scabies, resulted from the conditions that some men 'on the run' endured and led to persistent itching, so unbearable, that one Volunteer was driven to bathe in Jeyes fluid in a futile bid to find relief.[75] A west Clare IRA officer opted instead to lie in bog water to relieve the pain, that would only later exercise itself though the manifestation of boils on the skin.[76]

The summer of 1920 saw the Clare footballers, led by James Foran, face Tipperary six times in friendly and championship action. A three-game saga in the championship had profound consequences for the eventual victors, Tipperary, and served to illuminate the darkened times in which Clare Gaels sought to continue their ancient game. Foran recorded the challenges of being an inter-country footballer, forced to travel outside the county to partake in appointed games. On the first Sunday of July 1920, Clare travelled to Limerick to face Tipperary in the Munster semi-final, in what was the first of three encounters. The levels of disruption recorded by Foran, provides an insight into the broader reality of life in war time Ireland:

> It was very difficult to travel around the country at that time … we travelled to Clonmel in four cars on Sunday morning. As we came to the corner of O'Connell Street in Limerick, there was a tank stationed there on the corner. An officer stepped out and held his hand for us to stop … There had been an ambush in Carey's Road in Limerick the day before. Some houses were set on fire. We were stopped and searched but nothing was found … Some miles outside Limerick we were stopped and searched again by an officer and fifty soldiers. We were ordered out and searched again … we were told to be on our way by the officer who was very unpleasant. He was only about twenty years of age … The next time we were stopped was at Pallasgreen. The road was blocked with sandbags at either side … We made our way to the Market Fields … There were about thirty RIC at the gate … very few spectators. There was a lot of tension and there was a feeling of danger in the air, during the match there was a raid by the RIC but they did not catch anyone. The match was a draw.[77]

After another draw, Clare were finally beaten by Tipperary in August.[78] As a result of emerging victorious from the long running saga on a score of one goal and seven points to six points, Tipperary went on to face Dublin in Croke Park, in a game that etched itself into the fabric of Irish history, on a day forever known as Bloody Sunday.[79]

It was a summer of volatility. On 23 June, seven British soldiers were held up in Ennis and disarmed in an example of an emboldened IRA.[80] Three days later, a high-ranking British officer, Major-General Cuthbert Henry Tindall Lucas, was captured by the IRA, while fishing near Fermoy in Co. Cork.

Having been held for a period in east Limerick, he was moved through an extensive IRA network to East Clare brigade area, where he spent a number of weeks under the guard of the local IRA. The limited resources of the east Clare rebel army were put under immense strain during the period of Lucas' captivity, through the provision of whiskey, conversation and entertainment for the forty-one-year-old general, as well as the manpower to guard the captive. Eventually, the IRA guard was intentionally relaxed, enabling Lucas to escape, a liberation which was as much relief to his captors in the IRA, as it was for Lucas.[81] In 2011, I contacted the granddaughter of Gen. Lucas, who outlined the family tradition she inherited and learned of the respect he had for his captors:

> My grandfather's letters show the IRA Volunteers in a good light: that those who held him were kind and honourable men who were fighting for a cause. He appreciated that and true to his character made sure that others knew that these people were not the evil fiends that many in England wanted to portray them as. There was no Stockholm syndrome as some have suggested, my grandfather was still a British officer.[82]

The Lucas experience demonstrates the intricacy and effectiveness of the IRA network. However, despite such a network, many Volunteers were captured and imprisoned. For those left behind at home, usually women and children, there was much hardship to endure. The adversity often associated with IRA activity is reflected potently in the experience Norah O'Brien from Ogonnelloe. In private documents belonging to a senior Cumann na mBan figure, Kathleen Foley recorded the privation which O'Brien went through. Foley wrote how when four of Norah's brothers and their father were arrested, 'she and her sister had to go 'on the run' for a time, the house being searched daily and in the night'.[83]

By 1920, the women's republican organisation had strengthened considerably and, while not commanding the numbers recorded elsewhere, had a committed and active contingent.[84] It is beyond dispute that without the activism of Cumann na mBan members, the IRA could not have affected the war that they did.

There are many examples to illustrate the contribution of republican women in Co. Clare. For example, when the O/C of the Scariff Company, Seán O'Halloran was badly wounded in Cratloe, just two days after the incident on the bridge of Killaloe, it was Nan Hogan, the brigade O/C of Cumann na mBan who ensured his safety.[85] Helena Tuohy, the first captain of the Scariff Cumann na mBan, outlined her own activities in 1939, detailing how the first republican courts in the town were held in her home and that she acted as 'Intelligence Officer for the troops' (IRA).[86] Mary Ryan was O/C of the 5th Battalion, Cumann na mBan which comprised companies from Tulla, Kilkishen, O'Callaghan's Mills and Bodyke. Ryan records that from 1919 to 1920 her involvement was as follows:

> Worked hand in hand with the fighting men, sheltering, scouting, conveying arms, keeping and carrying same, supplied First Aid, mixed among enemy forces for purpose of receiving information for fighting men, receiving and delivering dispatches, took charge of arms and ammunition in Battalion Master's absence'.[87]

Ryan also recorded that on the night of 11 November 1920, she 'rescued three men of the Flying Column who were about to be surrounded by enemy forces by crossing a river in full flood at risk of my life to notify them of danger'.[88] Josie Gleeson, Bridget Slattery and Mary Moloney from Bodyke were active members of the same battalion. In the 6th Battalion area, sisters Margaret and Mary Moroney from Gurtavrulla in Caher maintained an arms dump, tended to wounded IRA men and sheltered others in a dug out on their family farm.[89] In the same battalion, Annie O'Mara from

Flagmount was known for her committed activism. Of Annie, whose sister Bridget was also involved, it was once recorded that the British forces, 'hated her as much as they did her brother Henry', a senior IRA figure in the area.[90]

Meanwhile, for many active men, the pressure from authorities resulted in departure from their native land. In Killaloe, one local poet, Timothy Moloney stood on the Ailvaun on the shoulder of Killaloe town overlooking Lough Derg and composed a poem, entitled 'Farewell to Killaloe'. Moloney had apparently been forced to leave the area as a result of his IRA activities.[91]

Characterised by some as a 'Black and Tan town', one local republican suggested that British money injected into Killaloe during the First World War, had developed a largely pro-British sentiment in the area and made it less than conducive for republican intelligence gathering. Efforts were made to break through the apartment information barrier, however, including the planting by the IRA of a man called Meehan in Crotty's Public House and Michael Fenton at the local post office.[92] Fenton eventually managed to steal and decipher police codes with the help of his sister Mary. He later received a seven year prison sentence, after he was captured with official telegrams. Despite Fenton's efforts, the vice O/C of the East Clare IRA accepted that 'I find it impossible to get any information out of this town as all the inhabitants according to my information are dangerous'.[93]

For republicans in the town, it became particularly precarious. An IRA group meeting at Matt Nihil's home on Hill Road, would have been captured were it not for the ironic intervention of an RIC constable called Mackey, who tipped off Fr Greed, a republican sympathiser, who then informed the republicans not to assemble. Mike Daly recorded in 1972 that the police had been informed about their movements by a local steamer man called Tom Lewis, whose home on

Thomas Street was not far from that of Nihil.[94] The IRA also recorded their concerns about Harry Lefroy, the manager of the mill in Killaloe and a former major in the British army who led recruitment in the town during the First World War. Lefroy was characterised by one Killaloe republican as 'very bitter' towards the national movement.[95] In addition, a message intercepted by the IRA between Hugh Tudor and G Company, discovered in 2019, instructed the latter 'that Major Lefroy's house was not to be visited.' The IRA communication concluded that if Lefroy was 'a friend of theirs, he is not a friend of ours'.[96]

The republican movement did have friends in Killaloe, however. Bella Lucas, a twenty-five-year-old member of the Ballina branch of Cumann na mBan, had some success in eliciting valuable information in the area.[97] In addition, while small in number, committed republicans like Jim Moloney of Kilroughil, maintained an active presence in the area.[98] A deliberate declaration was also made at the public house of Mary Flynn on Church Street, when it was painted in the republican colours, drawing considerable attention from the nearby British forces.[99] Her daughter Lil was an active member of Cumann na mBan, who later married the well-known republican Joe Clancy, before dying at a young age in 1931.[100] At the eastern side of Lough Derg, close to Killaloe, an active IRA network existed. Veteran republican, Dan Gleeson was asked to reflect on that period in 1978, by Uinseann Mac Eoin:

> During 1920 I'd say, all along that period in the winter of 1920 there was hardly a night but we were out, blocking roads, all kinds of activities. It was nearly full time ... you got home and you tried to get a wink of sleep and you tried to do something ... that was the story of the Tan war.[101]

On 9 August, news came through that Royal Assent had been

given to the Restoration of Order in Ireland Act, giving the British forces significant powers, including the use of court martials instead of criminal courts and replacing coroner's inquests with military courts of inquiry.[102]

The act had direct consequences for how the treatment of Rodgers, McMahon, Gildea and Egan was adjudicated, only a short few months later. However, at that time, the former three were part of an increasingly determined group of young men who were already planning their next major challenge to the British forces in east Clare. In Scariff, Rodgers, McMahon and Gildea observed closely the movements of the RIC. There remained in their town the last heavily fortified and occupied police barracks in north-east Clare. Over the summer it had been comprehensively reinforced as outlying RIC posts were abandoned. The movements of the police as well as details about the building were reported to brigade staff and plans were carefully formulated. In a secret factory in Dublin, explosive charge was being carefully inserted into the metal shells of large grenades. The fuse, striker, detonator, percussion cap and firing pin, were all slowly encased within a large serrated metal shell. With the safety pin and handle inserted, it was carefully put away with many others. Soon, a selection was moving covertly towards the county of Clare and into the hands of the East Clare IRA.

4

'HE GOT A SLASH HOOK AND WANTED TO GO OUT'

The Attack on Scariff RIC barracks

By the end of August 1920, the conflict nationally was intensifying. Increasing violence perpetrated by the Black and Tans, instead of having the desired effect of intimidation, seemed to instil a greater determination in the republican movement and their supporters across the country. On the eleventh of that month, sixty republican prisoners in Cork jail embarked on a hunger strike. Three of those, Michael Fitzgerald, Joseph Murphy and Terence MacSwiney, died due to the protest in October.[1] Both sides sought avenues to further their positions. For the IRA, it was necessary to have consistent activity. This was required both to evenly draw the attention of crown forces around the country and also to sustain the interest of Volunteers. In many cases, actions against British forces were frustrated by a last minute change of direction, as experienced on 18 August when McMahon, Rodgers and Gildea were part of an IRA unit that assembled close to Scariff, ready to ambush an expected contingent of Black and Tans who failed to show up.[2]

From mid-September 1920, a discernibly more aggressive position was adopted by the IRA, under the leadership of Michael Brennan who spent most of that time in the area. For Rodgers, McMahon and Gildea, a period of republican activism, which up to that point had involved military training, raids, implementing boycotts and informal intelligence gathering, was about to become a time of violence, warfare, murder and death.

By the end of the summer, only the RIC barracks in Feakle and Scariff remained occupied in the north east Clare district, with Scariff by far the most heavily defended. Such had been the intensity of attacks on RIC positions that in June the lord lieutenant, John French, determined the RIC needed men with military experience to help better defend barracks.[3] Before long, a Barracks Defence Officer had been appointed to Co. Clare. John Joe Fitzgerald spent time in the town of Scariff helping to fortify the barrack building. While there, the twenty-two year old former British army officer, was captured and wounded by the local IRA who shot him with his own revolver, before he escaped and was removed to Dublin for treatment (see p. 174).[4]

The RIC barracks in Scariff was a two-storey stone building, which stood between Moloney's drapery shop and Stephen Duggan's public house, regularly frequented by the RIC. The building was manned by between twelve and twenty police, comprised of both RIC and Black and Tans. Before Fitzgerald was forced to leave the area, he had reinforced the front of the building. Two steel shuttered windows flanked the doorway at the centre, which for some time before the attack had been permanently closed with sandbags and barbed wire. There were three windows on the second floor, which were also steel shuttered. It was obvious to all that the RIC were prepared for an attack:

> They had it actually turned into some kind of a fortress like. They really had. They had the floor kind of raised. The timber floor. It was raised off the foundation. So they had it taken out and that brought it down to a nice chest level at the window where 'twould be grand to put a rifle on it and shoot out, if the worst came to the worst. 'Twas good thinking ahead really.[5]

By mid-September, the IRA in east Clare decided to move on Scariff barracks. Their aims were twofold. Firstly, as part of IRA strategy nationally, the police were to be driven from rural areas for the IRA to establish bases of control. Secondly, and for the local IRA perhaps this was equally as important, their aim was to capture any intelligence and ammunition they could from within the barracks.

Life continued and as often is the case, young men in the uniform of the RIC were attractive to some young women of the area. One story recalls Alphie Rodgers observing a local woman approaching the barracks. According to his nephew, Alphie had been aware the girl was visiting a particular constable and that she was bringing him eggs concealed in her dress. Remembered as a 'happy go lucky' young man and 'a bit of a devil', the young girl was not concerned when Alphie beckoned her to come to his shop, which was located close to the barracks. Once inside the shop, Alphie is reputed to have laughingly picked up the girl and sat her down on the counter, breaking the eggs destined for the constable and sent her on her way, a far more gentle warning that was handed out elsewhere to young women becoming too friendly with police.[6]

Rodger's apparent jovial countenance masked a deeper commitment, which became evident over the coming days. It is during this action that McMahon, Rodgers and Gildea, by now battalion staff officers, seemed to elevate further in military significance.[7] While in the town, Alphie Rodgers managed up to that point to portray a public image that did not draw attention and was seen by the RIC as the popular son of a business man. However, there were indications of some covert activities, with one young admirer recalling years later that when attempting to evade attention, he tended to leave home by the back door and emerge onto the Feakle road through a small bow way.[8] Tommy Bolton, a seventeen-year-old Volunteer at the time, claimed that Alphie had used his position of apparent innocence and knowledge of the town to assist in the planning. He implied that Rodgers may have had the confidence of the police and was able to gather significant information, remembering that 'Of course he [Alphie] was very free around the police barrack. He was in the evening before they set up the ambush'.[9]

On the day of the attack, in Mountshannon, Paddy Muggivan and other IRA Volunteers opened cartridges and removed the pellets which they replaced with metal to form more cohesion and make them more effective as projectiles. Decades later, he told his son how they crossed over the mountain into Scariff and moved towards the town from the Fossabeg side, visiting the church beforehand. There, a local clergyman, aware of what they were doing, impressed strongly on them to return home. They continued on.[10]

The attack involved IRA Battalions from across the East Clare Brigade area from Newmarket to Kilanena. Peter Higgins, uncle of Ireland's ninth president was a participant.[11] Tomás Malone, who during Easter Week 1916 was involved in a shootout with the RIC at his home in Meedin, Co. Westmeath, spent much of the War of Independence in Limerick, under the alias 'Seán Forde', was also present, together with fellow Limerick IRA men, Nicholas O'Dwyer and Bill Hayes.[12]

All roads were blocked entering the district. The role of the Bodyke Company in the 5th Battalion area, led by the Gleeson brothers, Michael Tuohy, James Cox and Michael Moloney, was critical. That company created a particularly large roadblock to the south of Tuamgraney to ensure a contingent of the Oxford and Buckinghamshire Light Infantry based in Tulla did not get through.[13] If they breached that obstacle, a further barricade was set up closer to Tuamgraney, manned by armed republicans from Bodyke and O'Callaghan's Mills.[14]

The planned action was more ambitious and dangerous than any undertaken in the brigade area to date. Therefore, an arsenal deadlier than previously used was required. On the evening before the attack, rifles and bombs had been sent to the home of Michael Gleeson in Bodyke, concealed within a donkey and cart. Gleeson arranged for the ammunition to be stored in a disused home, between Bodyke and Tuamgraney.[15] The bombs had been brought to Clare by train and after arriving at Ballycar Station outside Newmarket-on-Fergus, were removed by Seán Murnane, who later arranged for their movement to the O'Callaghan's Mills Company. From there, Michael Lenihan carried them in a donkey's cart to Bodyke.[16]

The Military Archives of Ireland revealed the importance of Newmarket and in particular the Ballycar Company area to the attack in Scariff with the release of IRA Brigade Activity reports in 2019. The reports underline how large numbers of armed Volunteers moved through the area both before and after the attack. Others in the company were appointed to block roads, cut wires and scout for the men involved in Scariff.[17]

Key to the confidence in the operation was the operability of the large bombs, made in an IRA factory in Dublin. While confidence was high in the ammunition, the local IRA leadership were cautious that bullets recently procured had been deliberately planted by British forces for the IRA to use. It was established that bullets marked 'KN' or 'ZZ' had been tampered with by the British, so as to explode on firing and cause damage to the man holding the rifle.[18]

With all ammunition and strategy in place, on Saturday 18 September, large numbers of IRA Volunteers began to move from surrounding areas towards the town of Scariff. An operation of this nature is a useful illustration of the co-operative and collaborative nature of the conflict and underlines how the IRA depended on the support, passive or active, of the local population. In the days beforehand, a message was communicated to the inhabitants of the town, who gradually and with as little fuss as possible, moved from Scariff to surrounding areas:

The word of course came around nice and easy that there was something on. Everyone was advised to take it nice and easy and pretend you're goin' on a picnic or whatever, but get out of Scariff! So my grandmother and her family headed out to Carrowmore. The Hannons next door headed off someplace as well. Probably all headed out towards Moynoe. Gradually the town kind of emptied out so that there was no one left on the streets.[19]

While the town's residents moved away from Scariff like a slowly receding wave, others moved towards the town to help with the planned attack. Strategic positions were occupied throughout the town within sight of the RIC barracks. The barracks faced north against houses on the opposite side of the town, whose bases, because of the natural gradient in Scariff, were higher than the roof of the barracks, offering optimal rifle and sniper angles. Before long, IRA men had rifles positioned on the upper windows of those houses.

At her home in the town, thirty-six year old Helena Tuohy, the first captain of Scariff's Cumann na mBan Company, nervously waited with an assembly of first aid equipment.[20] Mary Ryan, the O/C of the 5th Battalion, was also involved in the preparation for the attack.[21]

Others who heard the news came forward and volunteered to help. Forty-five-year-old mason, John Melody from Poulagower in Scariff, offered to go up on the roof and to take off the slates so that the police could be burned out.[22] South of Scariff, fifteen-year-old Paddy Gleeson watched intently as men he knew to be republican Volunteers passed his house in Coolawn, Tuamgraney at approximately 8.00 p.m. The men had earlier spent time in Derrynaheila, on the border between Bodyke and Feakle, where at the home of Bridget Slattery, some fifty rebels were fed before moving towards Scariff, passing Paddy on their way.[23] The teenager became accustomed to the sight and understood the secrecy surrounding such scenes. He returned to his chores in the home of his aunt, with whom he had lived in Tuamgraney, after his mother Agnes died from meningitis in May 1913. At the age of 105, he told me how he established the following day, where those men had been going:

> That barracks was attacked of a Saturday evening and my aunt and myself used to go to Mass in Scariff and we went on Sunday morning ... I remember seeing the Volunteers goin' down where I was living [Coolawn, Tuamgraney] and they attacked the barrack ... I heard all the shots and everything.[24]

Before the attack took place, Alphie Rodgers, Michael McMahon and Martin Gildea sat quietly in the town of Scariff and waited. For Rodgers and McMahon, the town that had been their childhood playground was about to be transformed into a battlefield. They had been central to the organisation of the action. The three young republicans had already committed themselves to the cause of Irish independence. That concept was now becoming more real, as a strange feeling loaded with both fear and nervous energy, ran through their bodies.

As they sat in silence, from surrounding areas equally silent republican Volunteers were drawing closer. Tuamgraney IRA Volunteer Joe Noonan had made his way to a place known as 'Long's Barn', a derelict building in Coolawn between the villages of Tuamgraney and Bodyke, which looked directly across at St Coelan's ancient holy well, enclosed in a stone house in 1803. There he was met by approximately fifty IRA men, who Noonan helped arm with weaponry concealed in Long's Barn.

The IRA men assembled close by in the 'Evicted Field' (later the grounds of Bodyke GAA Club), where they were broken into sections. Before long, they moved slowly and purposefully towards Scariff. The section to which Joe Noonan was attached was slowed considerably by the backfire of a passing car and the nervous return fire of an inexperienced

Volunteer. By the time Noonan had reassembled his then scattered section and made their way to the bridge of Scariff, they could hear from over the hill of the town that the attack had already begun.[25]

At the other side of that hill, McMahon, Rodgers and Gildea had taken one final deep breath and emerged to take a leading role in directing the action. It had been hoped that with an element of surprise that the barracks would be overcome with relative ease. Through intelligence gathered locally, it was established that the police drank regularly in Duggan's public house, attached to the barrack building. The initial plan was to enter Duggan's through a laneway and there attack the police. The men selected for this action were part of the 1st Battalion, who had travelled twenty miles from the Newmarket area using various back roads, under the command of Paddy Brennan.[26] In Scariff they were led by his brother Michael through the laneway towards Duggan's.[27]

Sitting in a car close by was Tomás Malone. The Westmeath man had been directed to drive a car past the barracks and from within the vehicle to open fire on the policemen outside, which would drive them towards the gunfire of the unit approaching from behind the building. Waiting in his car, Malone heard a shot. A Volunteer had prematurely discharged his weapon, alerting the RIC to the impending attack. Malone paused and when a barrage of chaotic gunfire followed the initial shot, he knew it was too late and emerged from his car to join the fight.

As a child, Michael O'Gorman listened carefully as stories told in his home in Ballyminogue made some imprint on his young mind. He relayed his understanding of how the attack was revealed prematurely, firstly describing the ever vigilant condition of the RIC:

> They lived on the edge and they had the instincts of rabbits. They

knew there was something very quiet about the place. 'Twas a beautiful day. They had a plank and a couple of rocks outside the barracks and they were sittin' on it chattin' ... The boys [IRA] that were coming down to take part in the attack, they'd be coming down from back around the mountains, we'll say Clonusker and Cappabane and places like that but they were coming down Knockatulla, we'll say the hill by the church. One of 'em fired a shot up in the air and said 'it was for the republic we're goin to have'.[28]

Malone confirmed that when the shot was discharged, the RIC who had been outside playing pitch and toss 'scurried for the barracks'. Bodyke Volunteer Michael Gleeson also noted that 'things went wrong from the beginning' and that an accidental discharge of a weapon enabled the RIC to escape into the barracks and adopt defensive fire.[29] Feakle's Tomo Tuohy named the man who discharged the shot as Mick Hehir. However, Seán Murnane, who was part of a group that rushed Duggans, accepted that one of his party accidentally discharged his weapon.[30] Irrespective of whose gun the shot came from, the action had been announced. At that time the RIC, although vigilant, had been easing themselves into a Saturday evening, seemingly free of disturbance:

Jack Farrell lived in one of the houses that are there across from where the Medical Centre is now ... They had the six boys [crown forces] lined up. The police were just sitting there chatting away and they were smokin' and they had no notion of going anywhere. They had no idea that the boys [IRA] had their guns trained on 'em from across the way. Jazus when the shot went off, the six of 'em got up and they ran like rabbits down the bow way.[31]

When the firing began the garrison was called on to surrender with safe passage promised. When the response to this suggested clemency was a barrage of gunfire, the IRA in various positions around the town were ordered to commence firing on the building. From the Market House, Rodgers and Gildea squeezed their trigger fingers and ordered those with them to do likewise. 'Brud' McMahon had just left with Joe Clancy and Martin 'Neighbour' McNamara to guide them towards the back of the barracks.

Within minutes of the firing, Sgt Michael Sullivan and Const. Edward Broderick had been shot and wounded.[32] Sullivan was shot in the chest but managed to make his way into the barracks from where he organised the defence of the garrison, while Broderick, a former British solider from Kildare, was wounded in the lung but also survived.[33] McMahon, Rodgers and Gildea were later implicated in shooting the policemen, despite no evidence to support the claim. One English journalist, staying in east Clare at the time, even made the assertion that McMahon and Rodgers 'were instrumental in saving the lives of the police' during the attack.[34] Likewise, there is nothing to verify this contention.

Before long, Very lights illuminated the sky above Scariff town to alert the British forces in Tulla, who upon later approaching the village of Tuamgraney would realise their roadway had been heavily obstructed by the Bodyke IRA.[35]

Positioned in a small laneway between Moloney's shop and the barrack building, Michael Brennan pulled a firing pin from one of the grenades that had been sent from Dublin. Brennan had waited for months to receive the explosive missiles. He only had to wait a further five seconds to put them to effect and energetically hurled the bomb over the ridge of the barrack roof, keeping it from sliding off with a light rope tied around the neck of each grenade between the firing pin and lever. The twenty-four year old hunkered down and internally counted five seconds. No sound came. No explosion. He released eleven more bombs, all to the same silent effect.

High above, Joe Clancy, accompanied by his fellow Kilkishen man and former British army colleague, Martin 'Neighbour' McNamara, were making their way towards the roof of the barracks. At that time, Michael 'Brud' McMahon stood at the back of that building, having directed the Kilkishen men through Moloney's drapery shop from where they gained access to ridge on the roof.[36] With Clancy and McNamara on the roof, McMahon quickly moved back towards the centre of the town, where his comrades Rodgers and Gildea were based. Clancy and McNamara smashed a hole in the roof but despite throwing at least seven bombs into the barracks, none exploded. Having been ordered not to burn the barracks, Clancy knew it was time to retreat:[37]

> Just before the signal to call off the attack was given, I went back to the roof and flung three more grenades into the barracks, but these also proved to be duds. As I was engaged in throwing these bombs the other men who were in the building with me withdrew from the place, leaving me locked in. I managed to attract the attention of a few Volunteers, and with the aid of a ladder put up by them, I got out.[38]

While Clancy and others were engaged close to the barrack building, Tomo Tuohy had been positioned in at a house on the north-west corner of Scariff town, where Mountshannon's Tom McNamara, Michael McCarthy and Michael Cleary joined him. There too were Tom Bleach, Joe McNamara (Kilkishen) and Tommy Walle who was in charge of the post. All men had rifles and had a clear line of sight to the barracks. While there, Tuohy, who had earlier removed the potentially dangerous bullets as instructed, forgot that he had placed them in his pocket. In the midst of firing, he inadvertently loaded one of the damaged bullets, which, as predicated, exploded, causing what Tuohy thought at the time was a minor injury to his right eye. Years later, however, his sight deteriorated entirely.[39]

The shooting continued for some time. Tuamgraney's Joe Noonan remembered stopping at one firing position where he asked local IRA Volunteer Peter Flannery to let him 'have a few shots' with his rifle, the contents of which Flannery had been emptying in the direction of the RIC barracks.[40]

While all this was taking place, the people on the outskirts of Scariff listened intently as they heard ominous sounds emanating from the town. In Coolawn, Tuamgraney two miles away, Paddy Gleeson heard the shots as they intermittently cracked into the still country air for over two hours. In Poulagower, approximately the same distance from Scariff, eleven-year-old Kathleen Minogue moved closer to her mother Bridget, as she too heard the gunfire and sound rockets from the attack, which she recalled in 2009 at the age of 100:

> I do, I remember it well. I do. You could hear it out from Coolreagh to Scariff. They blew it up, I think. It made a lot of noise anyway. I was at home when I heard it. My parents were wondering what was wrong.[41]

Inside the town of Scariff, Sonny Moore was in a public house when the firing started. He told Tony Muggivan many years later how one man insisted on joining the fight:

> There is a story told. Sonny Moore in Mountshannon, he lived in Scariff at the time … This man was there and he had a few pints and when the shooting started … they had to hold him back. He had got a slash hook and he wanted to go out and help the boys [IRA] and he as drunk as a fox! [laughs] A slash hook![42]

While the action saw key Volunteers move around the town to strategic positions, a central area of command based at the Market House was led by Alphie Rodgers and Martin Gildea, who were soon joined by Michael McMahon who had returned from assisting in the elevation of IRA men atop the barracks roof. There the three men directed a firefight within the town they knew intimately.

While the young IRA men concentrated their focus on the direction of fire, it is claimed that the eyes of an RIC constable were at that time focused on them. One local historian claims that an RIC constable was on a night off duty and drinking in a local public house and that he observed the action from an upstairs window; 'he saw those guys and he was able to give a full and accurate detail of the boys'.[43] That observation ultimately made the three republicans marked men as they were deemed responsible for the attack.

For over two hours, the RIC and Black and Tans put up a determined defence of the barracks until a number of sharp whistle blows signalled the action was called off and IRA Volunteers immediately began to peel away from the town between 10.30 p.m. and 11.00 p.m.

For those involved, it had been a failure.[44] The key element of surprise was removed by the accidental discharge of a shot. However, it was the failure of the bombs to affect the type of damage expected that ultimately meant the action was doomed. Even after the retreat had been called and Malone, with his west Limerick comrades, hurriedly got into their vehicle, he realised the operation was compounded by further mistakes. As the car made its way out of Scariff town and into the village of Tuamgraney, it began to stutter and slow down, eventually stalling and having to be pushed into the local workhouse. It transpired that a local Volunteer whose job it was to ensure that the car was filled with petrol for the getaway had inadvertently poured in oil instead and was forced to return to Scariff to seek out petrol, Malone and his comrades encountered a now-emboldened police force that had emerged from the barracks and began shooting indiscriminately:

> The police had come out of the barrack at this time. They were very brave when they thought everyone had gone, and they were firing all-round the place … as soon as we started to shoot, they all scuttled back into the barracks very quickly.[45]

The day after the attack, Michael Gleeson examined the remaining bombs back in Bodyke and noted that the detonators had not been inserted, making the supposedly explosive devices redundant.[46] Others claimed that the deficiency resulted from the striking pins being too short, which prevented the detonators from exploding.[47] While the IRA leadership were examining the faulty grenades, it became apparent that a second act of the RIC barrack attack was forthcoming:

> There was a sequel to this ... The following day, when the boys [IRA] dispersed, a whole lot of Crossley tenders arrived up from Killaloe, to help the police escape from Scariff. So as a reprisal for what happened they said they'd set fire to the town hall ... 'twas the local Volunteers and one very active Volunteer named Vincent Scanlon from above in Ballyminogue ... when the Black and Tans set fire to the town hall, the boys opened a really heavy fire on them and they wouldn't let 'em out. So because the hall was on fire, they were kind of caught between a rock and a hard place [laughs] so they had to put the fire out themselves! So eventually, a Crossley Tender came down the hill, or an armoured car and they cut across in front of a line of fire and they escaped.[48]

The *Daily Herald* reported that 'Black and Tan raiders' first destroyed a motor garage and confirmed they were only deterred from burning the Town Hall, located at the foot of Scariff hill, when 'the local company of Volunteers suddenly mobilised, opened fire and drove the marauders from the village'.[49] Joe Noonan, John Dillon, Denis Nihil, Joe Malone and Michael Brady, are also recorded as firing on the would be arsonists, from a position later known as the 'dock road'.[50] When, the following morning, young Paddy Gleeson walked past the barracks on his way to mass, he observed the after-effects closely. The sounds he had heard the previous night; made by the men he had seen pass his house earlier that evening, now had greater meaning. Nine decades later he told me how he and his aunt 'used to put the ass in at Michael Duggan's yard and as we walked down, we walked on the mortar and lime off the cill that the bullets knocked off.'[51]

The first effect of the attack was to increase dramatically

the levels of British force activity in north east Clare, with multiple violent raids across the area. Before long, a large cordon encircled the town, within which the inhabitants were harassed and beaten. All shops with Irish over their premises were 'obliged to obliterate them'.[52] Although not an initial success, the withdrawal days later of the RIC from the barracks and its subsequent destruction by the IRA had the effect of removing a regular police presence from the area. In total, over £1,270 worth of damage was done to the barracks, owned by Margaret Hynes, a sixty-eight-year-old farmer and widow with a number of properties.[53]

The week after the attack, the Scariff Board of Guardians passed a resolution expressing their support for a boycott of Belfast goods.[54] No mention was made of the attack. However, at a local level the effects were very real. All Volunteers from the area who had been involved were advised to go 'on the run'. The family homes of McMahon and Rodgers became the subject of intense and aggressive raids, in a clear indication that their sons' involvement was noted and they had now, with Gildea, become wanted men. On one occasion, when British forces were beating in their door in Scariff town, eighteen-year-old Gertie Rodgers was handed a revolver to conceal, which she did by quickly placing it in the ashes of a fire range in the home.[55] During a separate raid, Gerald Rodgers was forced by the crown forces to the centre of Scariff town and made to sing 'God Save the King'.[56] The home of Michael McMahon's uncle in Middleline outside Scariff was targeted repeatedly. John McMahon was warned that if he helped his nephew, his house would be burned, and his family shot. Among those staying in his house was Frank McMahon, Michael's younger brother.[57] Meanwhile, republicans intensified intelligence raids on mail cars in east Clare and Scariff post office was stormed on 24 September, where official documents were taken.[58]

Given the intensity of such raids on houses suspected of supporting the IRA, Volunteers primarily remained in man-made dugouts, dotted carefully around the countryside. In Sillernane, Mountshannon, a substantial dug-out of approximately eleven feet square and six feet high was made in a lime kiln on Pat Noonan's farm.[59] In townlands across Tuamgraney and Bodyke, many IRA men were sheltered in the weeks that followed. Rodgers, McMahon and Gildea stayed for a time in the loft of Glebe House in Tuamgraney, a former Protestant rectory building bought in 1912 by Denham Sparling.[60] 100 years earlier that building had been attacked by Ribbonmen, rebels of a previous generation (see p. 51).

While Alphie Rodgers was beginning life 'on the run' from crown forces, the wrath of his sibling was more challenging to evade. Days after the Scariff attack, a letter was on its way from his sister in Belgium, within which the young rebel was excoriated for not taking the time to write![61] Alphie had written to his sister many times, even sending her a selection of shoes just months before.[62] There was no time for letters now. From that moment until eight weeks later when a loud knock shattered their sleep, Rodgers, McMahon and Gildea were wanted men. There were killings, long journeys in dark nights, house dances, bravado, worry, laughter, danger, loneliness and bravery, until all emotions were distilled into fear and panic on 16 November 1920.

5

'THE BOYS BEGAN TO FIRE'

Taking the War to the Crown

Two days after the attack in Scariff, in Dublin, District Inspector Peter Burke died after he was shot by the IRA, an incident that led to the burning of large parts of Balbriggan. Burke had earlier served in north Clare when he led a party of RIC that found the body of IRA leader, Martin Devitt in a bog outside the town of Ennistymon, following his killing in February.[1]

In the same week as Burke's death, the area of north-west Clare where he had been stationed, was the scene of unprecedented violence following the Rineen ambush, discussed below. In the same week, resignations from the RIC continued as certain members found they could not continue a war against their fellow countrymen.[2] Others undoubtedly left as a result of intimidation. Since June, ten RIC men had resigned from barracks in Scariff, Broadford, Mountshannon and O'Brien's Bridge.[3] Across Ireland in September, the IRA killed thirty members of the force, including Black and Tans.[4] Indicating the increasingly levels of violence in Co. Clare, nine of these men were shot dead in the county.

The attack in Scariff left an area of approximately 180 square miles from Woodford in Co. Galway to Tulla and over to Killaloe, without a regular police presence.[5] West of Scariff, a large garrison of the Oxford and Buckinghamshire regiment was stationed in Tulla and in Killaloe to the south, a substantial stronghold of RIC and Black and Tans was based, expanded following the Scariff attack by those police who had been stationed there. Raiding parties were frequently launched from both Tulla and Killaloe. However, the danger of such raids was mitigated partially by an increasingly proficient IRA warning system, based on a network of trusted scouts observing British movements. Other methods to impede British forces were used also. Trees were felled, trenches dug, roads blocked and stone barricades were erected, all with the effect of creating somewhat of a safe haven for IRA men 'on the run'.

The British forces were deeply frustrated by these actions, as was seen in their actions towards the general populace. In Feakle, Mae Tuohy recalled one occasion with British forces threatened to shoot her father, on the suspicion that he had been involved in felling a large tree close to his house in Kilbarron, between Tulla and Feakle. John Powell was saved by the dust on his tools, evidence that they had not been used in downing the large obstacle.[6]

The attack on the RIC barracks in Scariff was a watershed for the broader experience in north east Clare and represented a dramatic escalation of the conflict. From 18 September to 16 November, there were several serious incidents involving republican attacks on crown forces. The intensity of activity in the area was in large part attributable to the presence in east Clare of Michael Brennan, who remained sheltered in Bodyke for much of late September and October. Those two months proved critical for Rodgers, McMahon, Gildea and, ultimately, Michael Egan.

'Practically no Sinn Féiner now ever sleeps in his Own Home'

Just four days after the attack in Scariff, as crown forces raided and burned houses in the north-east Clare area, a major ambush was executed in north Clare. This occurred on the road between Lahinch and Miltown Malbay at a place called Dromin Hill, also known as Rineen. Six members of a Black and Tan/RIC patrol were ambushed and killed by a considerable, if poorly armed, IRA force comprised between fifty and sixty Volunteers from the 4th Battalion, Mid Clare IRA Brigade.[7] The resultant reprisals later that night by

British Army and police in the three north Clare towns of Ennistymon, Lahinch and Miltown Malbay left five civilians and one active IRA Volunteer dead. In less than twenty-fours, twelve people were killed in an area of just 2.7 miles.

The fight in Rineen represented a significant moment at a national level and was the largest military defeat to date with the crown forces losing six of its members. The ferocity and violence of the reprisals was also symptomatic of a tendency amongst the British to inflict maximum damage on civilians and to apply what can be termed, 'collective punishment'.

The killings in north Clare, sent shock waves throughout the county. Some doors began to more slowly open to IRA Volunteers 'on the run' while others hardened in their support of the republican movement.

The violence of Rineen was brought to the area of Flagmount when it was revealed that one of their own people, Joseph Sammon, a thirty-four-year-old farmer on holidays in Lahinch at the time of the reprisals, was shot dead by crown forces. According to a number of reports, Sammon was shot as he ran from a burning building.[8] Two witnesses later testified, however, that they had seen Sammon in the custody of the military in Lahinch after being taken from Walshes boarding house, which carries the clear implication that the Feakle man was murdered in cold blood.[9] Sammon had been born in America but returned to east Clare as a child, where he grew up in Poulatrumpa, Corlea in the parish of Feakle.[10] His body was returned to his native parish by motorcar. Sammon left his fifty-seven year old widow Maria and a daughter, who was just weeks away from her fifth birthday.[11]

The terror of Lahinch was likely also circulated in the Scariff community through the experience of a number of other people from there who had been holiday in Lahinch at the time. Fifty-four-year-old bachelor, Michael Rodgers, had been staying at Vaughan's Hotel in Lahinch when crown forces burned it. He received £40 in compensation for the loss of his property.[12] Also staying at Vaughans were seventy-five-year-old Patrick McAllen from Scariff and his thirty-one-year-old son, Patrick junior, who ironically was in Lahinch 'for the good of his health'.[13]

In the aftermath of Rineen, the inspector general of the RIC was satisfied that reprisals 'had a most satisfactory effect on the whole county' and happily declared that 'practically no Sinn Féiner now ever sleeps in his own home'.[14] Back in east Clare, the IRA Volunteers involved in the barracks' attack, though not sleeping in their own beds, were not quelled, as the days that followed underlined profoundly.

Although the War of Independence was primarily under-stood through the local experience, increasingly, the national and local moved closer together. On 23 September, the Scariff Board of Guardians called on all public bodies and local authorities throughout Ireland to boycott Belfast until the 'pogrom' had ended.[15] During this time, four different ambushes on the RIC in Feakle were prepared, none of which came off.[16] IRA strategy and guerrilla warfare generally places an onus on outlying activists to maintain a level of action that negated the ability for enemy forces to concentrate heavily on any one area. It was therefore been in line with IRA strategy for the east Clare Volunteers to ensure that sufficient attention was drawn to their area. Within days of Rineen, the IRA leadership in east Clare were mobilising for a series of actions that would focus British energies on the area.

On Saturday 25 September a large armoured car sat in the centre of Scariff Town, encircled by a group of watchful military. Young Gertie Rodgers maintained an outward com-posure as she walked away from the imposing spectacle. In her hand was a quickly scribbled note stamped with a Royal seal, that functioned as a travel permit, when the following day Gertie travelled to Lisdoonvara to collect her mother from the north Clare town.[17] Lt M.W. Spicer, the British officer who signed the note, could discern from the young woman's countenance that she was not enamoured by their presence in the town. What he did not know was that while signing that note, Gertie's older brother Alphie was at that time moving with an Active Service Unit of the IRA, in the direction of Broadford and towards some of Spicer's colleagues in the British crown forces.

'Held Up by a Group of Armed Men' – Attack in Broadford

The late Seán Crowe from Broadford, attended throughout his life to all things history and folklore. A poet and source of local knowledge, Crowe was engaged in tradition surrounding the struggle for independence. As a result, when his father John spoke about the period, he listened carefully. When John Crowe recounted how on a late September evening in 1920, while on his way to the village of Broadford, he became embroiled in the periphery of an incident which brought war to their village. Seán Crowe outlined his father's story:

> Well I used her him telling of a particular evening that he was going to walk down to the village of Broadford ... he used to smoke a pipe, maybe 'twas for tobacco. Just as he was coming out, there did a lorry pass ... there was a man from Broadford driving for McDonnells by the name of Tommy Murnane. He was delivering goods from McDonnells up to the big house, the lodge. He said to my father, 'are you going to Broadford? If you are sit in here with me,' he says, 'we'll be up as far as the lodge with the messages and you'll be back down along with me' ... He sat into the front of the lorry with him and they went up the avenue and they were up half ways when they were held up by a group of armed men. They were asked where they were going and they said what was happening. So the armed men anyway, one of the leaders said, they'd have to keep 'em. They couldn't let them go until whatever they were going to do was over. So Tommy Murnane pointed out to these men that if they were held, his employers would know there was something wrong. So after consultation, they decided then that they would allow them

take up the messages to the big house but when he'd be coming back they'd have to take one of the group into Broadford. So they delivered the messages and turned the lorry around. The man was picked up. I believe he was a man by the name of Martin Vaughan from up in the mountain. He was part of the group. There were IRA men ... They took the man into Broadford and they dropped him outside McDonnells.[18]

Sometime later, in the dark of night, the IRA unit moved to the edge of Broadford village, closer to their enemy. Twenty-two-year-old John Crowe, having travelled with Murnane and Martin Vaughan, a thirty-two-year-old IRA man and native of Caherhurley, made his way to Tommy Marsh's forge, a common meeting place in the village:

My father went down to the forge. There was people there after the smith working, they'd meet and have a chat. There was a number of men in the forge, Tommy Marsh's Forge. So in the meantime anyway, this Vaughan man ... there was no street light that time of course. There was a peeler having a drink inside in McDonnells. But apparently he was friendly to the national cause and there was no heed paid to him. But this Vaughan man went down to Brien's pub and there was peelers inside. He got a bottle of stout, that was what I was told and he left. But the peelers got wary of him ... in the meantime, the [IRA] men had come down at the back of the street.[19]

Tuamgraney's Joseph Noonan was among a small group mobilised earlier that evening under Comdt Seán O'Halloran, who marched to O'Callaghan's bog in Bodyke to meet with others for an as yet undisclosed action. Noonan recorded that approximately twenty men assembled, including Alphie Rodgers and Michael 'Brud' McMahon.[20] After Noonan and the IRA unit quietly moved into Broadford village, they assembled at a place then called 'The Lever' at the northern end of the village street. Having received a report from Vaughan, they began to move:

At this point, Martin Vaughan, who had been sent into the village earlier to ascertain if any R.I.C. or 'Black and Tans' were out of barracks, reported to Michael Brennan that some R.I.C. were drinking in Will O'Brien's pub and that two Black and Tans were out with girls … about 9 p.m. we saw the R.I.C. leaving O'Brien's and coming towards us. We moved to meet them, walking lightly down one side of the street. When the police were within a few yards Michael Brennan advanced on to the middle of the road and opened fire.[21]

Writing in 1954, Brennan recorded how at that point he:

Walked in front with James Hogan … and just below the barracks we met two men. It was very dark, but they stepped in front of us and peered into our faces. As they did I saw a reflection of light from a window glinting on the peak of one of their caps and I realised they were R.I.C. men. I pulled a gun at once and fired at one of them and James Hogan followed suit. Both men turned and ran down the street.[22]

Standing on the street that night were Michael McKenna and eighteen-year-old Martin Marsh, who watched, stunned, as the scene of violence unfolded:

A man told me that was standing in the street, Michael McKenna that he was watching. He was standing outside what was Mary Doyle's that time, himself and a man, Martin Marsh. He heard the peelers walking up the street and when they came up as far as Danny Moloney's that time, the light was shining out the window and when the light shone on the buckles, the boys began to fire. He got rooted to the spot but the man that was with him ran into the local shop, Mrs Barron's at the time … Michael McKenna was rooted to the spot and he saw the boys firing. One particular peeler, he ran up the street in front of him and there was an IRA man a distance back and he trying to shoot him.[23]

Inside in the forge, a number of men stood silent and uneasy as they listened to the hard crack of gunfire, the scurried sound of frantically running feet, followed by an impatient silence:

They were still in the forge … The next thing, somehow they knew that it was Brennan came in and he stood at the door with a gun in his hand and he said 'who's there?' and the reply was 'friends'. So he turned his back and went away. That's what I was told.

It is probable that John Crowe and the other men in the forge clearly indicated their 'friendly' position but it is more likely that a search was made. In fact, one of the participants later recorded that as 'the attack took place opposite a forge into which we thought the two police might have escaped. A thorough search of the forge and of the ground at the rear was made but there was no trace of them.'[24]

Const. Michael Nealis, who testified later that he had been with Brogan, as well as Const. Brennan when confronted by what he claimed were at least fifteen men.[25] Nealis affirmed in court how the IRA men 'fired at us and I saw Constable Brogan fall and Constable Michael Brennan knocked to his knees'.[26] It was also claimed that when Brogan was first wounded, he 'dragged himself to shelter nearby', after which 'three or four more shots were fired at him then, which completely finished him off'.[27] Joe Clancy, the training officer for the East Clare Brigade, was also involved in the Broadford action:

After shooting at Const. Brogan, Brennan and myself went into O'Brien's public house further down the village. As we were going in a policeman was about to get out by the back door, whereupon both of us fired at him and, though he was wounded, he managed to elude us and get back to the barracks.[28]

One piece of local tradition describes the fleeing policeman escaping:

The peeler went in Murnane's gate, ran down the back and that Brennan had followed up and his gun jammed. The peeler was running and Brennan was after him and the peeler told it afterward that Brennan rose his hand and was drawing down for to hit the peeler with the gun. But the peeler knew the run of the ground and when he came to the bank of the river he jumped in and came up the other side … whether Brennan knew the depth of it or not, he didn't jump in and he came back.[29]

With the help of a Kilkee native and teacher, John Haugh, the IRA were soon out of the village. In Broadford, quietness descended in the wake of panic and noise. Whispering inside the forge, John Crowe and the other men slowly and cautiously emerged from Tommy Marsh's forge, only moving as far as a horse car which sat close to the forge, unaware they were feet away from a dead body:

> They fired the Verey lights in the barrack for the military in Tulla. The men who were inside in the forge came out, including my father. There was a horse's car outside and they sat down on the horse's car for a few minutes before they decided what to do. But 'twas dark of course and they paid no heed. But there was a peeler under the car and they didn't know he was shot dead. A man by the name of Brogan – 'Brogan a peeler'. They knew that when the military would come down from Tulla, they wouldn't have a hope, so they made their way home as quickly as they could.[30]

The following day, it was reported that many people in Broadford 'vacated their homes in a state of terror' and that 'every conceivable vehicle' was used to carry as much belongings as possible to safety. Later that day it was recorded that 'refugees were pouring into the Clonlara district'.[31] Earlier, hurlers from Sixmilebridge, on their way to O'Callaghan's Mills had been ordered out of motor cars, their hurleys broken by police and forced to walk home.[32] However, although crown forces demonstrated a show of force in the street of Broadford the night of the shooting, the reprisals seen elsewhere did not materialise.[33]

The attack in Broadford led to the death of Const. Michael Brogan and the wounding of Const. Michael Brennan, a former British solider and member of the Black and Tans. The press reported that Brogan was shot dead at 9.15 p.m.[34] Const. Brogan, who was forty-one when he was killed, was born in Attymon, Loughrea on 16 September 1879 and joined the RIC in 1905.[35] His parents, Thomas and Mary, were both Irish speakers. Brogan served in both Kilkenny and Roscommon before transferring to Clare where he had been stationed in Ennis before arriving in Broadford.[36] He was buried in Loughrea on 28 September 1920.[37] Brogan's father later testified in court that his son was his primary support and had regularly sent him money which helped support 'a delicate brother' who lived at home in Attymon. He received £503 in compensation.[38] Speaking at the same sitting, Sgt Martin Turnbull, a forty-eight year old native of Mayo, declared angrily that 'it was a pitiable thing to think that men who are a credit to the Irish race should be murdered by Irishmen, if they are Irishmen'.[39] It is worth noting that two years previously, Turnbull had been involved in the shooting of an unarmed man, John Ryan, in Castlefergus in March 1918 during a cattle drive.[40]

The attack in Broadford also involved Loughrea native, James Hogan. Four months earlier, Hogan had been appointed professor of History at UCC.[41] A short time into his tenure, he left Cork, joined the East Clare Brigade and spent the following years immersed in the creation of history, before returning to UCC where he dedicated over four decades to its teaching. His father, Michael F. Hogan was a native of Coolreagh in Bodyke and his cousins, James and Michael were both also present in Broadford that night.[42] Hogan was born and raised just five miles from Martin Gildea, who was also a member of the IRA group in Broadford. There is a remarkable irony that both Gildea and Hogan were born and raised approximately five miles from the birthplace of Michael Brogan in Attymon, who the IRA group shot dead that night.[43]

While Rodgers and Gildea were present in Broadford for the attack, McMahon had to wait on the outskirts of the village with Tommy Walle, who had taken ill. As they sat and waited, McMahon and Walle heard the crack of gunshots reach over Violet Hill and to the townland of Claremount where they waited in the dark to see what those sounds meant. When they reunited, his comrades had now been involved in the first killing of an RIC man in east Clare.

'Looking for action' – O'Brien's Bridge

Four days after the Broadford attack, fifty-seven-year-old John Ryan and his seventeen-year-old daughter, Annie May, tended their bar in the main street of O'Brien's Bridge. Given the nature of the troubled time, public houses were not visited with great regularity. The most frequent customers they had were the small section of RIC men based in the village. The RIC men frequenting the bar that evening continued their conversation while Ryan and his daughter busied themselves against the routine of the evening. Annie May then noticed faces peering in the window. It was unsurprising that Constables John O'Keefe and John Downey, who had been sitting at the bar, immediately turned when a noise was heard at the door. Pivoting quickly, they were faced with the rising hands of IRA men, including Michael McMahon, Alphie Rodgers and Martin Gildea.

Constables O'Keefe and Downey were shot at 8.30 p.m.[44] O'Keefe was a thirty-year-old married man from Skibbereen in Cork. John Downey was also a native of Cork and was aged thirty-five.[45] Downey and his wife Margaret had one son, who was six at the time of his death.[46] Dr Joseph Humphreys, the medical doctor for the district who had served in the Royal Army Medical Corps in the First World War, was called to attend to the scene, while a constable was dispatched to Killaloe for Fr John Greed, who administered the last rites to Downey.[47] It was claimed that Downey, who had been in the RIC for eleven years, had in the weeks before his shooting given notice of his intention to resign.[48] During the action, John Ryan's seventeen-year-old daughter Annie May was also shot 'clean through the leg above the ankle'.[49]

The attack in O'Brien's Bridge had begun early on

29 September, when a small IRA unit quietly made their way towards the village of Kilbane. Since the killing of Brogan, several IRA Volunteers had laid low in the Bodyke and Tuamgraney areas, mainly in the home of Paddy McDonnell in Kielta. Before departing McDonnell was told that 'There's another handy job', which he knew meant a further action against crown forces. A boil on the back of his leg meant that McDonnell turned down the invitation on this occasion.[50]

With the help of local republicans, the IRA, including Rodgers, Gildea and McMahon, moved out of Kielta in Tuamgraney. Leaving early on the morning of 29 September, they first travelled through a boggy area known as 'The Lane' in the mountain townland of Caherhurley. The men then crossed Cowmnagun River, leaving Moylussa Mountain on their left and moved into the Sliabh Bearnagh range. After reaching the top of Carrownagown Hill overlooking Kilbane, they descended in the direction of Cloonconry townland, situated in the 3rd Battalion area. On the previous day, the O/C of that battalion, John O'Brien, was arrested with his brother Jeremiah in Ogonnelloe.[51] In Cloonconry, the IRA men approached Jackie 'Bishop' Ryan, who was to replace O'Brien as O/C.[52] In March 1955, Ryan placed his own memories of the event on record:

> The Brigade O/C (Michael Brennan), and three IRA men who were afterwards murdered while prisoners by Auxiliaries and RIC on Killaloe Bridge Michael McMahon (Brod) [sic], Alfred Rogers and Martin Gildea arrived in my house around 11 o'clock in the morning. Each man had a rifle and a revolver. After a meal they opened a conversation with me on the subject of where they would get something to shoot. On my suggestion, it was decided to go into O'Brien's Bridge about three miles away where there were usually Black and Tans and RIC drinking in the public houses during daytime.[53]

The testimony of Jackie 'Bishop' Ryan is illuminating with regard to the increasingly aggressive position adopted by Michael Brennan and partly as a consequence by the IRA under his charge in east Clare. Ryan remembered that 'Brennan was in the mood that if this opportunity had not presented itself he would have gone right into the RIC barracks rather than leave the place without getting one of the enemy.'[54]

Police administrative records show that earlier that day, Constables Joseph Clegg, George Dawson and Robert Niblock, all Black and Tans, had just arrived at O'Brien's Bridge barracks to begin a posting in the area.[55] In the approximately eighteen months the war had raged up to that point, little had occurred in O'Brien's Bridge.

Within hours of their arrival, however, they were introduced to the violence of the conflict in dramatic fashion. As the recruits settled into their new surrounds at the RIC barracks, the IRA unit, including McMahon, Gildea and Rodgers were moving steadily towards O'Brien's Bridge. According to Denis Cusack, who was then a twenty-five-year-old in the townland of Artaggle, the men passed by close to his home. From there they moved on by Spaights, travelled down by the canal at the back of the Mill in O'Brien's Bridge and under the arch of the bridge in the village.[56] The Volunteers then quietly moved to the door of Ryan's public house attached to that barracks, where, beside the entrance, they gently placed their rifles against the wall. With a final nod to his unit, the leader of the group approached the two-part door and lifted his left hand towards the latch, his right tightly enclosing a revolver, which he slowly elevated. Alphie Rodgers, Michael McMahon and Martin Gildea steadied their nerves, gripped their handguns and moved silently behind him:

> I pushed in the door armed with a revolver. As I did, two RIC men swung round from the counter and faced me. I fired at once and there was a burst of firing and I found my right arm numb.

> We retreated, collected our rifles and moved out of the village. I couldn't use my right hand and I could not understand what had happened.[57]

During the shooting, Michael Brennan was hit in the right arm. From the testimony of Jackie Ryan, it seems that he was mistakenly shot by Martin Gildea. Both Rodgers and McMahon were reported to have been at either side of the O/C with Gildea bringing up the rear.[58] Reports indicate that eleven shots were fired and that Downey, who was shot through the heart, died immediately while O'Keefe, having been shot in the stomach, died two hours later.[59]

The IRA group made their way back towards Kilbane, having to assist the weakening Brennan, until they arrived at the home of thirty-eight-year-old Pat Clancy and his wife Bridget in Artaggle later that night. In the distance behind them, over the village of O'Brien's Bridge, Very lights were already drawing attention to the action. At one point, while Bridget was dressing the wound, when Pat Clancy realised the severity of the injury, he ran upstairs to where an earthenware jar had been stored safely. The Volunteers gave a sigh of relief at the vision of what they thought was poitín or a similarly effective substance. The young men were not accustomed to war or killing and awaited the calming effect of the distilled beverage. It was not intoxication that was offered, however, but spiritual cleansing in the form of holy water![60]

At that time, British forces had already arrived in O'Brien's Bridge and began firing shots into several houses, leading to the inhabitants of the village to flee to the outskirts of the area. Through the intervention of the local RIC sergeant, further reprisals were avoided, for a time.[61] Masked and armed crown forces returned a month later, however and, with the help of the RIC, burned at least six houses in the area, fired indiscriminately into homes and beat up several local people.[62]

Back on 29 September, having left Clancys in Artaggle, the IRA men involved in the attack moved to Kilbane where they spent time in the home of Fr Murray. On the top of the mountain separating Kilbane from Caherhurley, McMahon, Rodgers and Gildea informed their commandant that they could not walk any further, having at that point walked for ten hours straight. Brennan departed with other members of the group and moved towards Hogans in Caherhurley. Jackie 'Bishop' Ryan had earlier made his way towards Gunnings of Newtown and from there to the Cratloe area where he spent a considerable period 'on the run', staying in a disused house owned by thirty-six-year-old Larry Ryan in Ballymorris.[63]

Having rested, Rodgers, McMahon and Gildea wearily emerged from the shadow of the Sliabh Bernagh mountain range and moved northwards towards Whitegate, where they spent the following month. They had now been involved, directly and indirectly, in at least three serious IRA actions, including the shooting dead of three constables and the wounding of others. The actions the men took part in were at the hard edge of republican strategy. In both Broadford and O'Brien's Bridge, the RIC had little chance to defend themselves and died relatively brutal deaths. Such was the nature of guerrilla warfare, however, and for McMahon, Rodgers and Gildea, the reality of physical force was accepted.

By November 1920, the RIC were front and centre of the enemy forces for the republican movement. In fact, the day after the O'Brien's Bridge action, the October edition of *An t-Óglách*, the official organ of the Irish Volunteers, foregrounded the central role of the RIC. It underlined how 'the operations of the Black and Tans' would be practically 'impossible without the assistance of the old RIC', who they characterised as 'the real agents and instigators of the campaign of savagery'. The editorial went on to insist that 'without their local knowledge the Black and Tans would be helpless; it is they who mark out men for murder and houses for destruction'. Strikingly, it charged that 'The wretched cut-throats and looters of the "Black and Tans" do not deserve punishment half as much as the cowardly Irish spies of the old "R.I.C." who remain to carry on the dirty work against their countrymen.'[64]

With the IRA in east Clare, putting that call into action, across Bodyke, Tuamgraney and the broader north-east Clare area, the intensifying violence drew more and more people into the trauma of conflict.

'Mobilised under a Local Leader'

Few would escape the consequence of revolution and the British empire's determined attempt to quash it as both sides became increasingly hostile. The *Clare Champion* editorial of 23 October articulated the polarised and entrenched position the country found itself in, declaring; 'The government evidently believes that it will intimidate the people by violence, and the people, it appears, believe that the Government is, or will be, defeated'.[65]

As a result of his wounding in O'Brien's Bridge, Brennan was forced to remain in the Bodyke area for a number of weeks, during which time moving between Scanlons, Hogans, Gleesons, McDonnells and Slatterys in Derrynaheila. This escalation of activity in east Clare had been noted in Dublin by the British authorities. T. J. Smith, the inspector general of the RIC, asserted in his monthly report for October 1920 that 'more desperate men were on the run and were believed to be mobilised under a local leader Michael Brennan'.[66] Such intelligence was put into effect when, on 8 October, two lorries of British forces from Limerick, 'in long coats and soft hats' arrived at his home in Meelick, where his widowed mother and sister were living alone and burned the house to the ground. As well as being a leader of the East Clare IRA, Michael Brennan was at that time chairman of Clare County Council. His brother Austin was chairman of Limerick Board of Guardians and the oldest of the Brennans, Patrick, was clerk of the Limerick Union.[67] All three were 'on the run'.

At the time, Paddy Gleeson was a fifteen-year-old boy living across from the McDonnells, a known republican house. Paddy told me how, on one occasion, he had called to Hogans in Caherhurley with a newspaper when a local Volunteer called with another man who, it seemed to the young Gleeson, was important; 'I was there of a Sunday evening when Eddie Stewart and my teacher Joe Doherty was there as well when they brought in Brennan. That was the first we knew of Brennan or saw him.'[68] He explained that it soon became apparent that the British forces were made aware of the leading IRA man's presence in the area:

> I heard the lorries passing down. I had a dog outside and I heard the dog barking. They took their lorries or Crossly tenders down as far as Coolawn Well and they walked it back to McDonnells. I heard my dog barking and I got up to the window and here they were going towards McDonnells.[69]

On 25 January 1921, Margaret McDonnell, a fifty-eight -year-old widow, and her daughter Bridget, spoke at Ennis Quarter Sessions. They outlined their experience over the previous months when their house in Kielta, Tuamgraney was repeatedly raided and finally burned by British forces.[70]

Although the McDonnell home was raided a reported eighteen times during the War of Independence, the scenes of enraged crown forces became a more regular and frightening occurrence in early October in Kielta, following the Broadford and O'Brien's Bridge attacks. Particularly severe and brutal raids were recorded on 3, 17 and 22 October, as well as 22 November 1920, before the force finally came and burned the house to the ground in December.[71] Paddy McDonnell remembered how on one occasion he found himself on the roof of his house as the crown forces below were raiding:

> There was a trap door in the ceiling. I shoved up the door of the ceiling and I got to the top of the house; but I couldn't put back the trap door. They knocked off the front door ... they were savage and all drunk that night ... I got back to a fireplace and I lay there. I had my rifle with me. 'Is he there?' I heard them shout. 'No he's not' ... 'Oh God,' says I to myself, 'what will I do?' Some of them could go first for I'd shoot them and then they'd murder mother and the girls.'[72]

Paddy Gleeson watched as his townland became the scene of increasingly violent and frantic raiding by crown forces, clearly aware of rebels in the area. At the age of 105, he remembered clearly:

> I was coming on down with my little parcel. A lovely fine night around seven o clock. And when I was comin to Coolreagh cross, Hogans was only five or six hundred yards away, I heard the lorries and the tear-away at Hogan's ... I looked around and I saw nowhere to go and there was a big tree and up I went. I went up on the tree with my messages. Sat down above and hung up my messages and the Black and Tans were all around and raiding Hogans and raiding everywhere and I was a witness to the whole lot of it and still I stayed above on my tree sittin' down.[73]

On another occasion, ominous sounds disrupted the slumber of young Paddy Gleeson. There was trouble once more at McDonnells:

> The Black and Tans arrived to McDonnells and they put Mrs McDonnell and the daughter out with the only thing they had on 'em in bed. We heard knocking at the door at 1.00 a.m. ... So the next thing was I was above at the window looking over and I heard hand grenades and bombs being thrown at the house and big blaze and the house went up ... The daughter told me that she had brought a suitcase of clothes as far as the door and they shoved her out without it. We heard 'em going. They had the house on fire this time. My aunt slipped over and pulled the trunk of clothes out of

the fire. I went over and I knew the back kitchen and there was a pig after being killed a day or two before and I saved the barrel of bacon and a few other things.[74]

Bridget McDonnell also recalled that having arrived at the house in which Paddy Gleeson was staying, she 'went upstairs and on looking through the window, saw her own house in flames'.[75]

While attention was focused on the Bodyke area, in nearby Feakle, the local IRA was preparing to follow their leading comrades in the 4th Battalion.

6

'Praying Hard that their Houses Wouldn't be Burned'

Ambush in Feakle

In early October 1920, while McMahon, Rodgers and Gildea were making their way towards Whitegate in the hope of shelter, attention was being drawn to the parish of Feakle. Hostility had been growing in that area between republicans and police. On Friday 1 October, Const. Sidney J. Longham, arrived at Feakle barracks. Four of his Black and Tan colleagues had reached the village two days earlier and their arrival to bolster the existing crown forces considerably worsened tensions in the area.[1]

A week into their stay, the new Black and Tan recruits learned from their colleagues about the dynamics in Feakle and surrounding areas. Names like Pat Houlihan, Seán Moroney, Joe and Jack Tuohy, Tomo Tuohy and others were surely referred to in disdain as leading 'Shinners'. By 7 October, those men and more prepared to introduce themselves to the crown forces in person.

With Michael Brennan recovering from wounds, Henry O'Mara, Tomo Tuohy and his brother Michael, together with Pat Houlihan, took command of preparations for an ambush on the local crown forces. Several had been previously prepared but did not come off. This operation saw Volunteers based in three principle positions: at Keating's house at the fork of the road leading to Tulla, in both the local post office and Nugent's house to which it was attached, as well as behind the graveyard wall. The ambush site was less than a mile from the RIC barracks. The positioning of the IRA meant the RIC, walking in pairs approximately eight paces apart, would move into a triangular trap. In place from early that morning, the

IRA Volunteers waited, rechecked their weapons and sought to regulate their breathing.

At approximately 9.00 a.m., thirty-eight-year-old Tom Moloney left the post office he ran with his seventy-five-year-old mother Anne.[2] He had earlier opened the door to IRA Volunteers, including Joe Moloney, Pat Houlihan and Tommy O'Meara, who he directed to an upstairs window.[3] In the weeks beforehand, Moloney had been 'held up' by the IRA as he delivered mail to the RIC barracks so the police made the daily journey of just less than a mile to ensure their own post was not intercepted.[4] As he made his way towards the village of Feakle, the RIC emerged onto a road known as the 'Barrack Line' and headed towards the building Moloney had just left. Ahead of them, young Martin Maloney, a scout from Kilanena, sprinted towards Keating's house where he informed the waiting Tomo Tuohy that the police were approaching in the expected formation.

According to one participant, as the leading policemen, Sgt Doherty and Const. Stanley passed Nugent's house near the post office, nineteen-year-old Jack Tuohy fired on Stanley with his shotgun.[5] In the area, Stanley had gained a reputation for his treatment of republicans, with a claim that even his wife accepted he had become obsessed with 'murder'.[6] The previous evening Tuohy had sustained a savage beating from Stanley and so when he saw the forty-six-year-old native of Cork, he opened fire.[7] The ambush only lasted minutes with both Stanley and Doherty fatally injured in the initial gunfire. Constables McFadden and Murphy, who had been walking only yards behind, although slightly wounded, managed to escape into an adjacent field while the RIC men bringing up the rear fired on the attackers.[8]

As the retreating RIC men were reaching the barracks, Const. Stanley's forty-year-old wife Ellen was standing outside, drawn from her home by the sound of gunfire. From her home attached to the barracks, she could make out the shape of her husband's lifeless body.[9] William Stanley had been living in Feakle for over ten years with his wife, whom he married in 1909. They had four children, John Joseph, William, Albert and Catherine, who was two when her father was killed. Ironically, at one point, both Stanley and Joe Sammon, who had been killed in Ennistymon, lived close to each other in the townland of Corlea. Within a matter of just fourteen days, both were dead.[10] Stanley's oldest children, John Joseph and William, were attending the local school the day their father was shot and after the ambush had to walk past the scene. In a bid to reduce the trauma, when passing the site of the action, the children were instructed by the local teacher to walk in single file and to only look towards the graveyard, thereby keeping their eyes away from the dead body of their father.[11]

Sgt Francis Doherty was from Co. Leitrim. Doherty had been previously based in Scariff, where as mentioned on p. 49, he had become embroiled in the defence of Moynoe House and had been involved in several violent confrontations with local rebels. However, according to one of east Clare's most active IRA men, Doherty was not without compassion for local republicans. Paddy McDonnell recorded that at one point, Doherty travelled to his farm in Tuamgraney to warn him that there would be a warrant out for his arrest and encouraged him not to sleep at home. Later, when Joe Nugent from the Feakle Company came to McDonnell to borrow rifles in advance of the Feakle ambush, he pulled his fellow IRA man aside:

> When Joe Nugent and others came for the rifles I asked him what police went for the raid. 'The Sergeant from Scariff,' he said. 'I have a little matter to mention to you before I give you the rifles.' I knew the old sergeant was near his pension at this time. I told him all about the sergeant … 'spare Doherty', I said.[12]

Although McDonnell claimed the men IRA ordered 'hands up' in a bid to spare Doherty, this does not seem to be the case and the forty-six-year-old sergeant was shot dead without warning.

The local curate, Fr Patrick O'Reilly, was called to the scene shortly after the shooting and immediately attended to the men. The young priest waited with the bodies alone from 10.30 a.m. to 2.30 p.m. until the military arrived, saying later of the experience that it was 'a horrible ordeal and I hope I shall never have to endure it again'.[13] Despite the administration of care to the dead, O'Reilly, a thirty-three-year-old native of Corofin, was identified as sympathetic to the rebels and was that night attacked by the same forces. O'Reilly later wrote a detailed account of the incident which chronicled a night of fear for the people of Feakle, during which he was dragged from his house at 6.30 p.m. and 'thrashed soundly' with the stock of a rifle and sticks.[14] At the same time, Fr Jack Kennedy, the curate of nearby Kilanena was passing Feakle and was forced from his car and threatened to be shot.[15]

I interviewed Conor Tuohy from Gurrane in Feakle in 2012, who had spoken to many who remembered the ambush and the events that followed:

> I was speaking to Brud McGuinness and he was goin to school. A lot of people thought it was unnecessary. They [Doherty and Stanley] were fathers of children who were goin to school in Feakle. I remember Brud saying that he was goin to school that morning and how they had to tippy toe out. The bodies were kind of in the way. They had to walk around them you know. They were still there … We always heard the stories of the burning of the houses in Feakle and the burning of the post office … The Black and Tans came along as reprisal.[16]

Soon after the ambush, local people fled to the outskirts of Feakle in fear of reprisals. In Kilbarron, a four-year-old Mae Poll (later Tuohy) watched innocently as old women nervously assembled in her home, less than two miles from where the ambush occurred. In 2011, I asked Mae to describe her childhood memories of the scene:

> I remember the people saying that Feakle was goin to be burned ... There were several people who came down and stayed here all day and all night like. I remember 'em being in a back room ... I do remember 'em and I can see one woman on her knees with the shawl around her head. A lot of the older people wore shawls then ... They were inside in that room, kneeling down in circle, praying hard that their houses wouldn't be burned.[17]

As Mae listened quietly to the sound of prayers in hushed unison, in the village of Feakle, IRA Volunteers were preparing to occupy houses which they expected would be attacked by the crown forces. While they were making their way towards the village with reinforcements from the surrounding area, they observed the burning houses in the distance and realised they had been forestalled.[18] From New Zealand, Fr Martin Bugler wrote in 2014, to communicate his mother's memory of taking in some of those who suffered from those reprisals:

> In retaliation the Tans decided to burn down Johnny and Bridget Nugent's house, next door to the Post Office. Bridget had only barely rounded Pepper's corner when she saw her Bridget go up in flames. With two infants she walked to Ballycorban and found temporary shelter in a shed at Costello's gate, across the road from Conheadys. So my mother and her sisters were the closest of many helpers in their time of need.[19]

A week after the burnings, the *Wicklow People* newspaper quoted one observer in Feakle, who angrily declared; 'Women with babies in their arms fleeing their burning homesteads are a pathetic site to see'.[20] Nine decades later, I listened carefully as one of those babies, carried away by his mother Bridget from her own burning home, spoke forcefully about his early introduction to British rule. In ninety-year-old Seán Nugent's story, there was no doubting who lit those fires. The

RIC reporting of the incident provides a strong illumination of the potential for 'official' records to contain falsehoods. The RIC county inspector for Clare first reported that 'about 100 men' were involved in the ambush and claimed that 'after this, the whole of the able-bodied male population of Feakle fled to the hills'.[21] The figure involved in the ambush was less than thirty, according to the O/C of the Feakle Company, Thomas Tuohy.[22] When reporting on the destruction of homes in the aftermath of the ambush, official RIC reports recorded that the home of Timothy Kelly was burned when a party of 'unknown men' entered the village.[23] They also claimed that 'strange men' burned the furniture and outhouses of Michael Considine of Ayle and that the same 'unknown men' burned the home of Anne Moloney on 8 October.[24] Tuohys in Dromore were among other to have their homes burned beyond repair.

The reprisals continued over three nights with much of the village abandoned.[25] In Furnacetown, another Moloney family were convinced that the crown forces too would burn them out. Both Joe and Mattie, members of the IRA, had participated in the action at Feakle. As Joe's daughter Nuala, who was born in 1926, explained to me in 2011, the presence in their home of a respected medical doctor saved them:

> There was a Dr Stuart from Ogonnelloe staying in our house, as a lodger … He was the doctor for the RIC and he was terribly involved behind the [IRA] scene. They [crown forces] thought that he was their doctor and he was supposed to be very anti the IRA and that kind of thing. That's what they assumed! That's why our house was spared.[26]

The fires that illuminated the skies around Feakle were lit by Black and Tans and members of the RIC. Few of the Black and Tans knew their way around the parish of Feakle. For that, they needed assistance. That assistance was principally offered by Const. John McFadden, a native of Derry who had lived most of his life in Donegal before joining the RIC, like his father Patrick and brothers before him. He had been stationed in Feakle on 17 May 1919 and was intimately familiar with the area, by October 1920.[27] McFadden was shot at and wounded during the ambush that day. He dragged his colleague, Const. Peter Murphy over a gate, from where they made a getaway under fire.[28] McFadden later 'led the Black and Tans to the houses of Volunteers to carry out reprisals'.[29] He was subsequently awarded the constabulary medal for 'gallantry action' in Feakle and promoted to sergeant. Following his promotion, he was moved from Feakle and eventually ended up in the west Clare town of Kilrush fifty-five miles away from the East Clare IRA Brigade, safe for a time.[30] Nine months later, McFadden was shot dead by members of that brigade, who had travelled to attack British forces in that area.[31]

During the reprisals, the home of Fr O'Reilly was raided and after the curate was badly beaten, an effigy dressed in priest's clothing was burned in the street. It was believed locally for a time that it had been Fr O'Reilly who had been burned to death. While the effigy burned, the Black and Tans, accompanied by the RIC, were heard singing 'the rebel Padre is roasting'.[32]

Inside, O'Reilly was crouched in the middle of his kitchen floor while shots were fired in his windows periodically. He later wrote how he expected death and that he 'said the rosary a few times and thought of the Lord Mayor of Cork [Terence MacSwiney] ... I thought of my dear parents and all my dear friends'.[33] The young priest recorded that after 1.00 a.m. 'the attackers knocked at the door very violently', noting that he wisely remained still on the cement floor of his kitchen, instead of opening the door, which moments later was split by a rifle bullet. At 3.30 a.m., O'Reilly crept out to the back of his house and remained hidden in a nearby shed. From there he could hear 'the crackling sound of the burning and the thud of collapsing roofs and falling slates' as homes through Feakle were burned by crown forces. From there he made his way to a safe house in the countryside above Feakle. The following night his house was bombed once again.[34]

Bridget Nugent was married to one of the men involved in planning the attack. She was forced into hiding after the incident with her three children. With her husband a wanted man and himself 'on the run' Bridget, then pregnant, spent a number of months moving from house to house across the Feakle area, during which time she was pursued by the police and military. She was sheltered at the homes of Mrs Conheadys and William Jones. At one point, Bridget was given an abandoned cottage by Rody Costelloe, to which her husband had returned under darkness to help furnish and make somewhat liveable. At 2.00 a.m. on the first night that she rested with her children, the house was raided by Black and Tans and RIC led by Const. McFadden, who tied her to the gate, while his colleagues burned the cottage down.[35] By the side of his bound mother was her two-year-old son, Seán, whose anger at her treatment was palpable ninety years later. What was then incomprehensible noise, heat and fear, decades after was a deeply embedded anger, manifest in Seán's characterisation of the men responsible as 'the most desperate bastards of the worst order'.[36]

While the actions of the British forces in exacting such vicious reprisals and in particular the role of John McFadden left a bitter taste in Feakle, it is important to note that the police were angered by what had happened to two of their colleagues. The military inquiry which met following the ambush in Feakle claimed that Doherty had a rifle wound at the back of his head and several bullet wounds, while Stanley, it found, was killed with a shotgun at very close range. It also claimed that Sgt Doherty had a dog with him that was shot and wounded as it stood beside his master, its three legs being broken.[37] The inquiry also claimed that the IRA used expanding bullets.

The escalating tensions were exasperated by the presence in Feakle of fifty-five-year-old, Fr Michael Hayes, who was known for his anti-republican sentiments. While it was not unusual for parish priests to take a stance against the IRA, the vitriol attributed to Hayes was noteworthy, declaring that the ambush party were a 'murder gang' and that he would not desist until the last of them 'was swung by the neck'.[38] Hayes had a fierce animosity towards women republicans and in particular, the Moroney sisters from Gurtavrulla. One IRA leader recorded how Hayes was 'nasty towards them and inflicted every petty punishment he could', including regularly denouncing them from the alter.[39] Such was the nature of his public attacks on the republican movement and those who supported them (many of whom were in his congregation) that his mass service was eventually boycotted.[40]

Conor Tuohy spoke to me about the moment when the congregation in Feakle, including his own father, decided enough was enough:

> I know my father and a few others on one particular Sunday, Fr Hayes was speaking from the alter, telling them off for their activities against the forces and that. He stood up with others and walked out from his mass and didn't go back to that church for a long time after. For mass they used go over to Clonusker church.[41]

The late Seán Nugent remembered hearing a story about his uncle Joe, a member of the local IRA, more directly confronting Fr Hayes during one particularly harsh sermon on the evils of republicanism. According to Nugent, his uncle removed his coat and approached the alter from the pews, at which the hitherto bombastic priest retreated to the sacristy.[42] In 2014, a Roman Catholic priest and native of

Scariff, wrote to me to convey his knowledge of the period. Fr Martin Bugler referred to the aggressive position adopted by Fr Hayes and described one occasion when a local republican was sufficiently aggrieved to write to the bishop of Killaloe:

> One of 'the lads' [IRA] wrote to Bishop Fogarty reporting that he (and presumably others) was refused Holy Communion. The Bishop replied that it must have been a mistake, which drew a blunt and unassailable 'he went from my right side to my left side'. No possible mistake![43]

Eventually, the bishop visited Feakle to find only six people in attendance for Sunday service.[44] In October also, Fr Hayes' housekeeper, Johanna Slattery was captured by the IRA and transported to her native Tipperary, with a warning that if she returned she would be shot.[45] Slattery had, on the apparent instruction of Hayes, 'become very curious about the IRA' and was reporting their activities in the area.[46] On her way back from a trip to Limerick, Slattery was forcibly removed from her motor car. She was later taken to Cloonamerrin in Mountshannon where under the cover of darkness, forty-year-old David Minogue brought her across Lough Derg to Garrykennedy. From there, Jack Ryan took her on a horse and side car to Nenagh where she was put on the outbound train.[47] Notices were soon posted around east Clare, asserting that if Slattery was not returned, 'prominent Sinn Féiners would be shot at sight'.[48] The threats were ignored. Nevertheless, Slattery was later brought back to Fr Hayes, under an armed British escort.

Nationally, the month of October saw significant incidents, including the killing of four RIC constables in Roscommon, the death on hunger strike of Cork republican Michael Fitzgerald, as well as Seán Treacy, who was killed in a gunfight on Talbot Street, Dublin on the fourteenth of the month. Meanwhile, Rodgers, McMahon and Gildea enjoyed the breathing space which such intensity, particularly in Feakle, three parishes away from where they were in hiding, had offered. In Feakle, more violence was to come.

'Shot at Sight' – the Shooting of Martin Counihan

In Feakle, by late October 1920 a tense atmosphere weighed heavily on the community. In such environments suspicions can rapidly intensify and those seen as in any way to be supportive of British rule became increasingly isolated within the community. By 26 October, the War of Independence was becoming a global issue. In Brixton prison in England, the lord mayor of Cork, Terence MacSwiney died after seventy-four days on hunger strike.[49] Within the relatively enclosed world of a rural parish in 1920 like Feakle, however, the local experience remained primary. The day after MacSwiney's death, on a small road between Feakle and Bodyke, the ferocity and tragedy of the war was played out to dramatic effect.

Martin Counihan, a fifty-three-year-old process server, was making his way from Ballinahinch bog with his fourteen-year-old daughter Nora. Four Volunteers, reportedly digging potatoes in the townland of Annagh, noticed Counihan's approach and decided to act. Suspicions surrounding Counihan had been discussed at an IRA Brigade council meeting chaired by Vice O/C Tom McGrath held in the days beforehand and it was decided that his arrest and court-martial was merited.[50]

Soon, the now-masked IRA men confronted Counihan.[51] His daughter later explained that she and her father had filled a creel of turf and were returning home when 'men came out on the road'. She said in court three months later that her father 'went on his knees and asked them for God's sake to let him home to his wife and children'.[52] In response the men tied a black strip around his eyes and 'took him back the road' while Nora ran to Feakle where she alerted the police. She told the court that the next time she saw her father was in his coffin.[53]

After Nora had left running towards the village of Feakle, Counihan was taken deeper into the townland of Coolreagh, where he was given a court-martial of sorts. According to one of the Volunteers who was present, Counihan was questioned about his alleged spying:

> He admitted having given information to the R.I.C. about the I.R.A., adopted a defiant attitude and said he would whenever he got the chance again notify the police of anything he heard or saw concerning the I.R.A. He was sentenced to be shot and the sentence was carried out that night. I was in charge of the firing party. Though he received the contents of two shotgun cartridges and five .45 revolver bullets, two of which through the head, he managed to make his way to Bodyke three miles away, where he died.[54]

At the time of the incident, Paddy Gleeson was a fifteen-year-old boy living in Coolawn, close to the townland of Coolreagh, south-east of Feakle, less than two miles from where Counihan was shot:

> Poor old Martin Counihan. He had a crowd of children shur … he came down with a little girl, seven or eight years of age with a cart of turf from Coolreagh bog. There were Tuohys digging spuds above in Kilbarron and they were in the Volunteers and they followed him down and shot him inside in Coolreagh bog … They considered that he was a spy and they followed him down to a bog in Coolreagh … Listen to this now … They shot him and they went away at the Clonmoher side of Coolreagh bog, not the Coolreagh side. He came to [regained consciousness] and worked his way out through the bog, thought bog holes and everything out to Coolreagh road. He came on out here to Coolreagh cross and hit for Bodyke. He hit for Noonans. He knocked and this Jack Noonan opened the door and he fell in dead. They brought down Canon Mac.[55]

In an interview with Mae Tuohy, who was born in 1916 outside the village of Feakle, the killing was talked about and Mae, who was just four years of age at the time, heard the story debated, albeit with great caution, over the following decades. Mae accepted that the local IRA 'had their knife in him' because he had given information to the British forces about local Volunteer activity.[56] She also remembered hearing that Nora Counihan ran to the church and prayed at the alter that her father would be safe.[57]

From 2012 to 2015, I corresponded with the grandson of Martin Counihan. It was a delicate and charged correspondence, which only after a period of time began to fully reveal the impact the incident had on the Counihan family. In October 1920, the death of Martin Counihan left a wife and nine children bereaved and his death echoed through the generations of that family and remained palpable when his grandson wrote to me and defended his honour. Liam Counihan, a former US government auditor, died at the age of seventy-nine in April 2016 in New York. He was born in Manhattan in 1937, the son of Martin Counihan Jnr, who was twenty-five when the IRA in Feakle killed his father.

Liam knew Nora, the daughter who ran to alert the police and spoke to her often about that day. Liam was insistent that his grandfather was not an informer and that his death was instead the result of a local grievance.[58] The Tuohy brothers of Dromore, Joe and Jack, were deemed responsible and remembered in America, to where the Counihan family emigrated, as 'cursed Blackguard Brothers'.[59] The family tradition that the funeral of Counihan was 'overflowing with loving neighbours and friends' is unlikely given the context, but the presentation of his grandmother Katherine as 'distraught and weeping as she clung to her 'children for consolement [sic]', seems a more-than-credible image.[60]

Liam's correspondence was sincere and loaded with feeling, reflecting the emotional inheritance which he accepted from his father and his aunt Nora. One of his final communications described the passing of Katherine, Martin's wife, at the age of ninety-seven, forty-one years after her husband's death:

Grandmother Katherine, wore her widow's weave until her death at 97. On her final day, she, still alert as when first married, and putting down her sewing, called to Nora, with great urgency, to get Nora's brother, Michael (her son who helped bring her here to the USA) to come by. Soon, thereafter, she called Nora and Michael into her bedroom, kissed and hugged them, and said goodbye, asking them to wait outside the door and then lay back her head, a few minutes later, they heard her cry out for her Martin and thereafter they entered.[61]

The case of Counihan is one of those events which underlines the tragedy of the war. To the Counihan family, the death of Martin left a deep wound, which was worsened for them by the publicly accepted reason for his death. At a human level, his death was brutal and final, whether he was a spy or was not. A wife was left widowed and nine children without a father. In truth, it is challenging to exonerate the Feakle man against the allegations made against him. Much of the available evidence points to a man who, at the very least, was taking significant risks to demonstrate his opposition to the republican movement. Counihan is listed in the 1911 census as an agricultural labourer, having previously been described as a Process Server in 1901.[62] In 1920, at the time of his death he seems to have retained the previous role as process server or Civil Bill officer.[63] The post placed him in regular contact with the British machinery of justice and carried a social stigma and certainly did not favour the fifty-three-year-old in a time of such heightened political tension. In August 1919, the people of east Clare were warned by an IRA proclamation that anyone seen speaking with police would be 'shot at sight'.[64] When fourteen months later, Martin Counihan openly associated with the police in Feakle, he was knowingly placing himself in danger.

For the IRA, such activity was dangerous to ignore. It was argued by Liam Counihan that the nature of his job meant that he had to liaise with the police. However, the allegations against his grandfather related to the nature of the conversations and the suspicious pattern of police raids that seemed to follow. As the only one present to provide a testimony, Tomo Tuohy's statement is significant and he was quite clear on the motive to shoot Counihan. That a court-martial was held and that the execution was ordered, as Tuohy suggests, is challenging to believe, however. Counihan was confronted and shot within a short period of time. Typically, while IRA court-martials were not drawn out affairs, they required some time for the accused to offer some defence. In addition, given that Counihan's daughter had been released or escaped from the scene, it is more likely the IRA Volunteers involved decided on the spot, if they had not decided already, to execute Counihan. Critically, the fact that he survived the shooting draws attention to the botched and most probably hurried nature of the affair.

Amidst the increasing tensions in Feakle in the weeks and months beforehand, it has been claimed that Counihan adopted a firmly anti-republican position. It was also said that he had been one of the six parishioners who continued to attend mass with the anti-republican Fr Hayes and was seen speaking frequently with the police. Counihan also was one of two Feakle people who attended the funeral of Doherty and Stanley following their shooting by the IRA earlier in October.[65] It was later recorded that the fifty-three year old was 'very busy visiting different areas where he thought active members of the I.R.A. were being harboured'.[66] In areas like Coolagree and Laccroe where an IRA network existed, he was seen watching known IRA men at work, and soon after crown forces descended.[67] In Tuamgraney, Paddy McDonnell noted that Counihan had been long suspected of spying for the British. Once, having arrived back to his home in early October 1920, McDonnell noticed a distinctly red bicycle, which he recorded was believed to have belonged to Counihan:

Wasn't it a fellow from Feakle, Counihan, who was watching the house. I hadn't left it long when the Auxiliaries came from Killaloe ... There were some fellows coming from a dance in Scariff and they passed this fellow. He had no light on his bicycle and one lad who was curious went back to get a match by the way. Someone also had seen him [Counihan] coming out from Scariff, out of the barracks ... they found out that he was a process server ... they connected it up for this was his bicycle, a red bicycle, which he had bought from a postman and it was conspicuous ... He came into Coolreagh Bog on the next Monday and two lads shot him there; but didn't he keep his entrails inside and he walked in the two miles to Bodyke.[68]

Perhaps most significantly of all, the RIC county inspector's October report for 1920 refers to the incident in which 'a man named Counihan who was friendly with the police was cruelly murdered'.[69] It reported that he was 'kidnapped in Dromore with his daughter' and that four disguised men shot him. The report also recorded that Counihan died approximately two hours after being shot, having 'stumbled into the public house of Noonan's bleeding and dying'.[70] The county inspector's admission that Counihan was 'friendly with the police' is noteworthy. For a senior police officer to place on record such a declaration that at a time of unprecedented polarisation between the people and the police, certainly supports the contention that Counihan was either (a) knowingly placing himself in grave danger or (b) providing information about the IRA to the local police. While an understanding of the impact on Counihan's family is important, the irreparable damage done by those willing to provide information to British forces cannot be ignored. Counihan knew that his activity would potentially lead to the deaths of republicans, as well as the savage raids and burnings of the homes he identified. Yet he continued regardless.

One of the men involved in his death recorded that Counihan was 'defiant' at the end. Another IRA officer remembered that 'the lads [IRA] told me that when they moved him out a bit to shoot him, it never took a shake out of him.'[71] Such bravery in the face of his death provided little comfort to a family bereaved. Neither did it soften the generational stigma of a family member shot dead on the allegation of spying. The death of Counihan and the way he died was communicated throughout east Clare and whether the allegations were true or not, no one was left in any doubt about the punishment for informing. Michael Collins once declared that 'spies are not so ready to step into the shoes of their departed confederates'.[72] In north-east Clare, however, it seemed they were. It remains profoundly ironic that the execution of an alleged spy made McMahon, Rodgers and Gildea, then sheltering fourteen miles away in the Whitegate district, no safer from the damage of an informer.

The day after Martin Counihan's violent death, in the townland of Meenross outside Scariff town, sixty-one-year-old farmer James Treacy died. Unlike Counihan, no reference was made to Treacy in any police report and months later, the registrar, Daniel Reidy, simply recorded that his death was the result of 'carcinoma of stomach'. Treacy had suffered for nine months and towards the end of his life was bedridden for some time. Weeks earlier, as violent raids intensified across north-east Clare, British forces arrived at his thatched home close to the River Shannon, where he lived with his wife, Margaret, and five children. During the raid, despite his obvious frailty, James Treacy was manhandled and viciously thrown out of his bed, while the British forces searched for guns or evidence of republican activity. It is difficult to dismiss the obvious impact of such an attack on an already feeble man. His daughter Mary, who was there during the raid, spoke often of 'how weak and frail he was and how cruel they [British forces] were when they barged into their home'.[73] Such actions were typical. When crown forces were readying to burn the thatched home of Thomas Duggan in

Ahaclare, near the village of Broadford, his brother James, a seventy-five-year-old invalid, was severely beaten in the jaw with the butt of a rifle, when his infirmity caused a delay for the impatient arsonists.[74]

By late October 1920, as the conflict reached an unmatched level of violence in east Clare, at least 117 members of the crown forces had been killed nationally. As the month of November dawned, assaults on the British intensified. During one night, 31 October, at least fifty-two policemen were attacked across the country. Six members of the RIC were killed, eight wounded and five taken prisoner in counties as far apart as Kerry and Donegal.[75] The following day, eighteen-year-old Kevin Barry was hanged in Dublin.[76] As October 1920 came to a close, the inspector general of the RIC, Thomas J. Smith sat at his desk in Dublin to compile a report for the previous month. He recorded that the number of 'outrages' which were 'attributable directly or indirectly to Sinn Féin' within Co. Clare, had increased to fifty-eight.[77]

There had been much violence affected by both the IRA and British forces. For those connected to the republican movement, it had been a month of immense tension and disturbance. On both sides, intelligence gathered through various means meant that combatants became increasingly familiar with their enemies. Word spread across the East Clare IRA Brigade that Joseph Henry Booth had been replaced in Killaloe by a new district inspector named Gwynne, a Black and Tan known to be 'a proper scoundrel'. Almost thirty-five years later, one east Clare IRA man revealed that three different ambushes were set to kill Gwynne, at 'Flynn's Mill in Raheen, Hogan's Cross between Tuamgraney and Bodyke and 'The Sweep', a quarter of a mile outside Tuamgraney on the Killaloe road'. In each case, the enemy took another route. Safely behind the walls of Killaloe RIC barracks, Gwynne was emboldened further by the arrival of eight new Black and

Tan recruits on 30 October.[78] With an increasing force, the Black and Tans commandeered a large three-storey house on Main Street in Killaloe owned at the time by Surgeon General Nihil.[79]

The days were darkening in east Clare. The war, it seemed, was finding new and more fearful dimensions. As the war entered the month of November, in Whitegate, three Volunteers had established a regular shelter in Williamstown. Just over eleven miles away by water, Gwynne, Col Andrews and their forces were preparing their next move.

7

'SOLD AND TRACED'

Shelter and Betrayal

Since the attack on the Scariff barracks in mid-September, republicans from the 4th Battalion area of the East Clare IRA had been 'on the run', staying in safe houses across the region or in abandoned buildings, dugouts and sometimes the open countryside. As the months moved on, and with the attacks in Broadford, O'Brien's Bridge and Feakle, more severe raids resulted in a reduction in available safe houses in the area.

Throughout the entire struggle, the safe house had been a vital dimension of the IRA's campaign, as civilians sympathetic to the republican cause offered their homes as refuge to active IRA men. For example, when Michael Brennan led IRA Volunteers, including Rodgers, McMahon and Gildea to O'Brien's Bridge on 29 September, they moved through a network of safe houses before and after the action. Paddy 'Brud' Skeehan, who was a child in O'Brien's Bridge at that time, described the impact of such activities on local homes:

> You had to have a sign about that width now [showing a sheet of paper] with all the names, the father, mother, workmen, tacked to the back of the door … If they called and checked and somebody was missing, you see, you'd have to account to know where was such a one. 'Twas in every house, the time of the Black and Tans … It was all about trying to track down people 'on the run'.[1]

As the battles intensified, safe houses became discernibly fewer, leading to republicans necessarily taking increased risks. On 30 September, following the action in O'Brien's Bridge, McMahon, Rodgers and Gildea parted with their Brigade O/C on the Sliabh Bernagh mountain range between Kilbane and Bodyke. The three Volunteers must have known that they had passed a watershed in their lives. They were told by their O/C that they were now men 'on the run' and were discouraged from returning home so for the following forty-seven days they lived the lives of outlaws.

How that period in their lives was lived and where, has been a source of debate. The degree to which they took caution for their movements and the weight they attached to the ubiquitous danger in the then war-torn east Clare, has been contested. At least five senior east Clare IRA figures have recorded their belief that the men had become somewhat careless about their movements. In the weeks before the shootings, Rodgers and McMahon in particular, were seen occasionally in the town of Scariff. Tuamgraney's Paddy McDonnell recorded how the three Volunteers 'were stopping out the country' but noted how McMahon and Rodgers who 'had big business houses in Scariff' had been seen returning to the town 'to look at their books'. He approached the two men on one such occasion:

> I was afraid that they would be captured and I knew what lay before them if they had been taken. I said to Brud and Alfie, 'Go away for a while, get out of Scariff area until the column is formed' … Brud MacMahon was very sincere and he was a grand fellow. 'Very well Paddy', says he. I said to him 'Now this is an order from your Battalion O/C and you must comply with it', for I wanted to frighten him at the time, for he had a girl. They went on to Whitegate where we couldn't get a Company started. They had friends there and this was a wrong place for them to go.[2]

Tom Hogan, a native of Tulla also met the men in Scariff town and told his son many decades later how he also advised the republicans to be more careful in their movements:

> He met the republicans who were executed, a week previously, marching into Scariff or coming down the street. They had been socialising and they were armed and he advised them to return to the countryside, that the danger being, if word had spread to

Killaloe. But they seemed to treat it lightly and said 'well Tom, if we meet 'em we'll fight 'em.'[3]

For the first weeks of October, while the war was intensifying in nearby Feakle, the three men spent time sheltering in a farm building in the townland of Boleynagough in Whitegate, owned by auctioneer and former rural district councillor, Michael P. Holland, a first cousin of Alphie Rodger's father, Ned.[4] At some point later in October, however, the men began to stay in the unoccupied staff quarters of a large hunting lodge in Whitegate, on the shore of Lough Derg.

Williamstown House was a typical rural sporting lodge, first built in 1834 by the City of Dublin Steam Packet Company.[5] Having passed through several owners, the property was in the possession of a wealthy mill owner from Huddersfield in England named Alfred Ernest Learoyd in 1920 and was situated only 100 yards from Williamstown Harbour.[6] IRA Volunteer Tom McNamara from nearby Mountshannon, also claimed that during this time, McMahon, Gildea and Rodgers:

> were carefree and gay and availed of every opportunity of enjoying themselves. Unfortunately, in the times that were in it, such a life in the case of men who were 'wanted' carried considerable risks, at dances particularly ... They drove around the countryside quite openly in a pony and trap and made it known from their movements where they were staying.[7]

The period that McNamara referred to seemed to have been late October and early November, just weeks before their capture. It is unmistakable now that their movements were observed by at least one person who made contact with British forces and drew attention to their presence in the area. The carelessness of the men inevitably expanded the number of people who observed their movements. It presented the opportunity for both a direct reporting of their presence by an informer and also the likelihood that 'loose talk' drew attention to their whereabouts as the RIC used casual conversation to obtain local information.[8] However such passive intelligence-gathering was impossible in November 1920 as a result of the boycott enacted the previous year, indicating further that their betrayal was a conscious act. There is no doubt the crown forces were actively seeking information and prepared to remunerate those who provided it. It is at this point that a native of Co. Clare, positioned in the heart of G Company, elevates to prominence in the story.

Adding further to the revelation that Irish men were intensely involved in the deepest levels of British warfare, is the presence in G Company of Capt. Patrick Cullinan, an ex-British army officer born in Newmarket-on-Fergus. In Newmarket, he was remembered for having 'taken a very strong British view on things and for dressing very posh and behaving like the proper British gentleman'. Annie McNamara, who was a neighbour of the Cullinans, told her son how Patrick, who converted to Protestantism, once removed Catholic religious pictures from his parents' home and was thrown out a result.[9] A former captain in the Leinster Regiment, he joined G Company as a platoon commander only weeks before the murders and was notably promoted to intelligence officer only two days after the men were captured and murdered.[10] His promotion to the third highest rank in the company cannot be ignored and neither can a possible connection to his role in the gathering of information on the whereabouts of the three IRA men, be overlooked.

On 9 November 1920, Francis William Dudley Fletcher, a fifty-five-year-old from Dublin and inspector of navigation at the Office of Public Works, received a communication from a senior police official. It seemed that McMahon, Rodgers and Gildea had been staying in Williamstown for at least a week at the time this communiqué was dispatched. Lt

Col Andrews, the head of the newly arrived Auxiliary force in Killaloe, had written to Fletcher to request the loan of an inspection steamer, *SS Shannon*. Andrews claimed that he required the steamer 'for two or three runs around the lake'.[11] Fletcher complied and the boat, which was then undergoing a boiler inspection, was placed at the disposal of the Auxiliaries a week later.

With the boat being repaired, McMahon, Rodgers and Gildea continued to shelter at Williamstown. In a statement made on 11 March 1956, Joseph Clancy, the brigade training officer of the East Clare IRA, claimed that he had been sent by the Brigade O/C to warn the three Volunteers:

> They were all very young and after going on the run did not take any precautions to conceal their haunts. The sleeping quarters which they had selected was in an old store in Whitegate, which they entered and left at all times of the day. It soon became common knowledge that they were staying there and I was sent by Michael Brennan to warn them to leave the place and be more careful about their movements.[12]

When Clancy, a native of Teeronea, Kilkishen made his statement, he was fifty-four years of age. Ironically, in 1920, although a veteran of the First World War, when he approached McMahon, Gildea and Rodgers, he was younger than all three. Paddy McDonnell also travelled to Whitegate to meet the men and was told by Paddy McInerney from the Mountshannon IRA Company that the men had been staying in Williamstown for approximately two weeks:

> They were in a coach house; it was very small and snug and there was a loft in it with a ladder by which they could go upstairs. They were up in the loft when I came there and I told them that I was going to form the [Flying] Column. 'You shouldn't be here,' I told them ... 'Are you armed?' I asked them. 'Have you sufficient stuff?' For they had two Webleys .43 I had a good deal of ammunition at the time. I gave Alfie 4 or 5 [rounds] of ammunition.[13]

McDonnell suggested that this meeting took place the night before they were captured and he instructed the men to be at his house the following morning. In that case, the implication is that if the men had been at Kielta to meet with McDonnell, they would not have been apprehended. However, his chronology is questionable. For example, he recounted how the following morning, he was told how; 'There was terrible work in Whitegate last night' and that 'Alfie and Brud were riddled by the Black and Tans.'[14] This does not match with the sequence, however, as to follow McDonnell's recollection, the men would only have been captured that morning and not been killed until late that night. It is probable that McDonnell was in Williamstown in the week before their capture but perhaps not on the night beforehand.

Tommy Bolton, a seventeen-year-old Volunteer at the time, remembered the incident in 1989 with a deep sadness and also suggested the men had been warned:

> Old George Sparling told 'em not to stay there [Williamstown]. He sent them an account not to stay there and he had only the account sent when they were caught. They had to come down on a boat, down Lough Derg and to come in and held 'em there so long and brought 'em out to the bridge, the four of 'em and shot 'em. Oh the Lord save us! That was the most desperate thing of all. I felt terrible for them. I knew them four young fellas well.[15]

'Sold and Traced through Galway'

During my research, I discovered evidence to indicate that the three men may have been more aware of the danger that surrounded them than is commonly thought. Firstly, it was revealed in a 1976 recording, discovered in 2020, that instead of staying at Williamstown for weeks, the three young Volunteers regularly moved between there and Islandmore, a 218-acre island on Lough Derg, less than two miles by boat directly from Williamstown.

Paddy O'Meara who was born in 1894, is recorded confirming 'shur every second night they were in Islandmore'.[16] He later told how in the dark of night, he would lead the men from Williamstown with a storm lantern to his boat and quietly row across to Islandmore.[17] The home of Paddy's father, Frank, was a safe house for the IRA generally. The island was a relatively secure hideout but with the only escape route a boat to either the Tipperary or Clare side of the lake, it was not a place that would be used for long. Paddy's sister, Ellen, told her son, Tommy Holland, how the home was frequently raided. She also recalled how the family were regularly fired on by British forces as they went to and from the island and would have to lie down in the hull of their boat until they were safe.[18]

Despite alternating their hideout, in the days before their capture, it is now clear that the men had realised the danger of remaining too long in the same area and attempted to move towards Galway for greater security. It has been possible, through a series of interviews undertaken between 2005 and 2020, to trace the movements of Rodgers, McMahon and Gildea from Williamstown to Ashbrook in east Galway, as they made a final effort to remove themselves from the threat of informers.

Born in 1930, Kathleen Mitchell was raised in Cappataggle and only heard about her uncle Martin Gildea when she returned to New Inn as a teenager; 'When I came back to New Inn then, Dad used to be talking about it. That the first time I heard about it and visitors to the house used to be talking about it'.[19] Kathleen remembered her father speaking about the lead up to Martin's death and revealed that he and his comrades had travelled to Martin's native townland of Ashbrook in the days beforehand. Gildea was aware that there was danger in travelling to his home place, as a previous occasion illustrated when he returned to visit his sick father on his own:

Martin's father was very ill and he was dying and my mother wrote to him. He was working in Sparlings in Scariff and she wrote and told him to come down to see his father before he died. So he came to Woodlawn station and an RIC man seen him. He went up home to Ashbrook and sometime my mother went out to get water. 'Twas dark and she saw [the RIC man] looking in the window. So Martin left on a bicycle for Loughrea to go back to Scariff.[20]

With increasing pressure to move from Williamstown, Martin and his comrades had little option but to move once more towards the east Galway area. Considering the testimonies associated with their time in Williamstown, it is likely the men decided to move sometime around 10 or 11 November. Having discussed the move with Michael P. Holland of Nutgrove, it was suggested that a house in Gorteeny over six miles away may have offered an alternative refuge for a time. However, the Page family, although sympathetic to the rebels, were frightened to shelter the IRA men, as their house was positioned close to the road and vulnerable to raids.

McMahon, Rodgers and Gildea then made the decision to move northwards in the direction of Gildea's home parish of New Inn. Having travelled over a further eleven miles across country, the three republicans arrived in the townland of Shangarry. There, the Geoghegan family were connected to the republican movement, with thirty-three year old Bernard an officer in the Loughrea Battalion.[21] Martin Gildea, who knew the family, hoped he and his comrades could rest for a while. However, with increasing crown force activity in the area, the Geoghegans were similarly not in a position to offer shelter for long. So, with little rest, Martin led his two comrades towards his native home in Ashbrook, New Inn, seven miles from Shangarry. He did so in the worrying knowledge that the last time he was there, he had to flee having been spied on. Joe Duane, the grandnephew of Martin Gildea, inherited family tradition associated with the incident. During a field recording in Gildea's native area, he described to me the journey to Ashbrook for Martin and his comrades:

> Martin Gildea would have known that country very well of course so he could find his way across that area easily. They went across Curra Bog and then from there went down through Glanaskehy bog on their way to New Inn and on out to Ashbrook towards Martin's home place. They couldn't go back to where Martin was raised at Ryan's estate because all the workers would have seen them so they went on to the old home place where Martin's father came from. They met some of the family there and they were not there long when they realised they were being spied on. They had to go out on the road again.[22]

Having arranged to meet his family at the ancestral home of his father in a place previously known as Bouilagh, the men are likely to have arrived sometime between 12 and 13 November. Having made it to the apparent comfort of Bouilagh, there was little occasion for reunion as the men soon realised their presence had been noted by forces loyal to the British crown. The three men then began a cautious move back southwards across the east Galway countryside. Having made their way to Tynagh, they were next seen in Power's Cross, having travelled twenty miles from Ashbrook:

> They were spotted around Power's Cross between Portumna and Woodford. They went in there looking for food and they were reported there as well. I think they had just got some bread and tea but they were followed there too so they had to keep going towards Clare. So they were ran out of Ashbrook and then on to Power's Cross and from there on to Gorteeny.[23]

In a recording with Michael Joe Tarpey from Woodford, it was revealed that the men passed through Power's Cross on Sunday evening, 14 November where they bought a loaf of bread and a pot of jam, before moving on in the direction of Gorteeny.[24] In November 1996, ninety-two-year-old Anthony 'Sonny' Hackett was video recorded by John Joe

Conwell in Co. Galway. In November 1920, Sonny was a fourteen-year-old boy living in Gorteeny where he worked in Hogan's public house. He was there at the same time as McMahon, Rodgers and Gildea were making their arduous journey through that locality. Speaking seventy-six year later, Sonny revealed that he actually met with the three Volunteers when they entered the town looking for shelter. His testimony also confirmed that they were being followed by police and underlined the danger and intense pressure that surrounded the wanted young men:

> The three boys arrived in Gorteeny … The man at the house at Hogans was a great man for the Volunteers.[25] He seen to them. He regulated where they would be for the night. There was a little house … the people that had this little house, they'd have pigs on the kitchen floor and they'd have bags of corn on the loft. This is in November now! So Hogan says to me, 'these boys', he says, 'they're goin down to the little house, will you show them the way?' 'I will of course', say I … So I brought them down and showed them where to go and they went upstairs and the pigs underneath them and they lay on the bags of straw and there was a couple of old blankets that I brought down for them … So around ten o'clock in the morning, I went down to them. To make sure they knew who was coming I started whistling or singing or something. So I went up the stairs and there they were the three craters, lying on the aul bags. They had the aul guns thrown around.[26]

That morning, while delivering a message to Woodford, Sonny saw six policemen on the road, evidently tracking McMahon, Rodgers and Gildea. He recounted that after entering Gorteeny, the police had a drink at Hogans and next made a peculiarly targeted search for the republicans. At one point the six RIC men were standing at the turn of a botharín, where they 'stood there at the corner and took great observations'. Strikingly, Sonny revealed that McMahon, Rodgers and Gildea 'were above and they behind the fur and they peeping out at them.' Having evaded their chasers, the three Volunteers moved cautiously out of Gorteeny and towards Whitegate, seven miles away. On their way, they encountered the grandfather of the late Dermot Moran, who recalled that meeting to his grandson many years later:

> My grandfather used to speak very sadly about how he saw the three of them on the road near Gorteeny. He knew them because he would have been in and out of Scariff a lot over the years. He had a few words with them but they said they wanted to keep going. I remember him saying they looked desperate tired. Shur they must have had a fierce distance walked. Ah, he used to get very sad when he'd speak about that and it would be very seldom he would. He used to say 'that's the last I saw of them on this earth'.[27]

After a round trip of over fifty miles to Ashbrook with little rest, they arrived, exhausted and hungry back at the Holland home in Nutgrove. There, a surprised Mary Joe Holland greeted them resignedly; 'For God's sake, what brought ye back down here?' Choosing not to explain the series of rejections and pressures that followed them, Alphie Rodgers light-heartedly responded 'Shur we couldn't do without ye!'[28] Having made an effort to move from danger, it followed them and pushed them back towards a place that should have been safe.

After a rest the three young men are next recorded on Monday 15 November, working in the Holland farmyard. Tommy Holland explained to me how the three men helped the Hollands prepare corn for transportation to the mill and also took wheels off a horse car that required mending. While the men set to work on the cart wheels, on the same day in Geneva, the General Assembly of the League of Nations sat for the first time. For Rodgers, McMahon and Gildea, the ideals of the League were of no assistance in north-east Clare. As the men busied themselves with the Hollands, a local man was seen looking in to the yard from the roadway, but soon moved on. At the time, it was not considered noteworthy. In light of what happened the following day, however, that spectre deepened profoundly in significance.

Deep into the month of November, darkness was never far away and the men retired for the evening. Before leaving Hollands, the three republicans had tea made by Mary Joe Holland, who instructed them to be down for breakfast early the following morning.[29] The horse cart was left unfinished. They never returned to complete that job and, a century later, the cart wheels remain untouched in Holland's farmhouse in Nutgrove.[30]

That night, McMahon, Rodgers and Gildea left with Tom and Johnny Holland, together with twenty-seven-year-old, Paddy O'Meara from Islandmore and headed to Williams-town House. Having played cards for a few hours, the two Hollands left for their home nearby. The three IRA men convinced O'Meara to wait until morning to return to his island homestead and they continued to play cards into the night.[31]

Eleven miles of water separated them from Killaloe, where at that time, Col Richard John Andrews and Lt Alexander Mulloy Faraday were in deep discussion about plans for the following day. Information had already come to the British auxiliaries about the three wanted IRA men and they had been told McMahon, Rodgers and Gildea had been seen in the Whitegate area in the weeks beforehand. It now seems obvious that a final message had come to confirm the rebels were once again back at Williamstown. The British decided to make their move.

Within the Lakeside Hotel, the prospect of capturing the three wanted republicans had fired up the enthusiasm of the Auxiliaries. As preparations advanced, a thirty-four-year-old former English solider who had been posted to G Company just weeks before, left the hotel and made his way across the bridge to Killaloe town. Herbert Pritchard walked directly ahead and entered a public house on Bridge Street. There, Ida Maloney, who he befriended since arriving in Killaloe a month earlier, was working. It is not known why, but Pritchard quietly revealed to Ida, the plans then being fine-tuned at the Lakeside Hotel. She left the pub almost immediately. Bella Lucas later recorded how on Monday 15 November, she 'received information from Mrs Maloney that the Auxiliaries were going to raid Williamstown House, Whitegate, where some IRA were staying.'[32] Bella then explained how she and her husband to be, Percy Lucas, franticly made their way to Garrykennedy by bicycle, where forty-five-year-old boatman, Jeremiah Gleeson provided a vessel to take them across the one-mile journey to the Clare shore of a darkened Lough Derg. Having arrived at Church Bay, they moved towards Whitegate. On the way they met thirty-six-year-old Patrick Burke, from Drumaan House, who Percy knew. Bella later recorded, 'I gave him the message to tell the boys in Williamstown House, the information I had'.[33] Bella and Percy then returned towards Church Bay. The young couple quietly moved out onto the waters of Lough Derg, happy that they had forestalled the Auxiliaries, who they believed would find an empty house in place of their prey. Later, Burke claimed to Bella Lucas that he had relayed the information to the men in Williamstown.

Whether Patrick Burke, who later became a Fine Gael TD, did in fact pass on that information, is difficult to confirm. It is certainly hard to believe that such a warning would go unheeded by the men, particularly having gone to such lengths to avoid danger the previous week. It would be astonishing that Paddy O'Meara, not a member of the IRA, would have stayed with them that night if he knew of such an imminent threat. What is known, is that information existed that G Company were coming to Williamstown, yet the men remained in a strikingly vulnerable position, even if they had not suspected the Auxiliaries would arrive by boat. Seemingly unperturbed, the three IRA Volunteers, with O'Meara, continued to play cards late into the night at Williamstown, before all four bedded down in the staff quarters and fell asleep.

Although it is now evident that the men had made efforts to safeguard themselves, it seems certain that in the weeks before their capture, the three IRA Volunteers had relaxed what were then vital safety precautions and had begun to flaunt somewhat their presence in the area. Although armed and aware of the danger that the period presented, the lack of police presence in the broader area, combined with the boldness of youth and daring that IRA activism stimulated, Rodgers, McMahon and Gildea took risks. The reality that there were at least four IRA dugouts within five miles of Williamstown, also suggests the men were perhaps not prepared to endure the type of rough outdoor experience that other republicans tolerated, a suggestion that led to the labelling of the term 'shop boys' on the men by some.[34]

Tragically, however, their final efforts to heed the warnings of their comrades and move from the area were thwarted by the very danger that waited for them in north-east Clare. It is possible that senior IRA figures like Clancy, McDonnell and McNamara did not know that the young men had attempted to remove themselves from danger, only to be forced to return. What is clear is that their return was observed and reported to the crown forces in Killaloe. A dramatic late effort was made to reach the three men with a final warning the night before their capture. This ultimately failed and so began the final chapter of their story.

8

'WITHOUT CLERGY, JUDGE OR JURY'

Capture and Death

In early November 1920, word had come to the people of Killaloe that a new force was arriving in the town. At first, it was felt that the anticipated officers would assist in controlling the Black and Tans whose presence had increased since the attack on Scariff RIC barracks.[1] Days previously, on 30 October, an additional eight Black and Tans had reached the barracks at Killaloe, further bolstering an increasingly aggressive police presence.[2] What arrived, however, proved a deadlier force and left a mark perhaps more indelible.

The previous weeks in east Clare had demonstrated both the determination and ruthlessness of the IRA. In the first week of November, G Company of the Auxiliaries arrived by train to Killaloe and established their base at the Lakeside Hotel in Ballina, Co. Tipperary, which had been commandeered by British crown forces from May 1916.[3] Their arrival in the county as one of eighteen companies nationally is undoubtedly an indication of the levels of IRA activity in Clare.[4] Crozier, the leader of the force, characterised such areas as 'hot spots'.[5]

G Company arrived at Killaloe with 109 officers, forming four platoons of approximately twenty-five, two Ford cars and six Crossley Tenders. The liaised closely with the RIC across the River Shannon in Killaloe, a garrison consisting of at least seventeen members of the RIC in addition to eighteen Black and Tans.[6] Forty-four-year-old Lt Col Richard John Andrews, a veteran of the First World War, commanded G Company. Andrews had previously spent a number of months in a Bolshevik prison camp, after he had been taken prisoner when the Fifth North Russian Rifles he was grouped with mutinied. On their first night in East Clare, G Company burned three houses and caused £13,000 pounds worth of damage.[7] Immediately, they set about stamping their dominance on the local population. One eyewitness wrote that following a day's demonstration of machine gun fire in Killaloe aimed at intimidating the locals, the colonel of the Auxiliaries strode through the town 'pushing his revolver against men whom he met, threatening to shoot, and insisting that all shops should be closed at seven o'clock.'[8] Andrews had been made aware on arrival about the increasing IRA violence in the area over the preceding two months. Five members of the RIC had been killed, one spy had been executed, and at least seven RIC barracks or outposts destroyed. Andrews' approach was evident from the beginning. A group of auxiliaries who were later transferred to Killaloe were told plainly by the colonel, 'The only way we will beat these bastards is to fight fire with fire. We will be fair where we can but as the IRA does not adhere to any principles of war, neither can we'.[9] A former British civil servant in the town at that time recalled the very public response:

> On the Monday afternoon I was walking across the bridge from Killaloe to Ballina – once it was a beautiful spot, it now seems to wear an ominous and sinister aspect – accompanied by my wife and another lady. All was quiet, but we saw a number of the Auxiliary Police coming down from the Lakeside Hotel towards the village of Ballina. They carried rifles and other arms and were led by their C.O. an officer who is distinguished by the title of colonel. He carried a revolver and walked in a strikingly determined manner. Orders were suddenly shouted, the troops spread out through the village, and there was a general hold-up. The men within sight were ordered to stop and put up their hands.[10]

Such public acts had an aim: intimidation. From their base at Killaloe, G Company launched raid after raid into the surrounding countryside. In most cases the raids were deliberately visible. During this time at Ballyvalley, north of Killaloe town, sixteen-year-old John O'Byrne had a view across Lough Derg to the Lakeside Hotel. In 1978, in a recording with the historian Seán Kierse he remembered:

> I was watching the Auxies at the Lakeside kicking football in the field beside the hotel. Suddenly there was the sound of gunfire … they disappeared into the Hotel and soon afterwards I saw ten or twelve tenders with the soldiers heading along the road in the direction of Scariff.[11]

IRA intelligence established that during such excursions, the Auxiliaries posted two men to the post office in Killaloe to ensure that no wires were sent hurriedly to warn outlying IRA units.[12] This was not the limit of their efforts to quell the local population, however. Soon intelligence work was underway and information began to come to the Auxiliaries about the whereabouts of wanted IRA men. The information pointed towards Whitegate and before long specific preparations were made. On Monday 15 November, the *SS Shannon*, was ordered to be brought to the Lakeside Hotel the following morning. It is evident that a final tip off came to Killaloe and meant that on Tuesday 16 November 1920, G Company moved out of Killaloe to pursue their prey and they knew exactly where to go.

'That Day of Sad Renown'

Day broke in Whitegate on Tuesday 16 November, just before 7.00 a.m. Twenty-seven-year-old Paddy O'Meara woke early in a room at Williamstown House. He glanced at the sleeping shapes of three men who late into the night before, he had played cards with, talked and laughed.[13] He shook away his tiredness and quietly put on his boots, before heading towards the shore of Lough Derg. Soon he was pushing his clinker-built cot into the water and steadily rowing towards his native Islandmore. For farmers like Paddy, there was always some work to be done. Inside a loft at the back of Williamstown, his young friends slept soundly. With his eyes fixed somewhere between the bow and the water and his mind elsewhere, Paddy had no idea he would be the last man to see the men live a carefree moment.

Before long, Michael Egan walked the short distance from his aunt's home at 'Sosie's Cross' towards Williamstown House, where he was employed as a caretaker. Twenty-three-year-old Egan began to work at Williamstown just months beforehand, when he'd replaced Joseph Flanagan, who had emigrated to the United States.[14]

As Michael Egan made his way to work, in Killaloe, Joe McEvoy, George Shouldice and Joe Hogan, the crew of the *SS Shannon*, had just arrived to their work.[15] The morning was not unusual and the men were ready to undertake their routine tasks when they were given an order to take the boat to the Lakeside Hotel. Hogan, the boat's deckhand, remembered the morning clearly over three decades later:

> We were all aboard early on the morning of the 16th November, 1920. About nine o'clock skipper McEvoy was directed by Mr Dudley Fletcher, the district engineer, to get the boat ready and bring her straight up to the jetty near the Lakeside Hotel – there was to be no delay.[16]

It was 9.30 a.m., when Hogan and his crew members moored *The Shannon* at the jetty close to the Lakeside Hotel, known then to locals as the Duke of York Quay.[17] Close by, forty-two year old storeman John Guerin and his young colleague Mike Daly were loading a canal boat, when they observed 'a crowd of men in civilian clothes, not uniform' walking from the Lakeside and boarding the steamer.[18] As Guerin and Daly watched the last of the men climb aboard the boat, inside Joe Hogan tried to maintain an outward calm:

> A party of about thirty Auxies with four officers came from the

hotel and boarded the boat. All the Auxies went down below to the cabins except three, who kept guard over the skipper and myself in the wheel-house. None of us – the crew – knew where we were going. Nobody on the boat could be seen. We were ordered to pull out up the lake and go ahead.[19]

Hogan had already fed water into a boiler which had begun to produce steam when the Auxiliary force boarded. Before long that steam had pushed open the valve on the side of the boat's piston cylinder, indicating that she was ready to move. With an audible hiss, the *SS Shannon* began to move out of Killaloe and into the waters of Lough Derg in the direction of Whitegate, where it arrived less than two hours later.

At Williamstown, Alphie Rodgers, Michael 'Brud' McMahon and Martin Gildea were still asleep, unaware of the encroaching danger moving steadily towards them. Less than four miles away from where they slept, in the townland of Derrycon, Mountshannon, thirty-two-year-old IRA Volunteer, Paddy Muggivan stood on his land and peered through a hand-held telescope, requisitioned by the republican movement for observing movements on Lough Derg. He was startled to see a steamer appear in his vision on the far shore of Lough Derg. His first thoughts were about his three IRA comrades in Williamstown House, close to where the boat was moving. The men were meant to have vacated the hideout, and the boat, he observed, was on the far shore of the lake, which indicated it would pass on and make its way up the Shannon. Nevertheless, Muggivan was worried. His son told me how this vision formed a perpetual regret on the memory of Paddy Muggivan:

The boat came up and it went on the far shore ... the far shore is deep there ... He had glasses here to watch the Shannon, a spy glass, the long one and he picked up the boat on the far side ... it didn't seem to come to Williamstown and suddenly it turned for Williamstown and he knew the lads were there but they were supposed to be gone out of it. He wanted to make sure so he ran to Pat Dinan's and Tommy was there. He was only about fourteen or fifteen and they went out and they saw the last of the boat coming in and the trees cut it off and he said 'They are going in to Williamstown'. Tommy Dinan offered to run to Williamstown but he wouldn't make it. They were supposed to be gone but they weren't.[20]

Approximately ten minutes later, the *SS Shannon* came into view of Williamstown House. On board, the deckhand observed, 'When the boat came opposite Williamstown House I was ordered to pull into the pier. The whole Auxie party, except one guard, got off quickly and, crouching, stole towards the Great House.'[21]

Inside, Rodgers, McMahon and Gildea slept. Having silently made their way to the front of Williamstown House, the order was given to enter by twenty-one-year-old American-born Lt John Alexander Faraday, who was leading the raid. In the kitchen of the house, Faraday first encountered Michael Egan. Egan was questioned if the three IRA men were inside the house. He told them no one was there. It had previously been believed locally that Egan was cutting a hedge outside the house when the Auxiliaries confronted him.[22] There too was Michael's younger sister, Annie, who had come that morning to visit her brother. Annie later testified that she was in the house when the Auxiliaries arrived and watched, frightened, as they roughly took her brother away.[23] For Michael Egan, who was not an IRA Volunteer and had no known previous engagement with the British forces, the presence of armed Auxiliaries must have been a frightening experience. Despite this, he continued to deny the presence of the three IRA men.

Before long, Faraday and the Auxiliaries under his command were outside the door of McMahon, Rodgers and Gildea. It is not known who woke first or what was said, but the glances exchanged among the three young Volunteers were undoubtedly fearful. A primal fear that sent adrenaline flooding through their systems, making their breathing hurried, their heartbeats rapid and their eyes wide. At the other side of the door, heavily armed auxiliaries screamed with frightening hostility. Inside stood three young rebels gradually realising the danger they now had to face. The only way out was to open the door to their enemies.

Faraday recorded in his statement to the British Military Court of Inquiry that he discovered Rodgers, Gildea and McMahon in the stable, 'locked in one room'. He told the court that they 'were undressed at the time and at first refused to open the door.'[24] He then noted that 'they did open when I threatened to fire through the lock'.[25] It was later claimed that the men were armed and that they had in their possession expanding or 'dum dum' bullets. Faraday gave further details of the arrest two days later:

> Rodgers was armed with an automatic fully loaded. Kildea *(sic)* had a revolver with three fired cartridges and two live rounds. They were expanding bullets. A cross had been cut in the nose of them. I searched all the men and found Sinn Féin propaganda and more expanding bullets on all of them. They all said they belonged to the IRA. Kildea *(sic)* said he had not left his room for a fortnight when he had been shooting birds … They both said they had the arms to defend themselves against the police and had them two years. Kildea *(sic)* said that he got the revolver from a man called Haren, an American, who has left for America. Rodgers said that his automatic had been given to him in a discharged condition. He refused to give the name.[26]

Captured, the three Volunteers, together with Michael Egan, were taken and forced to board the SS *Shannon*. Speaking just two months later, Annie Egan testified that the Auxiliaries 'took her brother and three other men away with them'. She recorded that they 'first tied them with ropes, then brought them to a boat and carried them off' and told the court at the end of her testimony that 'I never saw my brother again'.[27]

The four men, who later became known as the Scariff Martyrs, had been arrested under the Restoration of Order Act at approximately 1.00 p.m. on Tuesday 16 November 1920.[28]

Close by, two brothers made their way with a calm purpose towards a field on their land to cut scallops.[29] In that locality, the connection of the Conway brothers was always included as part of the story. Michael 'Hookey' Farrell grew up hearing stories of the War of Independence. He remembered being a small child in bed with his siblings when large uniformed Black and Tans came into his room to look for Volunteers 'on the run'. He too heard the story of the Scariff Martyrs and the connection of his neighbours, the Conways:

> They went in that morning into the back of where they were caught and they were cutting scallops [for thatching]. Didn't the Tans come in and didn't they spot 'em and they said come on, 'come on, come on, come in here to us' … shur the poor Conways nearly died. Shur they were as innocent as the flowers of May.[30]

In a hugely significant interview conducted by Brian Graney, a researcher from Maynooth University in 1953, John Conway, was invited to outline his memories of that day:

> On Tuesday, November 16th 1920 (I'll never forget it) my brother, Michael, my mother and myself had our dinner about twelve o'clock. Mick left to get Mike Egan to put a handle on the hatchet and I went out to cut scallops. I went along the road towards Williamstown House and walked right into the arms of the Auxies. They were dressed in plain clothes and spoke with English accents. I never expected them for I heard no lorries. They questioned me about the I.R.A. and the strangers who had been staying around the place. They searched me and found a bottle of milk in my pocket and tried to make me say that I was bringing it to the strangers. I had it for myself but when I wouldn't say I had it for 'the boys' they marched me away down to the pier where I saw the commissioner's boat.[31]

At Williamstown Harbour, Faraday had divided the Auxiliary section up with a group sent to the neighbouring houses to search for incriminating evidence. In Nutgrove, the Holland family were confronted by a section of aggressive Auxiliaries, who smashed and broke their way through their possessions. Fifty-eight-year-old Michael P. Holland and his wife Annie looked on as the Auxiliaries roughly searched their home and knew that their connection to the IRA men and the presence of incriminating documents in their home would bring consequences. They did not move, but their youngest daughter did. Mary Joe Holland crept out the back of the house with a biscuit tin in her arms, which she buried quickly. It has remained buried since that day.[32] The tin was reportedly full of republican court papers, which had been left in the house by her cousin Alphie Rodgers. Had the Auxiliaries located the documents, other members of the Holland family would have certainly been taken captive also.

Having found nothing incriminating, the attention of the auxiliaries moved to the many outhouses in the farm yard:

> They raided the house ... onto the house there was a dairy and onto the dairy there was a boiling house, where people used to boil a lot of stuff for pigs and Indian meal and corn and there was always a fire down. It was November and the door was closed but the boiling house was full of steam. And they always laughed at the idea when the Tans busted in the door, a big fog of steam came out and they could see they jumped in the air! They thought they were blown up! They thought it was a bomb![33]

Back on board the *Shannon*, an increasingly concerned Joe Hogan waited in the engine room, an Auxiliary's gun trained on him and his fellow crew members, George Shouldice and Joe McEvoy. Decades later he remembered that 'after about an hour they came back with four prisoners. They went off again and in about another hour came back with two more prisoners.'[34] At the same time, an understandably nervous

John Conway was marched towards the water's edge. There he saw his younger brother Michael from whom he had been separated when confronted by the Auxiliaries and also saw four other young men:

> On the deck I saw Mike Egan tied up in his own ass reins. Young Rodgers, McMahon and Gildea were tied up in the same way with the thick boat ropes. My brother Mick was also there but wasn't tied. There was about twenty-five Auxies and Joe McEvoy, Frank Shouldice, the engineer, and Joe Hogan, the deckhand, on board as well.[35]

After Conway was placed on the boat next to the other prisoners and when all the Auxiliaries had returned from raiding the locality, the boat's skipper, Joe McEvoy, was ordered to pull out from Williamstown. Much has been said about the men's experience on the boat. One tradition records that the men were repeatedly thrown into the water and dragged by a rope and that the hair of the boat's owner had turned grey by the time they reached Killaloe.[36] While neither is likely to have happened, the journey was certainly one of immense fear for those involved and has played out in the memory of east Clare for almost 100 years.

John Conway outlined his recollections of the boat leaving the shores of Whitegate:

> A bitter northerly breeze was blowing when the boat started off from the pier. We were all on deck. The Auxies were questioning us the whole way down and Alfie Rodgers, Brud McMahon and Martin Gildea kept saying to them that Mike Egan was not to blame. It was duskish when we arrived at the jetty at the Lakeside Hotel, Killaloe.[37]

Shackled with ropes, the men sat with their shoulders touching. Their heads only lifted to answer the many aggressive questions put their way by Faraday and other Auxiliaries. Passing ancient landmarks, the prisoners paid no attention to the landscape that enveloped them. To their right the monastic settlement of Inis Cealtra stood silent on the western shore of the lake, its round tower visible to the *SS Shannon* which straddled the territory of Tipperary and Clare while dissecting Lough Derg on its path to Killaloe. After two hours, just north of Killaloe town, they entered a narrowing where Lough Derg ends and the Shannon continues, and proceeded close by Beál Ború, reputed to be the childhood home of Ireland's High King, Brian Ború. The boat glided onwards, passing unknowingly over a thousand axe heads, which then remained concealed at the bed of the Shannon, deposited some 3,000 years earlier by unknown Bronze Age warriors.[38] From Beál Ború, the boat could easily be seen, progressing on its way and carrying within it another story in the ancient tale of Ireland's troubles. This was approximately 3.00 p.m. on Tuesday 16 November, 1920 and moments later the whistle of the *SS Shannon* was heard in Killaloe, before it came into view of the Lakeside Hotel. Close by, Mike Daly and John Guerin observed the boat they had earlier seen depart make its return. Both Daly and Guerin instinctively paused, moved towards the wall close by for partial concealment, and observed.

Having arrived at the jetty in Ballina, the two Conways were taken from the deck of the boat and placed in the hatch, while the other four prisoners were removed to the Lakeside Hotel, where they were placed in the dayroom. Before they were taken off the boat, Joe Hogan whispered to one of the prisoners; 'What the hell happened ye to be caught?' to which he 'said nothing but shook his head.'[39] Conway's recollection of the men's countenance would indicate they were painfully aware of moving inescapably towards a brutal experience.

Close by, John Guerin and Mike Daly cautiously watched as men began to emerge from the boat. Decades later, Daly recounted:

> When we got to the gate leading to Paddy Keogh's boreen, we saw the boat coming back and the crowd getting off ... I could see a number of men manacled from their necks down to their right ankle and the rope from the ankle was going back to the next fellow behind him and they were marching like that one after the other.[40]

Ominously, after Rodgers, McMahon, Gildea and Egan were led into the dayroom, notices were placed on that door, as well as other rooms to be used for interrogating the men, stating they 'were out of bounds to all personnel of the hotel'.[41]

After approximately an hour, the Conway brothers were taken to the hotel and into the dayroom, where they re-joined the other four, who were handcuffed. John Conway could see a change was discernible, remembered that; 'from the time they left the boat until we saw them again, Egan and Gildea looked like dead men – they were that shook and pale'.[42]

The prisoners were brought to the Lakeside Hotel at approximately 3.30 p.m. From then until 11.30 p.m., they were beaten and interrogated. Given the levels of injuries and blood which John Conway witnessed on each of the prisoners as they returned from a cycle of interrogation, it is apparent that the men were tortured. Conway detailed how each prisoner was taken out one by one to be grilled in isolation, thereby waiting their turn in rotation. After Michael McMahon returned from one period of 'questioning', Conway noted how he was 'very, very quiet'.[43] The fourth prisoner to undergo the interrogation was Alphie Rodgers:

> As we came in, the Auxies in uniform took them out of the dayroom one by one. They kept them out a good long time. Alfie Rodgers was the last to be brought back and he was pumping blood from the nose and face. I'd say he had lost all his blood before he was shot at all.[44]

Overseeing the punishment, were almost certainly Andrews and Faraday. John Conway testified to Andrews' personal role in his own questioning later that evening. Newmarket native,

Patrick Cullinan was likely present also. He evidently impressed his superiors since arriving only weeks before hand and days later was promoted to intelligence officer, a position which carried responsibilities for 'questioning' prisoners. The use of torture on republican prisoners has been noted elsewhere.[45] Typical methods included the pulling out of fingernails, the strained twisting of joints, mock explosions, as well as the most commonly used beatings delivered by especially chosen 'bullies'. Crozier also described the 'hardboiled' inquisition, involving the forced placement of hot hard boiled eggs in their shells under the armpit of the prisoner while interrogation continued.[46] Billy Malone, who was working at the hotel, noticed the signs pinned on certain doors warning all to keep away. It was not necessary for Malone to enter in order to establish what was happening behind those doors. When speaking to Mike Daly many years later, he recalled chillingly that from within those rooms, 'their roars could be heard in Birdhill'.[47] Given the later condition of their bodies, the observations of John Conway, as well as the screams heard from within the interrogation rooms, it is evident the men were subjected to a brutal experience. The use of the term 'torture' has been cautioned by some historians.[48] Technically amounting to the infliction of severe pain on restrained prisoners, the entirely subjective nature of such experiences, makes later reticence about the use of the term somewhat redundant, however. Certainly, if the imposition of intense physical trauma is the meaning of torture, then the four men in Killaloe were unquestionably subjected to it.

While all this was taking place at Killaloe, deeper into north-east Clare, Auxiliaries in Kilanena broke into the local Catholic church. There they took Fr Jack Kennedy, who was living in the adjacent house captive and after his collar was torn from him, Fr Kennedy was invited to fight, was beaten repeatedly and told he would be shot.[49] Thirty-seven miles away, the body of Fr Michael Griffin was lying in a bog in

Cloghscoltia near Barna in Galway, after crown forces had murdered him.[50] Fortunately for Kennedy, he was finally released twelve miles away from his home.

Back in Killaloe, after a long, agonising wait, John Conway and his younger brother were roughly escorted towards the colonel's office:

> Mick and myself were taken out into a small room where the Colonel – Andrews was his name, I think – cross-questioned us and threatened us. He showed us revolvers and ammunition and said they were found with the lads. He tried to get us to say we had seen the revolvers before and that we saw them with the boys. He wanted us to say that we were friends of Mike Egan, and that we knew the boys had been staying in Williamstown House for the last three weeks. We had nothing to tell him unless we started telling him lies. I had bad old shoes on me and one of the Auxies said that anyone would know from our dress that we weren't Sinn Feiners.[51]

At approximately 11.45 p.m., with the Conway brothers locked up in an unlit room deep in the Lakeside Hotel, Michael 'Brud' McMahon, Alphie Rodgers, Martin Gildea and Michael Egan were surrounded by crown forces and walked away from the hotel. Officially, the men were to be taken across the bridge to Killaloe, before transportation to Limerick prison. They walked within the fold of their enemy, cold, bloodied, hungry and scared, and after approximately five minutes made it to the edge of Killaloe Bridge where they were roughly pushed to the right in the direction of Killaloe town.

A darkened bridge lay before them and in the distance, Killaloe too was pitch black, its people under order that all lights be left extinguished. The young prisoners stepped into that blackness. Soon, sharp, loud shots began to ring out across the still Killaloe air. When the sound of gunfire eventually faded and as life left the bodies of McMahon, Rodgers, Egan and Gildea, different stories were already beginning to form.

Left: Denis McMahon and Edward MacLysaght in the 1920s. The murder of his brother Michael made Denis 'more inward as a person' *(Courtesy of MacMahon family)*. *Centre*: Denham Sparling who helped to secure the release of the bodies. Martin Gildea was his employee *(Courtesy of Gina Sparling)*. *Right*: Johanna (Siobhán) McMahon also confronted the crown forces in Killaloe about their refusal to release the bodies *(Courtesy of Niamh O'Hanlon)*.

Gathering at Raheen, Tuamgraney (c. 1914). Edward MacLysaght *(front row – 4th from right)*, Michael Egan *(front row – far right)* and Conor Clune *(back row – far right)*. Clune and Egan were murdered within days of each other in November 1920 *(Courtesy of Michael O'Gorman)*.

A staged photograph of G Company at the Lakeside Hotel. On the extreme right is Patrick Cullinan from Newmarket on Fergus, who was promoted to Intelligence Officer two days after the murders *(Courtesy of Auxillaries.com)*.

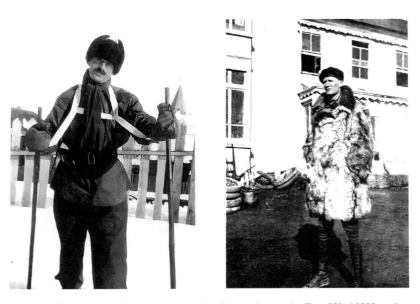

Left: Col Richard John Andrews pictured in Russia during the First World War, who was head of G Company of the Auxiliaries at the time of the murders *(Courtesy of Auxillaries.com)*. *Right:* Lieut John Alexander Faraday, who led the Auxiliary raiding party on the *SS Shannon* that captured the men, pictured at the Lakeside Hotel close to the time of the murders *(Courtesy of Ernest McCall)*.

The Scariff Martyrs

Michael Egan

Martin Gildea

Alphie Rodgers

Michael 'Brud' McMahon

The Rodgers family in 1919 with Alphie on the extreme left *(Courtesy of Arthur O'Donnell)*.

Alphie Rodgers with his sister Kathleen (Keesha) in September 1919, shortly before her departure to become a nun. They never saw each other again. Kathleen later took the religious name Sr Alphonse Columba, in memory of her brother *(Courtesy of the Rodgers Family)*.

Kathleen Mitchell, the niece of Martin Gildea who was at the Scariff monument's unveiling in 1945, pictured in 2016 before laying a wreath there in memory of her uncle. To her right is the late Dermot Moran, whose grandfather met the men shortly before their deaths *(Courtesy of Arthur Ellis)*.

Right: 100-year-old, John Michael Tobin from Laccroe in Feakle, at the grave of the Scariff Martyrs in 2012. In November 1920, he was at the funeral with his mother *(Author's Collection)*.

Below: The wheels of a horse car removed on 15 November 1920 by Alphie Rodgers, Michael 'Brud' McMahon and Martin Gildea at Holland's yard in Nutgrove, Whitegate. While they were working in the yard, they were observed by an informer. They were captured and murdered the following day *(Author's Collection)*.

Paddy Gleeson was in Scariff when the bodies were returned to the town, at their grave in 2008 at the age of 104 *(Courtesy of the Clare Champion)*.

Paddy O'Meara from Islandmore in Whitegate, photographed in the early 1920s. Paddy had sheltered the men in Islandmore and was the last man to see McMahon, Rodgers and Gildea before their capture (*Courtesy of Margaret O'Meara*).

Below: The *SS Shannon*, used by G Company to capture and transfer the men from Williamstown to Killaloe. The boat was later used by the Free State and is pictured here in Athlone *(Courtesy of Waterways Ireland Archive)*.

Below: RIC Sgt John Brennan was part of the escort that shot the men on Killaloe Bridge. His image is published for the first time in over a century *(Provenance withheld)*.

Right: Brennan in the early 1950s with his grandson in Roscommon. Discussions with his family in 2019 revealed that Brennan never spoke about his role in the Killaloe Bridge shootings. He died in 1953 at the age the of eighty-one *(Provenance withheld)*.

A Proclamation

TO ALL WHOM IT MAY CONCERN.

Whereas—It has come to our notice that certain individuals have been acting as **spies** for the enemy and giving information to enemy police ; and

Whereas—Numbers of evil-minded persons have been circulating **slanders** on the characters of various officials of the Republic, which slanders in every instance originate with enemy police ; and

Whereas—Some enemy policemen and civilians are conspicuous in their efforts to injure the Republic and its loyal subjects ; and

Whereas—Numbers of people have been giving information to enemy police and assisting them in their investigations by **answering questions from the police** as to their whereabouts and movements at particular times ;

We hereby warn all such persons in the Military area of East Clare that henceforward all such offences will be considered as High Treason and will be dealt with accordingly.

Any person charged with infringing this Order will be tried by Courtmartial, and if found guilty will be **shot at sight.**

We call upon all loyal subjects of the Republic to assist the carrying out of this Order by giving any information of which they may be in possession to the nearest Military authority.

By order,

The Competent Military Authority.

6/8/1919.

East Clare IRA Proclamation warning anyone seen talking to police would be 'shot at sight' *(Courtesy of Clare Museum).*

Left: Process Server and alleged informer, Martin Counihan was shot dead by the Feakle IRA on 27 October 1920. This is the first ever publication of his image *(Courtesy of Liam Counihan)*.

The monument to the Scariff Martyrs on Killaloe Bridge, erected in November 1923, with the Lakeside Hotel, where they were interrogated and tortured in the background *(Courtesy of Tony Cronin)*.

The earliest known photograph of the Scariff Martyrs grave, covered in funeral wreaths, taken shortly after their burial in November 1920 *(Courtesy of Gerry Quinn)*.

'I knew there was Dirty Work the Night Before'

Wednesday 17 November started like most in those years of fear and violence. As always, life continued and the people of Ballina and Killaloe emerged from their homes, workers to their work, pupils and teachers to their classrooms. Deckhand of the *SS Shannon*, Joe Hogan, woke from an uneasy sleep and made his way to the Lakeside Hotel:

> The Auxies wanted to keep me on board that night but my wife was sick and I asked Col Andrews to let me home. He did but I had to promise to come back the next morning. I returned in the morning and they offered me one pound a day if I'd stay with them. I refused. None of the crew had anything to do with the boat afterwards. Later it was sold and scrapped. I heard the shots on the bridge that night, and when I went back to the Lakeside next morning I knew there was dirty work the night before.[52]

With the Fair of Killaloe taking place that day, Tipperary farmers were making their way across the bridge soon after 7.00 a.m. Many later reported seeing 'blood and what looked like brain matter' on the roadway.[53] Maeve Hayes remembered how her mother's friend, Rosy Dwyer (later Horan) also spoke about seeing the blood of the young men mixed with straw and cow dung.[54] Mary McGrath recalled speaking with her teacher, Madge Fahy, who told how on that morning she had unknowingly walked over the blood of the slain republicans, while hurriedly making her way to teach at Ballina National School.[55] Across 2018 and 2019, I corresponded with the son of Madge Fahy:

> My mother was a teacher at Ballina National School from 1918–1964 and told many stories about this stormy period. The following morning, she crossed the bridge and witnessed an awful sight: blood mixed with cattle droppings. The cattle had been making their way to the November fair, which was held at 'the Green' at the top of the town of Killaloe.[56]

A young child, Gerry Gough, who with Michael Durak, also walked across the bridge that day, spoke seventy years later when he was recorded as part of a local history project:

> I remember the morning the four boys were shot on the bridge. I crossed the bridge that morning. There was a fair in Killaloe the same day the seventeenth of November ... But there was blood on the bridge ... couple of pools there maybe another farther over. We thought 'twas maybe a beast fell and cut itself ... There was an Auxiliary or two standing outside the barrack and you'd see groups of people talking here and talking there and the four bodies thrown in a heap outside in the back house in the barrack.[57]

At approximately 1.00 p.m. on the night before, after the shootings, Crossley tenders carried the bodies of the four young men towards the barracks at the centre of the town. John Conway explained that before he and his brother were handed to the RIC, he had witnessed the Black and Tans 'throw the body of Martin Gildea into the back of the tender just like you'd throw a dead pig'.[58] The treatment of the men in death has remained a potent dimension of the story. One local man remembered:

> I think they were thrown in over the cart into the lorry the same as bags and brought up [to] the barrack and were kept in there, some house in the back ... They were from Scariff mostly. They didn't give 'em to their relatives for two or three days ...[59]

The bodies of Rodgers, McMahon, Gildea and Egan were taken beneath an archway, which led to the back of the three storey RIC barracks, and were reportedly left unceremoniously in a shed. The following morning, when Bridget Doyle from Broadford arrived at Killaloe barracks where she was employed as a housekeeper and cleaner, she was unaware of what had taken place the previous night. Before she could commence her duties, she was beckoned by a number of Black and Tans and RIC men. Bridget tended to focus on her duties and kept a distance from the police, but did not think much when she was asked to accompany the men out to the back of the barracks. While walking across the small yard at the back of the building, one of the Black and Tans pointed at a small shed and said, 'Come and see the fine rabbits we shot last night'.[60]

Still unaware of what she was facing, Bridget began to get an uneasy feeling. One of the smirking constables then opened the shed door to a sight that left a profound mark on Bridget's memory. After Mary Faul moved to live with her grandmother Bridget in the late 1950s, she began to hear that story. Mary told me how her grandmother, who lived until 1986, occasionally returned to that morning and the image she saw in the shed, after which she left her employment at the barracks:

> She spoke about it with almost disbelief. That they could be so callous and cruel as to describe them as rabbits. She actually thought it was rabbits they wanted skinned. As she approached the door she said she got an awful feeling and when they opened it she saw the sight of the four boys thrown on the ground. She started to walk back and I remember her saying that she just said [to them] 'no, no, no' and tried to walk away before one of them grabbed her arm and forced her to look at the bodies, saying 'come and have a good look at what we do to Fenians'. It had a terrible effect on her. She couldn't get over how they were just thrown on the ground across each other in the shed. She was always very emotional when she would tell the story and I remember her clearly saying 'As long as I live, I will never ever get that sight out of my mind'. She would always describe them with this awful sadness in her voice as 'those poor lads'.[61]

The barbaric and sadistic behaviour of the RIC and Black and Tans who took pleasure in showing the corpses to a young woman demonstrated the levels of aggression and loathing for the republican movement within the crown forces.

Not all were emotionally aligned to this position, however. Before finishing night duty, forty-eight-year-old Const. Michael Fitzgerald, who had been based in Killaloe throughout the war, was sent with a barrel to the shed containing the bodies. Having returned home to his wife that morning he fainted, later describing to her the 'most sickening scene' he had witnessed in the shed.[62] In the 1950s, Tom Cooney who was born in December 1916, bought the house adjacent to the barracks and was told many times about the significance of the archway connected to his home, under which the men's bodies had been taken:

> The four Scariff boys who were shot on the bridge of Killaloe were laid out in our archway. They were brought in and then left out in the barracks. A man told me one day that 'the day the four Scariff boys were taken in there, I saw blood running out under your archway'.[63]

News of the four men's deaths only officially broke at approximately 3.30 p.m., when four telegrams arrived at the office of the local post mistress in Scariff. Const. Patrick Garvey of the Killaloe RIC delivered messages, which bluntly read: 'You are informed that your son ... (Name) ... was shot dead when escaping from custody last night. Gwynne, District Inspector.'[64]

Having read the devastating news and gathered her composure, thirty-seven-year-old Elizabeth Anna Burnett, a native of Longford, sent word for Fr John Clancy, CC, who she felt would reduce a modicum of the inevitable pain that the messages contained for their relatives and especially the families of Rodgers, McMahon, Gildea and Egan. The relations of the former three were aware of the danger that their son's activism attracted, yet nothing could have prepared them for such wreckage.

Decades later when a young Paddy Rodgers asked his grandfather Ned about his uncle Alphie, Ned glanced at his wife Nora, her head lowered and no more was said. The mention of Alphie's name was too much for his mother and this gave Paddy a glimpse into the pain that news brought on 17 November 1920. On that day, pain had come to four homes with an incomprehensible stealth and brutality. The silence Paddy observed had its origin somewhere in an indescribable sound. Decades later, Gertie Rodgers recalled to her son Arthur, the wailing noise that unnervingly filled the air in Scariff town, after her mother Nora's eyes lifted from the words on that telegram.[65]

Shortly after the telegrams were delivered, Denis McMahon (Brud's brother), Ned Rodgers (Alfie's father), Frank Scott and P.J. Hogan from Bodyke set out for Killaloe barracks. A fifth person travelled with them who has never previously been acknowledged: thirty-one-year-old Johanna Scott, who had married Denis McMahon in August 1919 and so was the sister-in-law of Michael 'Brud' McMahon.

In October 1914, Johanna, a native of Scariff town, had enlisted in the Queen Alexandra's Imperial Military Nursing Service and served in the front during the First World War. For 230 weeks, she was part of the British imperial system, until she returned to her native town in March 1919. She made her way home via Killaloe railway station, close to where she returned in November 1920 to confront her former colleagues.[66] Johanna was also the sister of Frank Scott, who according to family tradition was anxious to draw on her knowledge of military regulations when approaching the British forces in Killaloe.

The families had a sense that they would have trouble gaining access to the bodies. Johanna is reputed to have vocally expressed her indignation and quoted the various rules that the crown forces were breaking by not releasing the bodies to the families. Johanna later began using the name Siobhán and broke all ties with her former military service, in protest at what had happened in her locality.[67]

Having arrived at Killaloe at approximately 5.00 p.m., the relatives were left to wait a considerable time for District

Inspector Gwynne to arrive back from some other business.[68] When he returned, he curtly told them that the bodies would not be released and they were denied the right to see their relatives' remains. The time between the murder of the four men and the release of their bodies added dramatically to the tension. Stories of how the bodies were 'thrown into Crossley tenders 'like you would a dead pig' began to emerge. So too did the notion that some of the men may have been still alive when they were taken to the RIC barracks in Killaloe.

Mary Ann Kiely lived in a building less than fifty metres from the RIC barracks in Killaloe. Years later, she told her daughter, Maura, that on the night of the murders, she had heard moaning sounds from the back of the barracks. Kiely's recollections, if true, support the contention of R.C. Grey, that Michael McMahon may have still been alive when he was returned to the barracks. In addition, when Pat O'Donnell viewed the bodies, he contended that wounds 'were of such a nature as to ensure death but not to cause it instantaneously'.[69] All reviews and autopsies found no bullet wound to the head of McMahon, indicating that the twenty-seven year old may have been left to bleed to death beside the corpses of his comrades in the back shed of the barracks.[70]

As those bodies lay at the barracks, a community was mobilising to recover the men and to take them to their final resting place.

9

'If you were at their Funeral'

The Burial of Martyrs

They could hear the prayers and see the candles as a circle of dim light was gradually formed around the darkened cathedral in Killaloe. Their eyes followed the slow rhythmic motion, as the local people of Killaloe walked around and around the one-time palace of Brian Ború. Against the cold and the dreary silence, black flags, symbolising the British forces determination to continue their efforts, that had been placed around their vehicles by the Black and Tans fluttered. That sound was overcome by the collective prayer that floated from across 'the Green', reaching out from the gates of the cathedral.[1]

In Killaloe, on the night of 17 November, local parishioners assembled at the Catholic church less than 100 feet across from the RIC barracks. After encouragement from the local priest, parishioners emerged and began form a circular pattern around the church. The son of one of those parishioners explained in 2019:

> A lorry load of Tans and Auxiliaries arrived on the scene to observe the proceedings. They seemed stunned at the sight of the prayer group holding rosaries and praying aloud … To add insult to injury, the crown forces flew black flags from their lorries as they drove around.[2]

The days following the murders on the bridge were fraught with tension as the RIC withheld the bodies of the four men from their families.[3] Fifty-year-old Fr John Greed, a native of Bournea in Tipperary, was first to assist the relatives in making enquiries, but at the barracks all information was refused in such a way that Greed thought it unwise to sleep in his own bed that night.[4] After Johanna MacMahon and others had made determined efforts, the families later returned with forty-year-old Christopher Denham Sparling, Martin Gildea's employer, and a respected businessman from a Church of Ireland background. Sparling managed to establish from District Inspector Gwynne that the stated reason for their refusal to release the bodies was that a military inquiry had first to be held.[5] An agreement was made that the bodies would be released to the families the following night, Thursday 18 November.[6]

While the people of east Clare were gradually realising the horror that had unfolded, the war continued around the country. At 6.00 p.m. in Cork City on 17 November, RIC Sgt James Donoghue was shot dead by IRA Volunteers.[7] Earlier that evening, British forces had arrived in the town of Scariff and the press claimed that shopkeepers in the town were forced to remove signage printed in Irish and adverts for Irish goods were torn down. House-to-house searches were made, during which all males were marched to the outskirts of the town, searched and allegedly had possessions taken.[8] Later that night, in Cork City, British forces shot dead three people in retaliation for the killing of Sgt O'Donoghue: Patrick Hanley, Seamus Coleman and Eugene O'Connell, the latter two shot in front of their wives. In Broad Lane, where O'Connell was killed, sixteen-year-old Fianna Éireann member, Charles O'Brien was shot through the jaw but survived.[9] Back in Scariff, crown forces were still in the town. In a shocking act of cruelty, that night, they forced their way into McMahon's public house, where inside a family were still in a stunned form of grief. There, they compelled the family of the young man they had killed, and whose body their colleagues in Killaloe still withheld, to serve them drink. The outrageous affront of their presence was not enough, however. From the back of her shop, 'Brud' McMahon's mother Bridget was made to endure the sound of British forces taunting her with a loud rendition of 'Where is my wandering boy tonight?'[10]

The following day, as British forces were assembled within Killaloe RIC barracks to conduct a Court of Inquiry, Daniel Egan arrived outside of the building, aware that the body of his son lay somewhere within because, like the other families, Egan had been telegrammed to inform him that his son was dead. It seemed that the sixty-five-year-old operated independently of the other families in his enquiries about his son. Two months later, he told a different court in Ennis that after some time and repeated efforts, he finally saw his son. At the Ennis Quarter Sessions in January 1921, at which Daniel Egan spoke, Judge Matthias McDonnell Bodkin made a strong condemnation of the incident in Killaloe and criticised in particular the lack of information about the incident. The former newspaper editor, author and anti-Parnellite MP for North Roscommon, declared that 'murder is murder' and quoted scripture in stating 'the blood of the murdered cried to Heaven for vengeance'.[11]

Later in the evening of Thursday the eighteenth, after Daniel Egan had managed to see his son, family members once more left Scariff for Killaloe. They arranged for coffins and hearses to follow. It had been agreed to hand over the bodies after 9.00 p.m. that night. The police took the coffins and the habits for the bodies to the store at the back of the barracks where the dead republicans lay. After the remains were arranged in their habits, the relatives were allowed to see them. An argument then broke out over who would carry out the bodies, with the police insisting they take responsibility.

Meanwhile, a short distance below the town, at Killaloe bridge, four drivers dressed in black sat silently and held a tight grip on the reigns of their horses, adorned in plumes. A further crowd waited on the outskirts of Killaloe at a place called Kincora. The *Nenagh Guardian* reported that up to 1,000 people had assembled in the immediate vicinity in solidarity with the victims.[12] To deal with the deaths, a number of undertaker businesses, including Scotts and Moloneys of Scariff, Loughnanes of Feakle and Keanes of Mountshannon came together.[13] Thirty-five-year-old Stephen Farrell arrived from Mountshannon with four horses and an empty hearse. Close by sat a young Hughie Flynn from Loughnane's undertakers keeping four more horses under his youthful command. It was two weeks before Hughie reached his eighteenth birthday. The teenager sat nervously and waited amid a silent tension, broken only by the occasional sound of an impatient horse rocking back and forth or tossing his head before exhaling forcefully into the cold November air.[14]

At the RIC barracks, a tense standoff followed as the relatives refused to accept the bodies unless they were allowed to carry the coffins, with the district inspector reluctantly acquiescing to their demands. Neighbours then helped the relatives to carry the coffins down the steep hill of Main Street Killaloe and to the waiting hearses. According to one IRA officer, 'All Bodyke and Scariff went in a crowd for their bodies. Then the people stopped in Kincora for they were afraid to go in.'[15] Tom Hogan, a captain in the east Clare IRA, was, according to his son Con, involved in collecting the bodies of men and underlined the tension and emotion of the occasion.[16]

At 9.30 p.m., the cortège left Killaloe for Scariff church, ten miles away. The four horse-drawn carriages slowly conveyed the men back to Scariff and to where the mothers of McMahon, Rodgers and Egan waited. There too was Joe Gildea and his sister, Mary, siblings of Martin who had travelled from Woodlawn.[17] The crowd of people who waited outside the town of Killaloe blessed themselves in unison and moved in behind the cortège.

Following at a noticeable distance were a lorry of Black

and Tans and RIC, determined to maintain at least a vestige of power.[18] Slow moving hearses, illuminated with oil burning lantern lamps shone dimly forward towards the home of the victims.

Earlier that day, twenty-five miles away from Killaloe in Cratloe, former comrades of Rodgers, McMahon and Gildea, including their battalion O/C Seán O'Halloran, attacked British soldiers guarding a plane which had crashlanded. Pte Alfred Spackman died at the scene and Pte Maurice Robins died five months later from wounds received.[19] However, none of this registered with the grief-stricken assembly moving between Killaloe and Scariff. The cortège of four hearses followed by a 'fierce procession of cars' continued its slow journey. Among those who drove to Killaloe was twenty-seven-year-old Patrick Treacy from Meenross in Scariff, whose father had died only weeks before hand, a death expedited by a vicious attack by British forces during a raid on his home.[20] Approximately two hours later, having made its way through Ogonnelloe and moved down 'the sweep' into Tuamgraney, the hearses rounded the ancient rock outcrop in the village and moved off north eastwards towards Scariff. As the cortège approached the outskirts of Scariff town, it veered to the left at Scariff Union Workhouse, where the coffins were carefully lifted from each hearse and taken inside. It was a moment of some irony to see the remains of four Irish people arrive at such a place with so much attention. Just seven decades earlier, up to twelve bodies were daily carried out from there in hinged 'famine coffins', largely unseen, to be buried in Tuamgraney's grave of the Great Hunger, the 'Cathsaoireach'. The inversion of that historical experience was not lost on those present, but for now, present wounds were deep enough. Thirty-eight year-old Kate Young was a nurse in the Scariff Union Workhouse. Her grandson told me how she later spoke emotionally about that night:

> My grandmother would have been a nurse in the workhouse … She was in the hospital where the boys of course were brought in and cleaned up. They were brought up from Killaloe on this particular evening and there was a Dr O'Riordan in the hospital … They had to be washed and dressed … horrendous, horrendous, all you could do was cry … There wouldn't be a dry eye in the hospital. Everybody was horrendously upset over it.[21]

After the bodies had been cleaned and dressed, twenty-nine-year-old curate, Fr John Clancy, stepped forward and sprinkled holy water across the four men, in preparation for their conveyance to the church. Fr Clancy, who was born in Coolmeen in 1891, was the brother of Paddy Clancy, commander of the 1st Battalion of the West Clare IRA Brigade.[22] The young priest was living through what must have been one of the most challenging and traumatic weeks of his life, as the previous Sunday his former classmate at St Patrick's College, Maynooth, Michael Griffin, a twenty-eight-year-old priest, had been taken captive by British forces from his residence in Galway. Two days after Griffin's capture, Clancy had been charged with personally telling the parents of Alphie Rodgers, Michael MacMahon and Michael Egan about their sons' fate and, the following Saturday, he would officiate at the tensest funeral of his young ministry in Scariff. The day after that funeral, news broke that the body of his former fellow seminarian was found buried in a boggy field near Barna in Galway.[23] Later that evening, his cousin, Peadar Clancy was shot dead in Dublin Castle, together with Conor MacClune (popularly referred to as Clune), who on the previous day had stood in Scariff church grounds and watched him as he buried the Scariff Martyrs.[24]

In the darkness of Thursday 18 November, Fr Clancy attempted to maintain a calm composure, as he walked out on the road leading to Scariff town and waited for the coffins to be lifted into their hearses once more. The cortège then moved slowly towards the hill of Scariff, with Clancy and a number of priests walking ahead. A large crowd assembled at the foot of Scariff Hill, in direct contravention of the curfew and took the four men into the embrace of their community. The coffins were removed and a large body of men, including my own granduncles, Thomas, Pat and Michael Hill, shouldered the men to Scariff church.

There that night was a young boy from O'Callaghan's Mills and he and his friend witnessed the procession arrive at the chapel on that dark Thursday night and even at a young age appreciated the significance. Paddy Gleeson passed away on Sunday 14 November 2010 just days before the ninetieth anniversary of that funeral, at the age of 106.[25] A year before he had told me, as he'd done many times, that 'I was in Scariff the night the four lads came back from Killaloe'.[26]

Inside Scariff chapel, Nora Rodgers, Bridget McMahon and Mary Egan, together with the brother and sister of Martin Gildea, said their candle lit cycle of prayers over the bodies of their young sons and brother.

'If you were at their funeral'

Several interviewees attested to the traumatic effect of the killings on the local population. One interviewee declared that, 'It was tense and it was shock. These were young lads that everybody knew. They would have been very well known and very popular ... All of a sudden, they were dead and killed extremely violently'.[27]

Margaret Hoey's earlier powerful recollection, of how the news was disclosed at her home in Poulagower, was replicated all across the homes of north-east Clare. John Michael Tobin was an eight-year-old boy in Cooleen Bridge School when news broke, 'I remember the day they were shot. News came into the school beyond and the Master let us go home. There was great noise shur about it, four lads being shot'.[28]

Friday 19 November opened with a heavy feeling in Scariff. After autopsies were conducted and the absolution of the dead was complete, the bereaved families finally emerged from the church, leaving the four coffins, each with a republican flag lying on top, positioned close to the sanctuary, their feet towards the altar as was customary for lay people.

In Dublin that night, after the maid at 28 Earlsfort Terrace told the men standing at the door that there was no Fitzpatrick present, she stopped herself and remembered that there was a Mr Fitzgerald. The men, who were members of Michael Collins' 'squad' sent out to eliminate a British intelligence network across Dublin, passed her at the door, went to the room of Fitzgerald and shot him dead. It was the weekend of Bloody Sunday and Fitzgerald, although not the initial target, was deemed a British agent and killed. Ironically, John Joseph Fitzgerald had been recovering from wounds inflicted in Scariff, where he had spent some time while operating as a barrack's defence officer in Co. Clare earlier that summer.[29]

The funeral of the Scariff Martyrs took place at 11 a.m. on Saturday 20 November 1920, on a wet and cold day in east Clare. All businesses in the town were closed and blinds drawn.[30] In the days before, a grave had been dug within the grounds of Sacred Heart Catholic church in Scariff, large enough to receive four coffins. The townlands of east Clare emptied towards the church in Scariff and from Ballymalone in Tuamgraney came Thomas, Pat and Michael Hill. Patrick Minogue from Poulagower was at the churchyard early.[31] In Laccroe, Feakle, eight-year-old John Michael Tobin sat on a side car with his mother and with a jolt was moving towards Scariff. Eighty-two years later he offered me his memories:

> Oh God, I was at that funeral ... I was in it holding my mother's hand in case I'd be lost! Oh there was a big crowd. Cripes! Everyone who had a wish for 'em shur was there. They went in an ass and cars, it was the most plentiful transport or an odd horse maybe.[32]

In Poulagower, nine-year-old Kathleen Minogue was left at home but was told later how there was 'a desperate crowd there that day'.[33] From Galway, a series of cars left New Inn early that morning. The home place of Martin Gildea was well represented in Scariff:

> Every hackney car in Ballinasloe and Loughrea they hired them and were in Scariff for the funeral. The priest in Scariff asked Joe Gildea not to bring the body to New Inn, that when they died together to let them be buried together so that's why he's buried in Scariff. My father and mother went to the funeral. My father said 'twas terrifying. The Tans were firing shots. They were afraid. There was an awful crowd in the cemetery and on the road ... Someone told my father that he [Martin Gildea] had a girlfriend and that he saw her being carried out of the church ... Oh shur they were heartbroken and their father was dying at the same time but the parish priest of New Inn told them not to tell him that Martin was shot, because he was dying.[34]

In the end, it was decided to break the news to sixty-seven-year-old Michael Gildea. The man, who had many years earlier defied his local landlord to bring Martin's mother to America and begin a life together, was once more bereaved. His wife had died young, he lost an infant daughter and now his son had been brutally murdered. Michael Gildea, although infirm, insisted on coming to see his son buried. Intermingled with IRA Volunteers, some reportedly dressed as women, were children who were all handed crepe armlets to wear in memory of the men, while inside twenty-five priests readied themselves for the service.[35] Standing solemnly at the funeral, was sixteen-year-old Margaret Minogue:

> Era shur, there was a terrible crowd of people. But the military, there was all the Volunteers a lot of'em went to the funeral. Shur the military were there. They [IRA] had to escape from the funeral.[36]

Local press reported how, as the funeral was about to get underway, four motor lorry loads of armed British forces headed by Col Andrews arrived in Scariff and took up positions in the chapel yard and on the road.[37] Capt. Tom Hogan, who was disguised, was in attendance and described the scene to his son decades later:

> On the day of the funeral, thousands of mourners assembled for the final farewell and the Colonel [Andrews] stepped onto the wall opposite the cemetery and addressed the large gathering. He said if any had reprisals in their minds he would come back and burn the town of Scariff to the ground if there was as much as a hair touched on the head of any of his men.[38]

The press carried Andrews' warning that he would 'lay Scariff flat and kill all males.'[39] Finally, an uneasy silence fell on the massive assembly as the four coffins slowly emerged from the church door and were carried to the right, where they were laid near a large open grave, followed by the families, interlinked in each other's arms. Lil Fogarty, the girlfriend of Martin Gildea was carried out, inconsolable, from the church.[40]

Auxiliaries, Black and Tans and RIC jostled men while they were getting into position to bury the dead. Fr Clancy encouraged those present to maintain their dignity in the face of provocation. On the wall opposite, Col Andrews kept a detached watch on proceedings. As the rain poured down, two armed Auxiliaries stood on top of each pier of the church gate, bearing down on the mourning crowd.[41] Under the glare of those Auxiliaries, their colleagues, many of whom had been involved in the capture and torture of the four men, continued to threaten and intimidate the crowd. Conor Tuohy from Gurrane in Feakle told me in 2012 how his mother was one of those in attendance:

> I often remember her speaking about the day of the burial of the four martyrs in Scariff. She was there. I remember her talking about the British soldiers standing up on the piers outside the church, observing and looking through the crowds and also about the [IRA] fellas inside who were dressed up in women's clothes.

They knew they were sympathisers or there were some wanted men. They knew they were there but they went up in the belfry and where they put the trap door of the bell tower. They disguised themselves as ladies and went through the crowds … Oh 'twas very tense. Hugely tense. Very frightening as well of course. They [British forces] were there with their guns. They interfered very much with the ceremony and the actual burial and things like that you know. They imposed themselves strongly that day. [42]

While all this was happening, the parents, brothers and sisters of Alphie, 'Brud', Martin and Michael, fixed their eyes on the four coffins containing the lifeless bodies of their sons and brothers, knowing that soon their physical remains would be gone from sight forever. The magnitude of their despair and the deep, almost sickening, sense of finality, was their only buffer against the strain and fear that then surrounded them. A journalist from *The Freeman's Journal* was standing amongst the crowd and later described what he characterised as a 'pathetic' scene:

On one side, the aged father, brother and sisters of Martin Gildea, on the opposite side were the heartbroken mother, brothers and sister of Michael McMahon, while at the head and foot, stood the father, mothers, brothers and sisters of Alfred Rodgers and Michael Egan. [43]

Amidst the most unimaginable tension, the four young men were finally lowered to their graves. Even in those final moments of perpetual separation between the living and the dead, the British crown forces continued to impose themselves on the mourners. From left to right, first to be lowered beneath the earth was Michael Egan, followed by Galway's Martin Gildea. Michael 'Brud' McMahon and Alphie Rodgers were then laid to rest side by side. In the lead up to the funeral, the IRA had declared their intention to fire over the grave. At 100 years of age, one attendee told me, 'They were going to fire over 'em but on account of Sparling making such headway with getting the bodies back, they didn't want to make the story worse and they didn't fire over 'em.[44] That decision left several IRA men in the very dangerous position of holding weapons, encircled by crown forces, who were then readying to search them.[45] Over the crowd, Fr Clancy's voice was heard committing 'dust to dust', indicating the funeral was drawing to a close. As shovels of earth then began to land on the four coffins, Flagmount Cumann na mBan member Annie McNamara discreetly moved towards her armed comrades:

> I, with other girls, took their arms and concealed them on our person as the service was over … The officer in charge of the military ordered all women to leave … We passed through with those arms safely and kept them safe, until the military cleared away and we handed them back to the boys who returned to the grave to fire their volleys.[46]

The press confirmed that the Auxiliaries had earlier searched the church and forced some of the congregation to march in front of them.[47] Their search does not seem to have been sufficiently thorough, however. In an interview recorded in November 2008, Margaret Hoey, who was born in 1904, explained to me how she saw IRA Volunteers climb the inside of the spire in Scariff church where they hid from the British forces:

> Four of the Volunteers went up in the spire in the church. Oh they were terrible times … Oh of course 'twas huge. But the Tans were there searchin for lads they wanted and they were there! There was some of 'em up in the spire of the church. They were hiding at the funeral. Ya, the Volunteers were at the funeral but they were hiding because the Tans were there lookin for them … They stayed there until all was over and came down in the quietness.[48]

With wanted IRA men high up above Scariff town in the spire of the church, below, the lorries of British forces finally departed and moved towards Killaloe. Slowly, the crowds peeled away, leaving only the families at the edge of a grave. In time, they were gone too. When all was quiet, the IRA Volunteers descended from the belfry and after a momentary glance at the now covered and silent grave of their former comrades, they were gone.

It was an ancient custom that the sound of three musket volleys signalled a return to fighting, following a brief suspension to enable the removal of the dead from the battlefield. At a soundless grave site in Scariff later that evening, a small group of Volunteers returned and fired three shots into the air. They then concealed their weapons, moved away from Scariff churchyard, and returned once more to life and to war.

Soon after the funeral, a motorcar was making its way towards Dublin City from the village of Tuamgraney.[49] Its occupants spoke in Irish as the burble of its Ford engine faded from the east Clare soundscape. It is not known of what Conor Clune and Edward MacLysaght spoke, but the fate of the Scariff Martyrs would have inevitably been part of that conversation.[50] Conor had worked with MacLysaght at Raheen for many years and together, they had established a thriving Nua Gaeltacht. Later that night Clune entered Vaughan's Hotel in Dublin to wait to meet Piaras Béaslaí on Gaelic League business. While there, the hotel was raided by members of F Company of the British Auxiliaries and Clune, as mentioned earlier, was arrested and taken to Dublin Castle where his fellow Clareman Peadar Clancy and Dick McKee from Dublin were already held.[51] The following night, 21 November, all three were tortured and murdered.

Clune had only chosen to go to Dublin at the last minute owing to another employee, Pat Hayes' decision to stay at home to deal with the aftermath of the Killaloe incident. Hayes was a senior IRA figure and a member of MacLysaght's staff; in truth, this employment was cover to enable Hayes to conduct his role as adjutant of the East Clare IRA Brigade.[52] Clune's sister later claimed that Conor was an IRA intelligence officer. This contention was supported by IRA officers including Tom Hogan, Joe Clancy and Austin Hannan, the latter referring to Clune as a 'sort of free-lance liaison officer'.[53] However, MacLysaght later made a statement denying the reported implication that Clune was a lieutenant in the IRA. He also confirmed Clune's reason for being in Dublin that weekend was to audit the accounts of Raheen Rural Industries.[54] Decades later, MacLysaght's son William noticed a tear in his father's eye when Conor was discussed:

> Well, he would have a tear in his eye. He was very sad about Conor. He loved Conor. He had great admiration for him. The fact that he was such an innocent party. Poor Conor was not involved. He always felt, they were all at it [IRA activity] but Conor wasn't ... My father brought me years later to Dublin Castle. He showed me the mark on the wall where Conor was shot. I have the rosary beads that was put on his neck in the castle.[55]

The absence of Clune was also felt deeply by twenty-two-year-old Annie Brady from Tuamgraney, who local tradition indicates was going out with the young Quin man when he died. An Irish speaker, Annie remained unmarried for the rest of her life and decades later, she paid for a commemorative railing in Conor's name to be installed at the foot of the alter at St Joseph's Roman Catholic church in Tuamgraney.[56]

As with Clune, in the immediate period following the killings in Killaloe, a confluence of republican propaganda and local interest commenced a narrative surrounding the men. On 27 November, the *Clare Champion* described the four men as 'total abstainers and monthly communicants'.[57] It also stated that 'three of the men were Irish speakers and were of exemplary character'.[58] Both the emotional impact of their deaths and the inevitable republican propaganda that was elicited resulted in almost immediate endeavours to preserve the memory and the virtues of the Scariff Martyrs.

The families of all four were at that time deeply submerged in what one sympathiser described as a 'world of sorrow'.[59]

'World of Sorrow'

The deaths of the Scariff Martyrs on the bridge of Killaloe created two pathways, distinct but not entirely separate. The divergence lies between the families and the communities affected. Both grieved, but differently. At a collective level, before long, the murder of the men was transformed into a rallying call. Their memory became part owned by the communities of Scariff and surrounding areas. One local historian observed that the community 'had a great deal of sympathy for the martyrs, because they were really devout republicans'.[60] Over time, songs were written, monuments installed and commemorations organised. For some, it was a personal and silent trauma. For the families, the primary emotion continued to be pain. Margaret Hoey remembered some of the feeling in the area, 'Oh, there was terrible sympathy with the families. Mrs McMahon was a strong type of woman. But the Rodgers felt it terrible. They were a different type of people'.[61] For Alphie Rodgers' sister in Belgium, her father Ned, had 'been more badly hit than any'.[62]

Some of this pathos is captured in a private collection of letters I was given access to, written to the family of Alphie Rodgers in the aftermath of his murder. Correspondence from across Ireland, England and Canada, discloses the levels of sympathy with the families. From Canada, J. S. Rodgers wrote to Alphie's mother in the days after her son's death:

> The appalling tragedy of the death of your Alphie came to me as a great shock … I am sure you have the sympathy of all true lovers of Ireland and of liberty if not of all true lovers of humanity … The poor boys who are gone are now beyond the power of their persecutors and so let us pray for them that they may find favour in the sight of him who sees into the hearts of men and who will

reward the good and punish the wicked ... Poor Ireland is being martyred today and the sword of sorrow has pierced the Irish mother's hearts.[63]

The collection contains twenty-four private letters written between November 1920 and August 1922. In addition, a letter from Alphie Rodgers, one of those killed, written to his mother when he was a boarder in Mungret College, Limerick, has been preserved (see p. 2). In many of the letters, a intersection of nationality, pride and religion is noticeable and was crystallised in a notion of martyrdom. One Newmarket-on-Fergus writer put the tragedy firmly in this context:

> It is an awful time for the poor Irish, as our saviour knows what is going to happen, and it well for those who are gone to a better world and you may be sure that poor Alfie and his comrades have entered the mansions of the Blessed and it is a consolation for you that he died for a noble cause, and not as a tyrant or traitor.[64]

John Murphy, writing from Woodford in Galway, declared 'Human sympathy is of little use. Let us bear our loss for Ireland and pray for those who are fallen.'[65] From Maynooth College came the following commitment:

> I will not forget Alfy and his deceased comrades in my prayers. It is the least we may do for those who have suffered martyrdom for faith and fatherland as they have done. I feel sure God has already rewarded them for it'.[66]

John Fahy, the Jesuit rector of Mungret College wrote on 3 December 1920 to say how 'many here [Mungret College] remember the splendid boy Alfred was'. It had been a trying month or so for Fahy. A few weeks earlier, Fahy had written to eighteen-year-old Kevin Barry, who he had known from his time as rector of Belvedere College in Dublin.[67] The British hanged Barry on 1 November. Sixteen days later, Alphie

Rodgers was shot dead in Killaloe. As Fahy commented in his letter, the country was 'passing through terrible times'.[68] Another friend of the family wrote just three days after their deaths, remembering Alphie:

> I need not tell you how grieved I am at the loss of our darling Alphie. How fond we all were of your bright and funny boy and such a lovely boy. All his good qualities come up before me as I write and his funny stories. I cannot realise that he has been snatched so cruelly away from those who loved him so much ... 'Scariff will be the sorrowful town after poor Alfie'.[69]

The same sentiments were expressed to the other families bereaved. Years later, Edward MacLysaght recalled the shock that reverberated throughout east Clare in the wake of the incident. MacLysaght worked closely and considered Denis McMahon as his best friend, whose brother Michael was one of the four victims.[70] The emotional impact on the local community was also witnessed by the war correspondent and campaigning British journalist and author Henry Nevinson, who visited Tuamgraney in November 1920. Nevinson reflected later how, for him, areas of east Clare thereafter held a profound significance:

> Killaloe, where the night before I arrived four youths had been murdered by the British while crossing the bridge as prisoners. Scariff, where I saw their bodies laid out in the chapel and Raheen close by where I said goodbye to Edward [Mac]Lysaght as he started one morning in his motor to Dublin, having at his side the scholar and assistant on his farm, young Clune, who was to be murdered three days later in Dublin Castle. But those associations belong to the winter of the Black and Tans terror.[71]

10

'The Day Will Come'

Echoes of a Tragedy

In Dublin Castle in late 1920, the November report of the RIC inspector general for the county of Clare was being completed. The position of inspector general had been left vacant when, on 4 November, T. J. Smith resigned. His replacement, Hugh Tudor, had in effect directed the implementation of Auxiliary and Black and Tan terror in Ireland, as police adviser. Whether the words of Tudor or his deputy, C.A. Walsh, the report noted the 'wonderful change for the better' in the Killaloe area, occasioned by the arrival in the town of G Company.[1] It made no reference to the killings on the bridge.[2]

In east Clare, a heavy feeling of anger weighed on the community. Outwardly, a repressive environment continued, with G Company exerting an obvious presence. On one occasion from their base at the Lakeside Hotel, they fired across Lough Derg towards a cliff walk overlooking the lake, where Madge Fahy, the local schoolteacher in Ballina, was walking:

> My mother had a close brush with death as she went for a walk with Mrs J. C. O'Brien, the wife of the school principal. During an evening stroll on the 'Ailbhawn', shots rang out from close to the Lakeside Hotel, bullets were ripping up the grass at their feet. They fled for their lives to the laneway onto New Street.[3]

A dispatch from the East Clare IRA in the months afterwards warned in Killaloe 'any man going in there from outside is liable to be arrested'.[4] When soon after, Denham Sparling was driven through Killaloe by Tom Hogan, a twenty-four-year-old member of the IRA and employee of Sparling, they were stopped by the Auxiliaries. Sparling was soon released but Hogan was detained. His son told me in 2008 of his father's subsequent experience:

> The solider that searched my father took out his revolver, cocked the trigger and left the muzzle at the base of his ear; 'make one move now and your dead' ... They called him out and told him to get walking around that field and don't stop. He kept walking and walking and walking ... they kept him at that all night until it broke dawn ... dawn was breaking and he could see the top of Sliabh Bernagh mountain and he said 'what I wouldn't give to be on the other side of that mountain!' What they had planned was that if he made a break for it, they would have shot him dead.[5]

On the Monday after the shootings, the Auxiliaries spent almost two hours firing machine guns into the air of Killaloe, during which many older people were overcome and fainted.[6] Days later, Col Andrews and his men arrived in Kielta, Tuamgraney, where he informed the sisters of Paddy McDonnell, that he would return with 'his riddled corpse in a box'. Before leaving, Andrews commented to McDonnell's mother; 'Madame, give my compliments to your son and tell him I will shoot him when I see him'. During an earlier raid, one of his colleagues had declared he would shoot McDonnell and 'trample on his dead body', while another committed to hanging him with his own necktie.[7] A week later, one of the hidden tragedies of the period took place in Killaloe.

On Saturday 4 December, three lorry loads of British forces drove through the town. According to one source, the British forces had come from Bridgetown and were drunk. As they arrived at an area known locally as Royal Parade and ascended in the direction of Main Street, they began shooting. To their right, standing at the door of a public house ran by Edward Richardson, was a young female domestic servant.[8] In fact, the young woman, whose name was Ellen Kennedy, was so startled by the shooting that she went into shock and tragically was found some time later in her bed, where she had died. Her death register confirmed that Ellen first went into primary shock and only a half an hour later died of a cerebral haemorrhage.[9] Ellen was the daughter of Michael and Norah Kennedy from Clonsingle in Newport, Co. Tipperary. Born on 4 May 1900, she was just twenty years old when she became one of the forgotten victims of the British forces.

A further forgotten victim in the weeks after the Killaloe killings was Martin Walsh, a sixty-two-year-old from Caher in east Clare. Private James Arthur of the Royal Scots shot Walsh dead at the Clare Lunatic Asylum in Ennis on 29 November, claiming Walsh failed to halt when called upon. Walsh had been a 'liberty patient' at the asylum since August 1895, and even the press accepted that he 'did not understand an order to halt'.[10] Ironically, the British forces were chasing Michael Brennan who had left east Clare and moved to Ennis for safety.

In December, the Limerick postal authorities reported that owing to the frequent raids since November, mail cars would cease to run from 22 December to Tulla, Broadford, Whitegate and Killaloe.[11] In that month also, a party of police raided the premises of Fr John Greed and Fr Patrick Spain in Killaloe. Both priests, aged fifty, were arrested on the basis that weaponry was found in the house, including a sword, three bayonets, a knuckle duster and several rounds of sporting ammunition.[12] The priests were court-martialled in Limerick but later released when it was proven the objects were of an antiquarian nature. Also in December, Co. Clare joined Cork, Kerry, Limerick and Tipperary in having Martial Law declared within its boundaries.

As the year 1921 opened up to an uncertain future, the pain was still very raw in east Clare. A song was introduced to the community which began to draw from the surrounding despair in a bid to represent in tone and lyric the feelings of the people. Weeks later, the IRA struck the most significant blow of the war within the brigade area, when six members of a RIC/Black and Tan patrol were killed in the Glenwood ambush, between Broadford and Sixmilebridge.[13]

In the middle of February in the townland of Poulagower, a knock was heard at the door of the Minogue family. The same door at which news broke three months earlier about the Killaloe killings, now opened to three young men with strong English accents. This time, they did not portray the appearance of a raiding party. Having gained entry, they awkwardly asked for milk and food. A nervous Bridget Minogue obliged while her daughter Margaret nervously watched on:

> They came into our house lookin' for food and of course my mother was nervous and afraid of 'em but she gave 'em bread and milk and she had to taste the milk before they'd drink it ... Oh they were all shaking ... they deserted their regiment.[14]

Privates David John Williams, William Sydney Walker and Harry Morgan (real name Thomas Mullett) were soldiers in the Oxford and Buckinghamshire Light Infantry, who had moved from their Limerick base. Strikingly, for men claiming to have deserted their regiment, they moved away from Limerick with its rail routes and moved towards the east Clare countryside.[15] Having drunk their milk, the three men left Minogues and moved out of the townland of Poulagower. They were next seen in Ballycorban in Clonusker, where they approached the home of Martin and Ann Conheady, unaware that it was an IRA safe house and that local republican fighters were inside. In 2010, I spoke to the son of Mary Conheady, who at the time was twenty-seven-years old:

> Their home was a dead sitter for the boys [IRA] to hide away ... She would never have anything but the good word for them [IRA] but she would almost cry when she would tell of the thing that happened when three British [soldiers] who were obviously deserters turned up looking for asylum. The boys rightly pinned

them as it were and kept a guard over them to try and find out more about them. Is there a danger and so on? Now, three days later [begins to cry] I'm very emotional now. Beside Costello's driveway, there's another road going straight up the mountain. They brought them up and shot them. The local group decided it was too risky. All I know is my mother would cry each time she would tell me.[16]

The soldiers told the IRA that they were deserters from the British army. Republican veteran Seán Moroney recorded that 'during the trial it was proved that they had tried to and did in fact keep in contact with their own forces. The result was that they were found guilty of being spies and sentenced to death. The sentence was duly carried out'.[17] According to the nephew of one of those involved in the court-martial, the shooting of the soldiers may have been in revenge for what happened in Killaloe three months earlier.[18] Adding power to the latter suggestion was the reality that for a period of time before their execution, they were held on an abandoned house, which in the late 1800s was the ancestral home of Alphie Rodgers. It is certain that there was an appetite for revenge amongst the local IRA.

In the town of Scariff, intimidation continued of those seen to be in any way supportive of the IRA. Fr John Clancy, who had officiated at the funeral of the Scariff Martyrs, was deemed an enemy by crown forces. For a time, he was sheltered in the home of Helena Tuohy, a member of Scariff Cumann na mBan.[19] On 24 April, he was held up by Auxiliaries in the square of Scariff and marched with other men who had been 'rounded up' to the local church of Scariff. Against his protest, Clancy was prevented from saying mass and compelled to repair roads that had been damaged by republicans to impede British movements.[20] His nephew told me how Clancy had every reason to fear for his life:

The Auxiliaries took him in Scariff and drove off with him in the Crossley Tender a few miles outside the town of Scariff. They were mocking his breviary [liturgical book in the Roman Catholic church] the whole way out and after a few miles they threw him out and told him to walk back to Scariff. This was after the killing of Fr Griffin and Canon Magner and he was sure he was going to be shot but in the end they didn't shoot him.[21]

Twenty five year old MP, Oswald Mosley, discussed the issue in the British House of Commons.[22] It was dismissed by Hamar Greenwood, the chief secretary, who claimed that Clancy had chosen to 'accompany his flock'[23] Clancy wrote to the press to rubbish Greenwood's suggestion.[24]

On 8 June 1921, smoke billowed over the skies of Tuamgraney and Scariff. The British forces normally ignited such flames. However, on this occasion, it was republicans behind the ignition. In early June, a decision was taken by the local IRA to burn the workhouse hospital and other buildings, to prevent the British forces from occupying them in a bid to reassert a presence in the area.[25] Tommy Bolton was a participant in the burning and confirmed the intention of the crown forces:

> Oh 'twas goin to be. Shur I heard 'em to say it. There was a regiment of 'em coming out in it and the officers were going to take up this house … I was in the burnin of it and nearly burned in it! … the order came in kind of sudden. I was in the Caherhurley regiment under Capt. [John] Dillon … We got the orders to burn it and to burn the old Drewsborough House.[26]

In 2004 at the Lakes Nursing Home in Killaloe, Palkie McNamara from Scariff, who was five at the time of the incident, recalled clearly his memories of the burning:

> Well what I remember was actually I didn't know what was happening, I was in my own field playing and I saw cars pulling up at the school and people being carried in. They [IRA] took the patients out of the old workhouse because it was going to be burned down that night. I walked into the school and saw twelve or fifteen of them [patients] in a row in beds. So I heard afterwards that the workhouse was burned.[27]

On the same day as Scariff Union Workhouse and Drewsborough House were burned in Tuamgraney, Williamstown
House, where the Scariff Martyrs had been captured, as well
as Rinskea House close by, were also burned to the ground.[28]
Certain homes across north-east Clare remained decorated
with ornaments from the opulent surrounds of Williamstown
for decades after.

Two weeks after the burnings, on 29 June 1921, on a
remote road connecting the two rural villages of Bodyke
and Feakle, a local man was quietly making his towards the
Roman Catholic church in Clonusker, when the tranquil
sound of rural life was ruptured. Jim 'Birdie' Grogan's first
instinct was to run towards his home in the townland of Core.
Having jumped down from the lorry, Pte O.C.H. Biggs, of
the Oxfordshire and Buckinghamshire Regiment, aimed his
rifle at Grogan and fired, killing him instantly.[29] Dublin Castle
claimed that Grogan 'made for a scrub bush' and ignored calls
to halt.[30] Despite Grogan's father declaring to the court of
inquiry that his son had 'no intellect' and a 'weak brain', Biggs
suffered no punishment.

In July, after a final leaving party abounding with prostitutes
and alcohol, G Company left the town of Killaloe and moved
towards Corofin.[31] They arrived there with 'a big reputation
as seasoned and ruthless soldiers' and the sinister nickname
the 'Body Snatchers'.[32] Weeks later, the War of Independence
was effectively ended when the Anglo-Irish Truce was agreed.

'The day will come When all Will Know' – The Informer

In the local community where the murders occurred it
was seared into the historical consciousness. One aspect in
particular remained embedded in that memory, presenting
a strangely paradoxical curiosity: the informer. Equal to the
potency of their death in local memory is the betrayal of the

men by an informer, a person who has hung over the story of the Scariff Martyrs since the moment of their capture.

To understand the enduring nature of the informer story is to understand the place of the informer in Irish culture. A story was once told in the Broadford district about the arrival in 1798 of the North Cork Militia, notorious in the brutal suppression of the United Irishmen's rebellion of that year. Generations of attentive listeners heard of 'a brave man named Mr Barron', who was asked to give them information as to where rebel pikes and ammunition were hidden in the locality. After Barron refused to betray the local rebels, the story tells how he was brought to Broadford chapel gate and stripped. He was then tied naked to an ass car and flogged through the village of Broadford 'until they brought the skin off his back'. Critically, the story was always adorned by the presence of his 'patriotic sister' who 'walked by his side and gave him courage not to reveal the secret or not to be looked upon as a traitor.'[33] One commentator cautioned that 'the stain of their treachery would live in the folk memory ... there would be no forgiveness and their guilt would pass on to their children's children'.[34]

English writer Standford suggests an even deeper and ancient root for the reviled position of the traitor, particularly in Irish culture, pointing to the biblical character Judas.[35] As she played in her schoolyard in the late 1930s in east Galway, Kathleen Skehill (later Mitchell) heard some of her classmates call members of a particular family, 'the Tans'. What she passed off as childhood teasing, later carried a significantly deeper and personal meaning. Equally, her youthful recollections of a lame RIC pensioner held a greater significance, when she reflected back at the age of eighty-eight. The limping former policeman had an intimate connection with her family history and the betrayal of her murdered uncle, Martin Gildea:

> Well then, there was a strong branch of IRA in New Inn and they were saying they'd kill him because they knew he spied on Martin Gildea but they were merciful and they shot him in the heel so he was lame ever after. I saw him in later years limping. Years later, going to school his family were called 'the Tans'.[36]

Irish culture has few ways as powerful to capture and express the feelings of a community than in song. When the best known composition relating to the Scariff Martyrs was written, the story was raw. The emotional charge reflected in the lyrics, was based on just six weeks of anger when it was penned on Christmas Eve 1920. Such acrimony was based on the inescapable knowledge that information was passed to the RIC and Auxiliaries at Killaloe relating to the whereabouts of the three wanted men. The influence that the informer has had on social memory surrounding the incident is colossal, reflected in the concluding line of the song, which declares emphatically, 'the day will come when all will know who sold their lives away'.[37] However, the latter prediction is tempered by the fact that all known later versions of the song exclude the following charged verse, which is contained in the original song referring to the informer:

> May every curse fall on the wretch who sold their lives away,
> And may the fate of Judas, eer long be his, someday,
> And may the flesh fall off his bones and may his sight decline,
> May his cursed soul be tortured until the end of time.[38]

Throughout the War of Independence, intelligence rapidly became a key element in the arsenals of both the British and Irish forces. Both the gathering of intelligence and the prevention of information being released were equally critical. At least 184 civilians accused of spying were killed by the IRA throughout the war, including at least three in Co. Clare.[39] Exploration of the literature concerning the period in Clare indicates an inclination to partially ignore the role of the informer. For example MacLysaght, who wrote the earliest account of the conflict in east Clare, asserted that 'no informer was summarily liquidated'.[40] In fact, two of the three alleged informers executed in Clare were shot under the authority of the East Clare IRA Brigade and Michael Brennan. Moreover, the execution of Martin Counihan occurred in the same parish as MacLysaght. In Brennan's account published in 1980, the former O/C of the East Clare IRA also omitted reference to the executions, despite ordering the shooting of John Reilly, an alleged spy in Newmarket-on-Fergus in April 1921.[41] In addition, his second in command, Tom McGrath, presided over the meeting that led to Counihan's capture and execution.[42] In early March 1921, Brennan wrote to Dublin, requesting instruction on what action to take against identified women spies, describing 'one notoriously bad case in which a girl concerned has defied the volunteers', as well as 'another girl who has applied for a job as a woman [Auxiliaries] searcher'.[43] Within the 6th Battalion area, two retired lady teachers were identified passing information to police. In that case, the local IRA did not ask Dublin for direction and instead called to their home and after a stern warning, shot their dog.[44]

In nearby north Tipperary, the treatment of spies was acknowledged. Dan Gleeson, an IRA Volunteer from Ballymackey, declared in 1978 that 'of course there was severe punishment dealt out all along the line for espions [espionage] and spies'.[45] Despite warnings for such activity in east Clare, the capture and death of the Scariff Martyrs, came just three weeks after the East Clare IRA had executed Martin Counihan, for allegedly spying (see pp. 124–130). For one Scariff native, who experienced the period as a sixteen-year-old, information to crown forces was all too forthcoming:

> Families who had their sons on the run, they were worried. Terribly worried! They [crown forces] knew the houses to burn. They were getting plenty information from people who didn't like the local

Volunteers or didn't understand it at all. They were satisfied with England! People went to the police or the peelers as we used to call 'em. Oh they were getting plenty information![46]

Seán Nugent, who was born in Clonusker, Scariff in 1920, asserted more forcefully that north-east Clare was 'fuckin full of spies'.[47] This apparent ubiquity was evident in Broadford, where late in the war, four local people who had been identified as informers were marked for execution. It was recorded that the local IRA had already printed the warning placards to place on the chests of their corpses, only for the alleged informers to be saved by the Truce of 1921.[48]

'Who Sold their Lives Away'?

The curiosity about who the informer was is a loaded question and one charged with tension, deepened by the possibility that the informer was a local. The increased raids on mail cars in the Whitegate and Killaloe areas support the fact that the IRA made significant efforts to establish where intelligence was coming from.[49] No definitive evidence was found, either then or over the years that followed, but the curiosity as to the identity of the informer has endured, though such interest is usually counteracted by a reticence to know – at least at a public level.

As a historian exploring local history within a cultural context, such investigations can present challenges. In most cases, informers or spies operated on an individual basis, but the legacy of such action becomes the inheritance of their family. To be heirs to such activity carries an unfair burden, a recognition which in part explains some of the reasons why the British Home Office refused in 2015 to release archive material on paid Irish informants.[50] The intimate and localised nature of the War of Independence, within deeply interconnected communities, can result in linkages that draw the innocent and guilty together in striking ways, and are not always immediately apparent. What seems sincere and heartfelt can, in the cold light of history, manifest as deeply ironic. A correspondent writing to express deep and meaningful condolence can do so without knowing a sibling may have betrayed the men, or a subscriber to a memorial fund can offer his contribution, unaware of his father's possible role in the men's tragic end.

After deep reflection, I arrived at a position regarding the disclosure of the informer's name, were that person to be a local suspect, particularly with descendants of that person continuing to live in the area. While it can be argued the record yearns for completion, the benefit to historical knowledge would be far overcome by the damage and hurt to current and future generations who had no act or part in the betrayal. In any case, given the covert and invariably undocumented nature of British intelligence gathering, suspicions usually rested on likelihood and probability. Such measurements can be useful in the main, but with such a devastating allegation, would be insufficient and irresponsible. Careful examination of associated records and RIC reports, including available Occurrence Books, in which officers made notes of intelligence information, as well as RIC expenditure records, yielded nothing definitive.[51] Likewise, the Mulcahy Collection, housed at UCD, where the IRA named a list of suspected spies, provides no conclusive evidence as to the individual's identity. In truth, the effort to offer an irrefutable identification is challenged most powerfully by the reality that there was likely not one smoking gun, but several.

Across seventeen years of research, I have discovered the identity of at least twenty-one people in east Clare (including two in east Galway), who have been or can be put under some suspicion of spying. Eleven were recorded within local tradition, while seven were discovered in contemporary archival records and testimonies. The identification of two more potential informants, are based on my own conclusions. Seven further unnamed but identified figures have also been documented. In total, sixteen of those names identified are unique to this research with only five previously named in publications or testimonies. Nine individuals are named below, with others are referred to elsewhere in the book. Those named are discoverable to researchers. Six identified names, directly related to the story, have been consciously withheld on the basis that their identity is not discoverable on official records. Although it is likely that most were possibly guilty of spying, only some relate directly to the Scariff Martyrs story.

Over the decades, many theories have been put forward. Seán Crowe, who was born in 1926, was told how an RIC constable was heard speaking to a 'loose living woman' at the back of the chapel in the village of Broadford and that information disclosed in that encounter led to the capture of the men.[52] The suggestion that the sister of one of the men, fearing for her brother's safety, gave away their place to end their period 'on the run', was also circulated. That possibility ultimately led to deeply tragic consequences, as reflected in the conclusion. Another placed under an unfair suspicion was Michael Conway, who with his brother John, was taken aboard the *SS Shannon*. However, this occurred after the men had been captured, making the suggestion redundant.[53]

There are unknown figures that were noted in the local experience, like the 'tea man' tracked by Martin 'Ha Ha' Murray in Mountshannon. Murray, who carried messages for the IRA, encountered the man acting suspiciously in Mountshannon and having asked for a cigarette, touched the back of his coat which was dry. When the man claimed that he had walked from the Scariff side of Mountshannon after his car broke down, Murray knew he was suspicious, as a heavy rain was coming from that direction, which would have meant his back would instead have been saturated.[54] Over the months that followed, IRA HQ did note in a dispatch to the East Clare Brigade, the danger of crown forces 'dropping men in a wayside place and continuing on their journey'.[55] Although it was suggested that this happened in the days preceding the capture of the four men, the dating of the event is questionable. Equally, there was no known action taken against any travelling workers in the area.

When, on 18 September, Rodgers, McMahon and Gildea helped direct operations from the Market Square in the town, an off duty RIC man was positioned in the upstairs window of a nearby public house.[56] The constable was likely the individual who highlighted their role in the episode and made them wanted men. Significantly, on the basis of this information, the men were charged with having shot Sgt Sullivan and Const. Broderick in Scariff, despite evidence to the contrary.[57] However, this does not mean that the constable was involved in their final capture, nor in fact does it mean he was an informer, as his observations as a policeman were part of his duty. The role of over-zealous RIC men was not forgotten, however. An RIC constable in New Inn, Co. Galway, as well as a further local man in that area, were implicated in spying on the men when they returned to Martin Gildea's home place of Ashbrook. However, while not forgotten in that area for their role in pressurising Gildea and his comrades through their actions (the RIC man was shot in the ankle), neither had any role in their eventual capture in Williamstown.

Local loyalists like Robert Frances Hibbert, who had vocally declared his opposition to the IRA, as well as Francis Sampson who had multiple battles with local republicans, cannot be above suspicion. Ned Broy, who worked in Dublin Castle as a double agent for Michael Collins, recorded how loyalists and magistrates were a critical source of local information about the republican movement.[58] However, no definite evidence exists to link either man. A.E. Learoyd, owner of Williamstown House, also came under suspicion. A notice printed in a Dublin society journal, however, indicates that he was then in London for the wedding of his daughter Daphne Lorraine, to British officer, John Edward Conant, which casts significant doubt on the claim.[59]

In the late 1940s, Paddy McDonnell claimed that Jimmy McKeogh from Ballina had been guilty of giving information to the police about the shooting in O'Brien's Bridge in late September. Jimmy McKeogh was a forty-five-year-old merchant and owner of a substantial hardware business in Ballina. McDonnell claimed that it was McKeogh's wife, Emma, a native of Scariff, who was a relation of his own, that warned him that the information had been given and led him to go 'on the run' in Tipperary.[60] While McKeogh may have given information about IRA actions, he was unlikely to be in a position to know where the men were sheltered in Whitegate.

In his memoires, Michael Brennan claimed that a 'detailed investigation pointed to a local RIC pensioner as the probable spy'.[61] However, he also recounts that he refused to have him shot due to a lack of evidence. Brennan wrote that he had this man arrested during the Civil War and interned for two years as 'an irregular'.[62] Ó Ruairc suggests that the most likely man referred to by Brennan was 'a retired RIC sergeant named Blennerhassett'.[63] Further research shows, however, that John Blennerhassett was in 1920 a fifty-one-year-old still-serving RIC sergeant. A native of Kerry, Blennerhassett had been stationed previously in Kilrush before being moved to the Mountshannon and Whitegate area, where he had been for a number of years before the War of Independence. The family later moved to Tralee, where John died in July 1922.[64] Given that he died at the start of the Civil War, he does not match the man referred to by Brennan.[65] In fact, Brennan's claim does not seem to be supported.

Tom McNamara from nearby Mountshannon was un-equivocal that 'there is no doubt whatever that these unfortunate men were betrayed to the enemy by someone living in the locality.'[66] He recorded in February 1955 that soon after the Killaloe bridge incident, John Dillon and Jackie 'Bishop' Ryan instructed him, Charlie Turner, Joe Nugent, Pat Halloran and Donal Minogue, to shoot 'a man named Cahill in Killaloe said to be a spy'. While on route the action was cancelled without reason by Pat Duggan, the East Clare Brigade intelligence officer, and McNamara never learned why.[67] McNamara confronted another suspected informer in nearby Whitegate when he and Paddy McInerney raided the post office run by Richard Coppithorne. Coppithorne, a native of Cork and known loyalist was suspected of passing messages to British forces about republican activities. The telephone was disabled, and the postmaster warned at gun point against such activity.[68] This took place in late April 1921 and given no further action was taken against Coppithorne, it seems unlikely he was responsible.

Significantly, in secret communications between the brigade staff of the East Clare IRA and Republican headquarters in Dublin, discovered amongst the Collins Papers at the Military Archives of Ireland, intelligence pointed to 'the Postmaster in Killaloe', a Mr White who is described in one dispatch as 'a dangerous man'.[69] It was noted, for example, that in October and November 1920, a former British officer referred to as 'Captain Henry' had been given in formation by White, about an IRA arms manufacturing facility in Parnell Street in Dublin. Henry passed the information along, as a result of which it was raided and the arms found.[70] Given the timing and the findings of IRA investigations, it is evident that the Killaloe postmaster was supplying information to the British crown forces at the time of the Killaloe Bridge murders. James William White was in 1920, a forty-eight-year-old from Newtown in Co. Westmeath, who ran the post office on the Main Street of Killaloe, having taken over from his brother Richard in 1902. The level of White's spying was subsequently exposed by Mary Agnes Fenton (later Ryan) from Ballina, who was sent to Dublin by Austin Brennan to make enquiries about leakages in the area. The thirty-year-old Cumann na mBan activist discovered that across 1920 and 1921, White regularly sent reports to Dublin Castle via a Davis family, living in Mount Merrion. It was White who realised John C. Reynolds, an Auxiliary at Killaloe, had been giving information to the IRA and supplied the vital evidence that led to Reynolds' arrest.[71]

In November 1920, White was a critical agent for British intelligence. However, that intelligence had to come from somewhere. The answer to that questions lies back in north-east Clare; in the area the men were supposed to be sheltered. Characterised by Charlie Turner from Mountshannon as 'one of the dangerous places at the time', Whitegate had a reputation as somewhat unsafe for the IRA.[72] Three local people in that area have been identified across my research as potential informers. Given the delicacy associated with such information, they will be referred to here as Suspect A, B and C. All the accused lived within Whitegate. Beyond financial gain, it is challenging to identify a motive for the suspects. Suspect A was a member of the IRA; Suspect B was a farmer whose son was on the periphery of Volunteer activity, and Suspect C was from a house with apparent sympathies towards the British establishment.

One interviewee recorded how in the decades that followed, the father and brother of one of the four victims, notably ignored Suspect A, when they met at fairs and social gatherings. Suspect A had been arrested on charges relating to possession of weaponry shortly before the Killaloe incident and received a noticeably lenient sentence. The relevant Court

Martial Register shows that he was given just two months in prison shortly before the capture at Williamstown. At the same time, five others sentenced for similar offences, were given between one and two years in prison.[73] All three have been suspected of giving information to the crown forces, but which was the one responsible for the capture of the Scariff Martyrs, is more difficult to establish. The leniency with which Suspect A was treated when arrested in late October, would indicate he may have provided information. The time of his arrest correlates with the first indication the Auxiliaries became aware of the presence in Whitegate of Rodgers, McMahon and Gildea. However, since Suspect A's arrest, the three Volunteers had left Whitegate and only returned the day before their arrest, meaning further information was required from someone still on the ground. The seemingly hurried nature of the Auxiliaries journey to Williamstown on the morning of 16 November, strongly suggests information had come to them on the evening beforehand. A consistent oral tradition has emerged across many years which indicates that a local man was seen that evening, acting suspiciously in the area:

> I asked the question to my father and my uncle and a workman we had. They [McMahon, Rodgers and Gildea] were all working and doing the usual thing around the yard … But somebody came into the yard at Nutgrove, Holland's yard, that day … They just saw him and nobody said where did he go and nobody passed any remarks. Until later on when all was finished. 'What was he doing? Why didn't he come in? Was that the person?'[74]

The latter relates to Monday 15 November, when a local man momentarily watched McMahon, Rodgers and Gildea, as they worked in Holland's yard. Suspect A was then in prison. Suspect C did live in the broader area but was well known to the Holland family, which would make his presence far more conspicuous. Based on local tradition, set against the available evidence, the last person to see the men at Holland's yard was therefore, Suspect B.

It is evident that a final piece of information came to Killaloe, likely via the postmaster, James White, which confirmed the men had returned to Williamstown. If true, Suspect B continued to live on in the community for two decades in proximity to many intimately connected to the story. Local tradition indicates that he was later taken by the IRA to a mountain above Whitegate, where he was to be executed. It has also been suggested that it was only the profoundly ironic intervention of Suspect A, who as mentioned was a member of the IRA, that secured his reprieve. His actions were not the necessary inheritance of his family, however. In December 1945, his son's name appeared among 827 subscribers to a fund aimed at erecting a monument in honour of the men his father is suspected of having betrayed.

While an understandable anger has endured regarding the role of the spy, the inescapable reality was that all spies were ultimately in the pay or influence of an occupying government. When one follows the chain of command, the necessary elevation will take one to the upper echelons of British rule and it is there that ultimate responsibility must lie. When in 1921, Kathleen O'Callaghan, the widow of murdered Mayor of Limerick, Michael O'Callaghan, wrote about her husband's death, she referred to 'the boys murdered in cold blood on Killaloe Bridge'. O'Callaghan accepted 'one man's hand is fouled by pay for such deeds' but insisted that; 'blacker criminals planned these assassinations and they sit in high places.[75]

11

'Murder is Murder'

A Final Judgement

A communal consensus has long been established that the men were murdered. However, it is not enough to put forward that strongly held contention. A final and robust assessment, which ignores all previous declarations and steps back from the associated emotion is required. This will help to establish with as much conclusiveness as possible, what happened on that bridge that night. Here I will summarise the available evidence, foreground the British account of the incident and thoroughly examine the proposition that the men attempted to escape. I will then consider the counter contention that the deaths were planned and also the possibility that more British crown forces than was declared in the Court of Inquiry were present on the bridge that night.

The official British account of what took place on Killaloe Bridge on the night of 16 November, 1920, is based on the findings of a Military Court of Inquiry, held in Killaloe on Thursday 18 November, and housed in the British National Archives in London. By November 1920, the implementation of the Restoration of Order in Ireland Act meant that inquests were replaced with military courts of inquiry.[1] The inquiry held in Killaloe was therefore not judicial and only constituted an investigation of the incident, to determine if further action was required. Its findings are contained in a thirteen-page report, emblazoned with a handwritten note on its cover, which declares the men were 'shot by RIC while attempting to escape from arrest'.[2]

While the inquiry was taking place within Killaloe RIC barracks, the four bodies of McMahon, Rodgers, Gildea and Egan remained lying at the back of the building in an outhouse. Outside, Daniel Egan stood waiting to see his dead son.[3] Inside the building which separated Egan from his son, a three-man panel, made up exclusively of British military personnel, convened those assembled.

The president of the court was thirty-three-year-old John Francis Eastwood, a major in the Grenadier Guards, who was later a member of the British parliament.[4] Under Eastwood sat twenty-one year old Lt Aubrey Trevor Oswald Lees, of the Second Battalion of the Royal Welch Fusiliers, based in Limerick during the War of Independence.[5] His fellow member of the panel was Richard Crawford Warren, who, the same age as Lees, was a lieutenant in the Oxford and Buckinghamshire Regiment, stationed at Tulla. Seven months later on 28 June 1921, Warren died from wounds received the previous night, when a patrol he was leading was ambushed by the IRA in Tulla.[6] A day later, his regiment travelled to Feakle where they shot dead a forty-four year old civilian, James Grogan, in the townland of Core.[7] Like the sitting in Killaloe, the Military Court of Inquiry which sat to investigate Grogan's death, found no blame attributable to the men who fired the shots.[8]

While the court reported that seven men were involved in the escort that took the four men across the bridge, only five gave statements to the inquiry and among these, only four were on the bridge. The fifth witness, Captain Faraday, was the only member of G Company of the Auxiliaries to testify and gave evidence of arresting the four men. This means that the identity of at least three of the escort had not been revealed. According to the inquiry, it was not the Auxiliaries, as has often been claimed, but a combination of RIC and Black and Tans who fired the fatal shots.[9] Victor Stuart Gwynne, district inspector at Killaloe, gave evidence that the four prisoners were handed over by G Company of the Auxiliaries at 11.45 p.m. to a party of six police, under his command. Gwynne, a twenty-three-year-old native of Belfast fought for the British Army in the First World War and although technically a Black and Tan, in July 1920 Gwynne was posted as a district inspector to Killaloe on 1 October, possibly as part of an 'Ulsterisation' of the Irish police, which saw individuals with a strongly 'loyalist' sympathy appointed to senior positions.[10] While it has been suggested that the men were brought on a lorry to the bridge, the court recorded the men were 'on foot'.[11] Gwynne documented that it was a 'dark night' and outlined his version of the incident:

> As we crossed the bridge over the Shannon, the prisoners made a combined attempt to escape. They were ordered to halt and failing to comply with the order they were fired on by the escort. I personally fired twice. I should say about 8 other shots were fired. They fell at the shooting. I looked at the bodies and ascertained they were dead. I went to the barracks and brought down a Crossley Tender and took the bodies to the barracks.[12]

Thirty-five-year-old Black and Tan, Charles Edward McRae, a native of London, had been a sergeant in the Royal Army Medical Corp and had been based at Killaloe since April 1920. In his deposition, he claimed that the man he was in charge of (who he did not name) attempted to escape, and having called on him to halt, he 'fired at his feet and then at him'. He also claimed that he subsequently reviewed the bodies when they had been removed to the barracks. The third witness was also a Black and Tan, Samuel Hall, a twenty-two-year-old former miner from Derbyshire, who recorded a similar account, explaining how he saw his man 'dart off'. He informed the court; 'I then opened fire – I fired two or four shots in the direction in which the prisoners had gone'.[13]

Notably, Hall is the only witness to refer to handcuffs when he claimed the men were unrestrained. The final witness was John Brennan, an Irish member of the RIC and spoke of Rodgers, McMahon and Gildea, three men he had known for many years. A native of Wexford, Brennan had been based in east Clare for many years before the War of Independence. He was first posted to the east Clare district in 1893 as a twenty-one-year-old recruit to the RIC, the same year that Michael McMahon was born and was in the area for four years when Alphie Rodgers and Michael Egan were welcomed into the world. Brennan was previously in Bodyke barracks and seems to have been transferred to Scariff town in approximately 1913.[14] He had also been inside the barracks in Scariff two months before, during the Killaloe incident, when Rodgers, McMahon and Gildea were outside, centrally involved in the attack.

His presence on the bridge and his involvement in the men's deaths challenges many of the public notions about the Scariff Martyrs, principally that the men were killed by an exclusively English force. Brennan claimed that they marched the prisoners from the Lakeside Hotel and that after approximately five minutes 'they attempted to escape our custody'. Consistent with the other witnesses, Brennan claimed the prisoners were ordered to halt and when they did not, were shot. In fact, Brennan said that the escort 'called halt quite loudly' and 'heard it said twice'. In a significant admission, Brennan further recorded that he 'saw them fall and ascertained they were dead' – given the fact that it was a dark night approaching midnight, they must have fallen very close to the constable. Concerning the men's activity, Brennan told the court:

> I have known the men for 7 years. They were all members of the Irish Republican Volunteers and were engaged in the attack on the barrack at Scariff. They have been on the run since to escape arrest.[15]

It is notable that Brennan included Egan in his characterisation of the men as IRA members, given that this claim has never otherwise been made. For example, Faraday made no mention of Egan's membership of the IRA and Andrews, in questioning the Conway brothers, was only concerned with McMahon, Rodgers and Gildea.[16]

The panel accepted entirely the testimony of their colleagues. The findings were then sent to Victoria barracks in Cork, where they were signed off on behalf of Maj. Gen. Strickland, a man who had commanded the largest military barracks in Ireland and who the IRA had attempted to kill on several occasions.[17] They were predictably endorsed by the British government, whose chief secretary, Hamar Greenwood, spent the following weeks quoting and defending them robustly. According to his cabinet secretary, Sir Maurice Hankey, the British prime minister, Lloyd George privately welcomed the actions of his forces.[18] In addition, his secretary for war, Winston Churchill sought for the strategy of reprisals to be formalised and intimated a desire for more hangings. Crown forces oscillated between a public and private implementation of their leader's wishes.

'The Bridge was packed with Auxies, Tans and Peelers'

When Brian Graney interviewed John Conway in the 1950s, he knew the significance of his testimony. Conway, through his direct experience, was able to provide a level of detail and context that challenges, more than any other testimony, the British conclusions. At approximately 11.00 p.m. that night, following their own interrogation by Col Andrews, the two Conway brothers were returned to the dayroom at the Lakeside Hotel. As they entered the room, they passed the four other prisoners, who were at that moment being taken out and this was the last time they saw the men alive.

While McMahon, Rodgers, Gildea and Egan made their way under armed escort towards Killaloe bridge, John and Michael Conway ate a meal given to them by the Auxiliaries. They then walked down a long passage into a small room under ground level at the Lakeside Hotel, where they were given blankets and left to lie on the floor. Sometime later, from within that room, the Conways heard 'an awful hullaballoo away at the other end of the passage – shouting and roaring, and dancing and drunken men singing, "When Irish eyes were smiling".'[19] Although Conway did not hear the shots, at that time, Michael McMahon, Alphie Rodgers, Martin Gildea and Michael Egan were lying dead or dying on the bridge.

Conway's vivid recollection of his later walk across the bridge from Ballina to Killaloe, documents the brutality and horror of the night:

> Suddenly the door was burst in on us and Auxies shouted at us to get up quickly. Each of us was marched out between two Auxies – I was first – up to the bridge. These two Auxies weren't bad. The bridge was packed with Auxies, Tans and peelers. We were marched across it. We hadn't gone very far when an Auxie flashed a light and told me to walk [step] over the body – 'stiff' he called it. I knew it was the body of one of the four boys. About twenty yards further on there was another, and then another. The last body was right over the canal arch. There was a Crossley tender at Shannon View Hotel with the lights on, facing us, and I saw by its light that that was Martin Gildea. He was dead. He was handcuffed and his face was bloody. We were halted near the tender. The Tans used to come over to us, look into our faces and threaten us.[20]

Soon after that experience, Michael Conway left for New Zealand where three of his sisters were living.[21] Tragically, he died only five years later when scaffolding he was working in Timaru collapsed.[22] His older brother John lived in Whitegate for many decades, but seldom spoke about the Killaloe killings. As a young man, Michael 'Hookey' Farrell spoke to John Conway. Reluctant to speak about the experience, Conway only shook his head and commented in a low voice that the worst aspect of the whole ordeal was walking over the bodies during which he 'got weak', declaring in painful tones to 'Hookey' that, 'Jazus, Mike, I wasn't able to do it.'[23]

The testimony of Conway goes a long way towards demonstrating the temperament of the crown forces in Killaloe. Far from being subdued by the incident on the bridge, they seemed emboldened. When the Conways were handed over to the police at Killaloe, a series of beatings began. Speaking in 1953, Conway was clear that the beating and intimidation of him and his brother was not the preserve of English Black and Tans:

> After that we were marched up the hill by the same Auxies to the R.I.C. barracks, and taken into the dayroom. As we got to the barracks the tender passed us and went in the archway with the bodies … The day room was full of Tans. They jostled and pushed against us, but did no more. After a while they threw us into the black hole. We were beaten then, and it was by two Irish peelers – they struck us and knocked us down and leaped on us … Sometime afterwards a peeler came in with a baton in his hand. He drew at my face and I pulled back, but he got me on the point of the left cheek-bone and gave me a very sore black eye. In the morning I asked the man who came to see us for a glass of water. He said he was afraid to give it to us.[24]

'Attempted to Escape our Custody'

The notion the men were shot while attempting to escape is the central dimension of a contested narrative. One interviewee conveyed the rejection of the British account within the local east Clare community vigorously:

> They counted seventeen bullet holes in each of them. That was good shootin'! These boys were supposed to be running away trying to escape and each of 'em got seventeen bullet holes. That had to be a big patrol with very very accurate shooting, do you know, [because] between them because there was nare a spent bullet anywhere. They all hit home! Every soldier only fired one shot. Mighty! 'Twas no wonder they won the war![25]

Michael O'Gorman's angry reflection on the claims of the police echoes the broader disbelief at official claims the men were shot while attempting to escape. On 18 November 1920, the national press reported that Dublin Castle authorities received reports of a shooting at midnight of four Clare men who were attempting to escape custody.[26] Over the following days, both local and national press presented somewhat confused reports.[27] It was suggested that both Conway brothers (referred to as Connelly) had also been wounded in the shooting.[28] Almost immediately, alternative accounts to the official version were circulated locally. Critically, there were no other eye-witnesses to the event on the bridge, other than British forces.

However, testimony on sounds heard in Killaloe that night is important. Before the escort emerged from the Lakeside Hotel on Tuesday 16 November approaching midnight, there was no sound. No industry. No people on the street. The restriction of movement resulting from the war and consolidated by the arrival of the Auxiliaries to the town weeks earlier ensured that the bridge of Killaloe was a deathly silent place that night. However, sound travels further in cold conditions as when air becomes colder, it begins to condense, making it thicker and better able to transmit.[29] Additionally, sound travels better close to water. Conditions in Killaloe and Ballina in November 1920 were cold and wet. According to the monthly weather report of the Meteorological office of the United Kingdom for November 1920, Ireland received 110 per cent of its normal rainfall for that month.[30] The natural amplification due to the weather conditions, combined with the location of the shooting on the bridge as well as the military curfew, suggests that many of the local population in both Killaloe and Ballina were potentially aural witnesses to the shooting.

The houses of Denis Crowe, who managed the local office of the Board of Works, as well as those of Catholic priests, Canon Dan Flannery and Fr James Russell, were located on the Killaloe and Ballina sides of the bridge respectively. All three later testified to their aural recollections of the incident, which critically included hearing prolonged moans and cries in addition to gunfire. When Brian Graney undertook interviews about the incident in the 1950s, he was told that 'residents on both sides of the bridge heard before and after the shooting, the piteous cries of men in pain and the appealing wail for a priest'.[31] Both Canon Flannery and Fr Russell, although too afraid to try to intervene, gave conditional absolution to the men from their homes.

Crowe, whose house was closest to the Killaloe side of the bridge, was woken from his sleep by the moans and screams of men. He told Graney that 'It was pitiful to listen to them' and explained that he 'dared not put on the light for he knew if he had done so he would have been shot instantly.'[32] Crowe further asserted that he had been listening to the 'cries of the tortured' for over seven minutes when the first shots were fired. This supports the contention that the men were subjected to a savage beating and that they were bayoneted before being shot. Crowe also adjudged that the men were placed with their backs to the north wall and shot from close range. Some reports challenge the assertion the men were bayoneted. The correspondent for the *Daily Herald* for example, suggested that this belief was only 'owing to cries and groans heard by inhabitants near the bridge'.[33]

Canon Flannery, a seventy-seven year old native of Monsea in Tipperary, who was sick in bed at his home, close to what was then the Shannon View Hotel, sat up and declared to his niece Bridget; 'they are murdering someone'.[34] Local and national newspaper reports also claimed that residents of the town heard between fifteen and twenty shots over a prolonged period followed by 'shrieks and moans'.[35] Those noises carried deep into Killaloe town. From New Street, fifteen-year-old Micheál Hogan and two friends heard the commotion and, emboldened by their youth, crept to a spot where they could see the bridge, using the dark as shelter. In 1969, after his son Jack and The Shannon Folk Four were on RTÉ television, singing 'The Four Who Fell', Micheál revealed his memories of the incident. Out of sight of the British forces, Micheál claimed that he saw four men against the north wall of the bridge, faced by a large group of soldiers. Barrage after barrage of gun fire followed for an extended period and Micheál knew the men were dead.[36]

In Grey's account, shots were heard an hour after the prisoners were on the bridge.[37] When outlining details later in the British House of Commons, Hamar Greenwood recorded that the men were killed at 12.30 a.m., which is a difference of at least forty-five minutes from the official time recorded by Gwynne that the prisoners were taken from the hotel.[38] Joe Hogan, deckhand of the SS Shannon, also testified to hearing the shots.[39] Years later, in the town of Scariff, Mrs Burke, who had moved there from Killaloe having married a local chemist, disclosed to Gerald Rodgers that she too had heard the moans of his brother Alphie and the other men, which she insisted continued for some time and were interspersed by gunfire.[40]

Denis Crowe told Graney in 1953 that he had heard the sound of automatic fire, as he listened to the gunfire from his home near the bridge.[41] It should be noted that the sound of at least seven men firing rifles in quick succession could be mistaken for automatic fire. However, his testimony does not support the British contention that a short burst of approximately ten shots were fired. Critically, the Court of Inquiry is unequivocal that the men were shot dead upon their attempt to escape and that death was instant.[42] The latter clashes with local suggestions that protracted moaning and cries for help were heard on the bridge. All of the above lent credence to the claim by the *Irish Bulletin*, a republican newspaper, that halfway across the bridge, 'the constabulary fell upon their victims'.[43]

With increasing numbers of republicans being killed in

such a way, the notion that the men were shot 'attempting to escape' was challenged from the initial account of the incident.[44] In fact, the day after the killings, before news broke of what had occurred in Killaloe, Joe Devlin, together with fellow nationalist MP Jeremiah McVeagh, was questioning the British prime minister regarding the increasing number of prisoners shot while in custody and handcuffed.[45] *The Irish Times* commented that the deaths of the four men in Killaloe had brought to eleven, the number of men shot dead 'while attempting to escape from British custody of late'.[46] After details emerged, most newspapers attached little credibility to the official account, with the *Larne Times* in Antrim one of the few to seemingly endorse the British version.[47] One historian placed the number of prisoners shot dead by crown forces in similar circumstances at 108.[48] Concerns over such deaths were also noted by the American Commission on Conditions in Ireland, compiled during this time.[49] Even in the small village of Horsted Keynes in the south of England, attendees at a protest meeting were told about the shootings in Killaloe. The *Mid Sussex Times* reported how R.C. Grey, who had fled Clare owing to intimidation by Auxiliaries, gave an emotional address to the assembly, in which he explicitly accused the British forces of murder.[50]

In the British House of Commons in December 1920, Nationalist MP Arthur O'Connor, referring to Killaloe, demanded an outline of the instructions given to police and to military escorts in reference to prisoners under arrest and whether the order was given to kill before there was any warning or any attempt to recapture. Greenwood repeated the claim that the men tried to escape from their escort at Killaloe and were shot dead.[51] O'Connor pressed the chief secretary on the contention that the men were handcuffed at the time of their deaths but Greenwood avoided answering by declaring O'Connor had not included this issue in his private notice, at which Belfast's Joe Devlin shouted across the House of Commons to insist that 'they were all handcuffed'.[52]

Michael Brennan, then O/C of the East Clare Brigade, claimed the men were still handcuffed when their bodies were recovered.[53] MacLysaght wrote dismissively in 1954 that, given the 'liquidation' of the Scariff Martyrs, the attempts by the British to frame their deaths as the result of an attempted escape 'were such as to make this plea even more futile than was customary in such cases'.[54] His son told me in 2019 that MacLysaght never wavered in this conviction that the men were murdered.[55] Most critically, John Conway, whose vision was assisted by a Crossley tender facing onto the bridge, saw the bodies in the immediate aftermath of their deaths and testified that Martin Gildea was handcuffed.[56]

Conway's recollection that Gildea's body was close to the Killaloe side of the bridge in addition to Grey's statement that blood was similarly located, is also significant.[57] In their statements to the Court of Inquiry, four witnesses all stated that the men made their attempt to escape at the Ballina side of the bridge and were shot soon after with Const. Hall declaring 'when we got the bridge over the Shannon … I saw my man dart off'.[58] In addition, both Brennan and Hall further claimed that they saw the men fall, which on a dark night such as was admitted by his superior DI Gwynne, would have to mean they fell close by. Given that their testimonies assert that shots were fired almost immediately after the men 'made a combined attempt to escape' and that the men died instantly, logic would dictate that their bodies would have been found closer to the Ballina side of the bridge. The bridge of Killaloe is 200 metres (656ft.). When a local worker, Mike Daly found a substantial pool of blood the following morning and marked the spot on the wall of the bridge, he did so at 115 m (377ft) from the Ballina side which meant that the prisoners ran at least 115 metres before they were felled.

When considering that the fastest man every recorded, Usain Bolt, ran 100 metres in 9.58 seconds, it would be challenging to expect four prisoners who had been severely beaten for at least eight hours to exceed that distance in the time it would take to call halt and shoot, whether restrained or unrestrained, before being shot down.[59] Furthermore, the recollections of John Conway suggest that the bodies were spaced equally apart. This does not accord with a combined attempt to escape and instead suggested a planned execution.

'The Bodies were Riddled'

On the night of the killings, Charles Edward McRae, who had been involved in the shooting, claimed that he undertook a basic review of the bodies. His report claimed that one bullet hit the head of Gildea – three on the body of Rodgers, including two to the abdomen and one to the head – one in the abdomen of McMahon and one bullet wound to the head of Egan.[60] Two days later, Grey received a report from a nurse who he recorded 'had been a nursing sister all through the war.' That nurse was almost certainly Johanna MacMahon.[61] In the case of Martin Gildea, the nurse reported the primary wounds as follows: 'one bullet wound, entrance behind the right ear, exit side of neck, fired at close range, skin round entrance blackened'; for Michael Egan, 'one bullet wound, side of head'; for Rodgers, four bullet wounds were identified in the frontal bone (forehead), right cheek, left shoulder and liver. In addition, it was recorded that Rodgers' liver had ruptured, his right eye was black and swollen from what appeared to be a 'blow from blunt instrument'. Upon an inspection of McMahon, a bullet wound was recorded in the 'thigh, through and through wound, no bones broken, entrance from exit back' in addition to bullet wounds in the right buttock and abdomen'.[62]

Kathleen Mitchell, whose mother Mary was Martin

Gildea's sister, remembered her father speaking about his own observations at the funeral of the four men and in particular, of his brother-in-law, Martin Gildea. Paddy Skehill looked closely at his brother-in-law in the coffin, as he lay in Scariff church:

> Well they got a cruel death. They were fighting for their country and that was it ... Ah shur it's sad to think that he was butchered. I heard Daddy saying there was a big hole in his head ... Brutally murdered ... Martin Gildea had a big hole in his head. He saw it when he was at the funeral. A big hole.[63]

According to Michael O'Gorman, whose grandmother, Kate Harte, was a nurse in Scariff Union Hospital and who viewed the bodies closely when they returned from Killaloe, some of the bullets were fired from close range, based on the marks on the bodies of the men and that she felt the men were shot in turn 'brought over and pushed up against the wall'.[64] Paddy McDonnell, who examined the bodies as they lay in Scariff chapel at approximately 3.00 a.m. on the night 18 November asserted; 'They had bayonet wounds in their faces. Poor Brud had no face at all left for I saw them in the coffins. Alfie was fierce purple in the face'.[65] Despite being proscribed, an illegal and clandestine autopsy and inquest were held on Friday 19 November, after the coroner, Patrick Culloo from Tulla, formed a jury to view the bodies and directed Dr Patrick Holmes to carry out a detailed examination.

Holmes reported no less than seventeen bullet wounds in each of the bodies and that the shots were fired from close range.[66] Further evidence of 'singing' of the hair in the temples was found and in the case of Brud McMahon, it was established that 'the wounds were of such a nature as to ensure death but not to cause it instantaneously'.[67] Holmes was a physician and surgeon who was born in Athlunkard Street Limerick in 1881 and grew up in Knockballynameath in Co. Clare.[68] By 1920 he was living in Killaloe and had been working as a medical officer to the British forces in addition to his normal practice. Two months before the incident on the bridge, he had been called on to attend to RIC Sgt Michael O'Sullivan when he was shot during the attack on the Scariff RIC barracks.[69] This evident impartiality adds credence to his evidence at the autopsy of the four men.[70] Holmes' neutrality is reinforced by the reality that his predecessor, Dr Henry McKeogh had been removed from his position, when his tacit support for republicanism was established.[71] Pat O'Donnell, a twenty-nine-year-old IRA Volunteer from the town of Scariff who arranged the autopsy, claimed the method of execution was intentionally torturous. When speaking to Brian Graney in 1953, he remembered:

> Alfie's hair was singed at the temples where there was a gaping wound made. I'd say by one or more .45 bullets fired at point blank range. When I tried to lift Martin Gildea my hand ran through the back of his head. His hair was singed and there was a dreadful wound in his temple as if more than more than one bullet had been fired into the same spot. All the bodies were riddled and we were all satisfied from the wounds that the first shots were aimed low down and that the weapons, while being fired from, were gradually raised up. All the bullets went right through the bodies. There was an expression of a painful lingering death on Brud's face.[72]

Even when allowing for some possible exit wounds, Holmes' findings presented a damning contradiction of the British account. The results of his autopsy which, because of its illegal nature was undertaken in secret, was quickly disseminated across the community, verifying a brutal image of the men's deaths.[73] For example, the *Irish Independent* reported that such had been the severity of their treatment in British custody that the men were 'most unrecognisable'.[74] Both McRae and Grey's reports were based on cursory inspections, rather than the type of complete surgical examination undertaken by Dr Holmes in Scariff church.

'Bragging that they were going to Shoot the Prisoners'

The claim that the men were shot trying to escape has been shown to have serious weaknesses. In addition, the official suggestion that Egan was an IRA Volunteer, despite no evidence that he was, further undermines the findings. The suggestion that the deaths were premeditated must therefore be considered.

That contention was noted in 1923 when the *Nenagh Guardian* suggested that Andrews 'in conjunction with DI Gwynne, the Black and Tan stationed in Killaloe, planned the destruction of the four boys'.[75] With over 100 Auxiliaries based at the Lakeside Hotel, a number of people were employed as cooks and cleaners, mostly from the immediate locality and many who had previously served in the British army. Significant claims were made by many of them there, including the assertion that it was planned before the escort left the hotel:

> That night there were workers, local people who had been working in the Lakeside Hotel, making food and catering for the auxiliaries. Some of the workers had overheard in the bar that the prisoners were going to be shot. They knew that the men had been brought back that day and overheard them bragging that they were going to shoot the prisoners. Some of them went to Fr Russell who was the closest priest to the Lakeside and told him.[76]

John Fahy remembered hearing the story discussed in 1949, when on the bridge of Killaloe a commemoration was held:

> That day, I heard a girl comment about her father who had been in the bar in the Lakeside and that he always told her how he heard the Black and Tans betting about who would shoot the prisoners. She was certain about that.[77]

Fr James Russell later testified that he 'knew there were prisoners at the Lakeside Hotel and he lay awake', which supports the claim that workers at the hotel had informed him of the prisoner's presence there. Russell was the Catholic curate of Ballina.[78] A claim made by Russell to the Irish Grants Committee (previously Irish Distress Committee) in the late 1920s, revealed that he had been 'friendly with auxiliaries' and so he was boycotted by much of the local population and his house destroyed.[79] While contradicting the hitherto belief that his house was burned by British forces, it adds credence to his claims of hearing prolonged screams on the bridge and the suggestion that the action was premeditated and planned at the Lakeside Hotel. John Conway's clear recollection of hearing Auxiliaries 'shouting and roaring, and dancing and drunken men singing' in the immediate aftermath of the killings is also hugely significant and carries a clear implication that G Company were celebrating the killings on the bridge.[80]

'Paid to keep his Mouth Shut'

Perhaps the most dramatic and damning suggestion came from the highest ranking Auxiliary officer in Ireland at the time, Gen. Frank Percy Crozier. Crozier, who was commanding the entire Auxiliary force in Ireland, charged explicitly in relation to a member of G Company in Killaloe, that a 'blackmailer who had been dismissed from the force and sent to England by me was regularly paid to keep his mouth shut about the Killaloe Bridge Murders'.[81]

Crozier's allegation was raised in the British House of Commons in June 1921 by Samuel Galbraith.[82] The Irish Chief Secretary Hamar Greenwood referred to a previous discussion on Crozier's allegations, in which he had stood by the findings of the relevant military courts. However, inspection of the debate on the latter date shows that Greenwood made no reference to Killaloe.[83] Crozier's comments on Killaloe reflected on the tensions that developed between the various factions of the crown forces; after the killings on the bridge 'the regular RIC' complained that they had been left to 'clear up the mess' and 'explain' the deaths to the parents, which was 'not very nice'.[84] Crozier's contention carries an implication that the Auxiliaries may have had a more direct role in their deaths than official accounts might suggest.

The claim by Crozier that an Auxiliary was paid to purchase his silence about what took place on the bridge is a startling revelation. While there have been many attempts to discredit the former head of the Auxiliaries, the suggestion that members of G Company were at the very least aware of what took place that night cannot be ignored. Research indicates that at least fifteen members of G Company left the force in the months that followed. Ten of these, including Col Andrews, resigned.[85] The Internal Discipline Register of the Auxiliaries indicates that five were dismissed for disciplinary reasons. Of those five, two were posted to G Company in 1921 and so were not present in Killaloe in November 1920. This leaves three among the main Auxiliary group in Killaloe. Cadet A. W. Bromham, was dismissed in May 1921, while a month later, Head Const. Albert Griggs resigned on disciplinary grounds, with nothing in either of their story that would indicate they may have been involved.[86]

That is not the case with the third possible blackmailer, Percy George Wiles. A native of Islington in London he fought first in the Boer War in South Africa at the age of seventeen. At the outset of the First World War in 1914, he re-enlisted; 1918 he was a commissioned officer and in August 1919, he left the army with a gratuity of £1,500. It seems at this point that Wiles' fortunes began to change. Critically, from late 1919 to October 1920, he lost all his money after he established a bookmaker business at Epsom.[87] In October 1920, Wiles, then thirty-seven and in financial difficulty, joined the Auxiliaries and was posted to G Company at Killaloe. In April 1921, he was dismissed. After his return to

England, Wiles' life seemed to spiral further out of control and he was convicted under the Vagrancy Act in 1922, and imprisoned for three months. Removed officially from the army in 1927, he left his wife and later was tried for burglary and larceny with a criminal accomplice, Harry Cohen. This spiral continued until 1940, when he died in a workhouse in Manchester, of chronic alcoholism.[88] Despite repeated efforts to locate relations, none were found. Although technically dismissed after Crozier's own departure, Wiles matches the profile of a potential blackmailer.

A final potential candidate was Temp. Const. William Flowers, a twenty-three-year-old former labourer and solider, allocated to G Company on 9 October, 1920. As a driver, Flowers was registered differently to the main Auxiliary force. On 22 January 1921, he was transferred to the Veteran's Division in Dublin and two days later was struck off, with no reason detailed.[89]

It is not surprising that no record survives to confirm if and who the blackmailer may have been. If Crozier's allegation was true, it is far more likely that efforts would have been made to conceal such a strategy. For example, after the murder of Nicholas de Sales Prendergast, a hotel owner in Fermoy, auxiliaries who were aware of what had happened, were moved from the area. One of those, Leslie Shiner, was sent to Killaloe and later recorded how that incident and others were 'whitewashed' by British authorities.[90] However, both Wiles, because of his personal situation, and Flowers, because of the time of his dismissal, add to the possibility of such an occurrence.

'No use in Arresting Them'

Nationally, there are cases that demonstrate the capacity for British crown forces to use extreme violence and to make strident efforts to conceal them. For example, Harry and Patrick Loughnane were tortured and murdered by Auxiliaries based in Drumharsna Castle near Ardrahan in south Galway just two weeks after the Scariff Martyrs. Initially, the Auxiliaries claimed that the men had escaped their custody. It later emerged that the brothers had been severely tortured and buried in a shallow lake at Owenbristy near Ardrahan.[91]Also in Galway, Comdt Louis Darcy was shot dead and dragged behind a lorry and just days before the killings in Killaloe, Fr Michael Griffin was murdered and buried secretly by British forces and the blame laid elsewhere.[92]

Given the behaviour of their colleagues around the country, it is not surprising that G Company had the same capacity for violence. G Company contained within their ranks many who went on to infamy and who demonstrated their ability for ruthlessness. For example, George S.M. Nathan and William Harrison, who are alleged to have led a 'death squad' during this period, were stationed in Killaloe at the time. They are reputed to have, in March 1921, been responsible for the murder of Limerick mayor, Seoirse (also referred to as George) Clancy, as well as the previous mayor, Michael O'Callaghan and Westmeath native, Joseph O'Donoghue.[93] The role of Patrick Cullinan, from Newmarket, in the collection of intelligence, who had long declared his allegiance to the British imperial project is noteworthy. When Auxiliary Leslie Shiner was transferred to Killaloe in January 1921, it did not take long to establish the culture of G Company. On his first night a fellow auxiliary boasted that 'Andrews and Fara [Faraday] pretty much give us free rein in how we deal with the IRA and their sympathisers.'[94] Shiner observed Faraday declare, before his unit were sent to Kilkishen following the Glenwood ambush, that 'these IRA bastards and their sympathisers are going to cop it … it's payback time now'. Later, while his forces set houses on fire in that area, he was heard screaming 'You "Shinner" bastards, we are going to leave your land a smoking ruin!'[95] In March, the new head of G Company, Lt Col Hemming reinforced this approach when he yelled at a unit arranging to target the O/C of the East Clare IRA, Michael Brennan that, 'The man is a fucking murderer with blood on his hands. I want him brought back here for questioning, but if not, shoot him and his terrorist friends down'.[96]

Papers released for the first time in 2019 by the Military Archives of Ireland, reveal that as part of an attempt to gain intelligence and to prepare an ambush on the force, the IRA in east Clare captured Intelligence Books belonging to G Company in Killaloe. In the handwritten notes within, a dramatic insight into the inclinations of the British forces was disclosed. Describing the sister of a local IRA Battalion commandant as 'a Republican Bitch', the document betrays the position adopted by an alleged police force. Strikingly, in relation to members of the republican movement in east Clare, it declared that there was 'no use in arresting them' before bluntly affirming that instead, 'they should be plugged'.[97]

While four witnesses at the Court of Inquiry accept in their statements that they were involved in shooting the prisoners, the brightest light perhaps shines on RIC Sgt John Brennan whose aggressive stance against the local IRA was well known among republicans in east Clare. Mount-shannon's Tom McNamara recalled Brennan raiding his house on 22 September 1920.[98] Many years later, Tom's sister, Katy McNamara, who the following April watched as her home burned to the ground, recalled with anger the image of Brennan sitting close by, watching the house burn while eating biscuits.[99]

Accounts of Sgt Brennan demonstrate his negative position in republican memory. In one interview, however, it was claimed that Brennan once saved a local family when he intentionally covered a hiding place, which contained a rifle.[100] In a 1989 recording, a former Volunteer in the Caherhurley

Company of the IRA, angrily reflected on Brennan's role at Killaloe:

> Oh God help us. That was the most tragic thing of all. And 'twas one of our own. 'Twas one of our own Irish constabulary that shot 'em! The British men wouldn't fire on 'em! Yes, he was a drunken Brennan too! And the last that I heard of him was that he died mad in a lunatic asylum and 'twas no wonder he would.[101]

Tommy Bolton's affirmation that Irish members of the RIC were centrally involved in what had been for many years publicly declared the result of English cruelty is significant. The monument on the bridge pronounces in Irish that they were 'murdered by the army of the English'. In the early 1950s, when a posthumous application for an IRA Service Medal was made on behalf of Alphie Rodgers, it was recorded that he was 'shot by the Black and Tans'.[102] There were of course, in addition to Hall and McRae, fifteen further members of the Black and Tans based in Killaloe that night who could have been involved and whose aggression had been noted in east Clare since their arrival months earlier.[103]

Hall was imprisoned for two months in March 1921 after he and five Black and Tans seriously assaulted Const. Timothy Griffin at Killaloe.[104] When questioned, Charles Edward McRae insisted he only shot at the men after they attempted to escape. Notably, just two weeks later, the same man was one of a small group implicated in a violent raid on Bishop Michael Fogarty's home in Ennis, where it has been strongly claimed, the intention was to kill the prelate.[105] Revealingly, IRA intelligence documents within the Collins' Papers, labelled McRae 'a most aggressive person', who was transferred to Galway 'for his own safety'.[106]

However, the role of the RIC in their deaths has been previously overlooked and their inclusion must now be acknowledged. Two days after the incident, John Brennan, who had evidently been previously demoted, was awarded a £10 bonus and received a 'favourable record' on his RIC service detail. Such awards were given to those RIC personnel who demonstrated 'exceptional seal' in their duties and he was also reinstated to the rank of sergeant. While the timing is significant, it is probable the award was in relation to his role in the defence of the RIC barracks in Scariff, when it was attacked two months earlier.

While three of the escort were not named in the official inquiry, research has uncovered that in addition to Brennan, at least twelve of the policemen based in Scariff during the IRA attack in September were stationed in Killaloe at the time of the killings, including seven who, with Brennan, received awards two days after the murders.[107]

All were aware of the central role of McMahon, Rodgers and Gildea in that attack and so perhaps had a significant motive for revenge. Others whose names attract attention are Const. Peter Murphy, who had previously been involved in several violent actions against republicans. Murphy was awarded the constabulary medal on two occasions for his action against the IRA.[108] Sergeants Michael Harrington and Martin Turnball, who had both previously demonstrated their acrimony towards the republican movement, were also present in the town. So too was Timothy Brennan, who had been in Feakle for much of 1920, awarded a Favourable Record and promoted to sergeant. When Joe Noonan was later arrested and beaten in Killaloe, he identified both John and Timothy Brennan as key to his interrogation. He recalled how the latter, gave him 'a lot of punishment'.[109]

It is also striking that one of the police wounded in Scariff was Const. Edward Broderick.[110] The inclusion of Broderick as one of the possible shooters opens up a dramatic revelation. The Court of Inquiry recorded that among the crimes the men were accused of, was the shooting of Broderick two months earlier. This places an apparent victim of their alleged crimes in Killaloe on the night they were murdered.

Official evidence on the killings is limited and highly questionable. Local testimony too contains inevitable subjectivities. It has therefore been necessary to venture into the territory where conclusive evidence fades and informed judgement begins.

It is clear that when the varied testimonies and claims are assembled and placed against the evidence provided by the inquiry, a number of contradictions are illuminated which makes the British findings extremely challenging to believe. Even in the days after the incident, the national press recorded its own scepticism about much of the official version, including the peculiarity of transferring the men at midnight, as well as the contention that they were trying to escape.[111] But it is challenging to find even one contemporary commentator, outside of their own personnel, who seemed to attach any credibility to their version of events. Given the striking contradictions apparent in the British account, the whole version must come into question.

The contention that the men simply tried to escape the escort is not persuasive. By November 1920, it had been firmly established, both for civilians arrested as well as experienced IRA men, that whatever the circumstances, to run from crown forces was to sign your own death warrant.[112] They certainly would not have run if handcuffed.

From their own admission, the escort, who were apparently detailed to convey the prisoners across the bridge, were fully aware that they had at least three seasoned IRA men who had been involved in shooting some of their colleagues in the weeks previously and who had long declared their violent opposition to British rule, including its police force. When these men were captured in Whitegate, they were tied with thick ropes and shackled together, despite being on a boat, a confined space surrounded by thirty armed Auxiliaries and on Lough Derg, the third largest lake in Ireland. When the men were taken to the Lakeside Hotel, where over 100 Auxiliaries were stationed, they were put in handcuffs. Yet, according to British reports, later that night, a seven-man police escort taking these men across a dark bridge and into Killaloe town, did not deem it necessary or wise to restrain the prisoners.

That the RIC and Black and Tans were involved is certain. Given the presence of policemen who had in the months beforehand been attacked by the IRA, including Rodgers, McMahon and Gildea, the appetite for revenge is difficult to dismiss. It is also questionable that DI Gwynne, as well as others including John Brennan, did not have had a role in the interrogation of the four men at the Lakeside Hotel with Col Andrews. Brennan knew the men for many years and despite the probable work of Patrick Cullinan, the primary flow of intelligence had been to and from the RIC.

The possibility that certain members of G Company were also on the bridge and involved in the shooting, must also, I contend, be considered. That contention rests on some necessary questions. Why would Crozier make claims about an Auxiliary blackmailer, if no member of G Company was on the bridge to know what happened? Why would he suggest the RIC had to 'clear up the mess', made by the Auxiliaries?[113] Why were the Auxiliaries celebrating in the aftermath of the incident? When the Conways were taken across the bridge in the aftermath, why was it by members of the Auxiliaries, not RIC?

The broader version put forward by the British crown forces has been shown to contain many challengeable elements. Is it credible, for example, that with a force of at least thirty-four available to Gwynne and more than 100 at the disposal of Andrews, that just seven police were selected to escort four important IRA prisoners? Why take the risk of their escape? Why, if the escort left the Lakeside Hotel at 11.45 p.m., were their deaths officially recorded at 12.30 a.m. forty-five minutes later? In the end there are too many contradictions, too many questions.

Ultimately, there are only three plausible possibilities for what took place on the bridge of Killaloe.

Firstly, it is highly unlikely but not impossible that the prisoners made a combined attempt to escape and were shot as the Court of Inquiry found. The injuries reported in McRae's review and in the report issued to Grey, were not incompatible with wounds afflicted in the way the British recorded. However, in addition to the far more detailed autopsy of Dr Holmes, finding much worse injuries and other revelations which have been described, strongly challenge the British account.

The second possibility is that the men were not handcuffed and were encouraged to run to create a reason for their killing. This is more plausible but does not account for the above contradictions either.

Finally, and what I put forward as the most likely reality, is that the combined British forces lied about the men not being handcuffed and that they summarily executed restrained and tortured prisoners. Given the details outlined above, it is justifiable to conclude that the murder was premeditated and ruthlessly executed. The Military Court of Inquiry's findings are therefore considered a fabrication, invented by a combination of British forces, including the RIC, Black and Tans, Auxiliaries, in addition to the regular army command and endorsed by the British government.

It is far more likely that a considerable force was involved in the killing, comprising members of G Company, Black and Tans and Irish members of the RIC. The evidence suggests that as the republican prisoners crossed the bridge, they were surrounded and savagely beaten.[114] The conditions of their bodies indicate strongly that this beating including the prodding of their faces with bayonets and that they were beaten also with rifle butts. Although it was suggested the men's eyes were gouged and their fingernails pulled, this has not been proven. However, there can be no understating the severity of the brutal treatment they endured in their final minutes and in the eight hours before.

After a violent beating, it is evident that the four young men were then placed against the north wall of the bridge, close to where a monument was later integrated and the shooting began.

Epilogue

'Stored in the Annals Roll of History'

In the middle of June 1881, a forty-six-year-old Scottish suffragette found herself in the remote village of Bodyke in east Clare. From there, she was taken to the mountain townland of Caherhurley and into the thatched cottage of Mary Molony, who was sitting quietly by her open hearth fire. Weeks earlier, Mary's husband John had been killed by an RIC constable, during The Battle of Bodyke (see pp. 36–38) Both Molony's death, and the way in which the British judicial system protected his killer, left a deep wound in the area.

The endurance of such emotion was obvious to Jessie Craigen, who was in Bodyke as part of a Democratic Federation to document the incident. At first, Mary said little to the visitor and only after Craigen mentioned 'justice' did the grieving widow look up from the fire and angrily declare; 'There is no justice for us!'[1] By then, Mary had been aware that, despite the testimony of many, the RIC had ensured that no punishment would come to the man who struck the blows. A local man and witness to the Molony's killing, Patrick Slattery, had gone to great lengths to identify a sub-constable John O'Grady, the man responsible, including visiting RIC barracks in Broadford, Tulla, Bodyke and Feakle, where he was met with aggression from the police. In fact, Slattery was instead arrested by the RIC and charged under an evidently falsified allegation of attempted murder.[2]

In Caherhurley, Mary told Jessie Craigen that her husband John was a 'steady, good man' and explained how she saw him that night, 'in a deep sleep', lamenting that 'he never knew me or never spoke to me again'. Sadly, she described how 'it was like a dream' admitting that 'I often sit and think I hear his footsteps at the door'.[3] Mary Molony insisted that she forgave the man who killed her husband. Nevertheless, as she left Mary sitting by her turf fire, it was clear to the Scottish suffragette that the widow was part of an alienated community that harboured a deeply rooted resentment. After returning to the village of Bodyke that night, Craigen reflected on what she had experienced in Caherhurley and about her sense of that deep anger brewing amongst the people she had encountered. In a striking affirmation, she wrote that; 'Through sleepless nights and gloomy days, the people nurse their bitterness of soul till they hate us with that concentrated fury which is the surest pledge of war.'[4]

Twelve years later, in September 1893, twenty-one-year-old RIC Const. John Brennan, the son of a basket-weaver from Stonebridge in Co. Wexford, was stationed in Bodyke. Memory of Molony's murder at the hands of one of his colleagues remained potent. Echoes of the more recent Bodyke Evictions, which took place just six years before, continued also to reverberate in the east Clare parish, with sporadic outbreaks of tension between the local tenants and landlord, John O'Callaghan. In March of 1893, before Brennan's arrival, a serious confrontation had taken place as O'Callaghan executed a 'distress policy' which amounted to the forced seizure of livestock in lieu of rent.[5] Two months into Brennan's time in Bodyke, eight tenants were evicted, which led to further disturbances and in July of 1894, eleven cattle placed by O'Callaghan on evicted land were poisoned with arsenic. While emanating from a Land War, Brennan could have been in no doubt about the tension that existed between many of the people and agents of the British crown. He was also aware of which side of the divide he was on in this regard.[6]

When Brennan took up his post in 1893, Mary Molony was caring for her daughter, Catherine, who was then five months' pregnant and living in her home in the townland of

Caherhurley, where she was married to Michael Dillon. The following January, Catherine gave birth to her first son who she named in memory of his grandfather, John Molony.[7] For all the formative years of his life, young John Dillon had the company of his grandmother Mary and grew to manhood in Caherhurley with the killing of his grandfather as a constant backdrop.

When on 2 April 1911, census enumerator Thomas Geary travelled to their home, the family's strong nationalistic outlook was reflected in the registration of their surname as Uí Diullún on the national census. John Molony's widow forcefully recorded her own name as Máire Ní Maoldhomhnaigh.[8]

By 1920, John Dillon was the captain of the Caherhurley Company in the Fourth Battalion of the East Clare IRA, and had as his comrades, Alphie Rodgers, Michael 'Brud' McMahon and Martin Gildea. They were then engaged in a vicious fight against the forces of British rule that included John Brennan and the RIC. As underlined by one of his comrades, Dillon's intense activism had been largely driven by the murder of his grandfather many years before. He had been born into an aggrieved community that carried deep in their memory, past injustices and was culturally aligned with a tradition alienated from British rule. Brennan, through his employment, was a constituent part of that rule. At various times throughout history, such associations were not important, but at times of revolution, they were. One's alignment at particular moments of history can often determine where one's story is positioned in memory and historical consciousness.

Michael 'Brud' McMahon was three months old when Brennan arrived in east Clare. Four years later, Michael Egan and Alphie Rodgers were born. For all of their lives, they lived close to the RIC man, only interacting with him from 1913 when Brennan was moved to the Scariff RIC barracks. As the years moved on, they lived co-existent but separate lives – all

Irish men but with very different aims for their country. By November 1920, all had chosen their position: for Rodgers, McMahon and Gildea, it was freedom; for Michael Egan, it was a quiet life, and for Brennan, through his role in the RIC, a determination to crush the republican movement and return to the status quo of British rule.

Two months before the bridge killings, Brennan had been in Scariff barracks while an IRA force that included John Dillon, as well as McMahon, Rodgers and Gildea, were outside firing in. In the final night of their lives, Brennan was there with a gun in his hand, shoulder to shoulder with Black and Tans, pointing in the direction of Alphie Rodgers, Michael McMahon, Martin Gildea and Michael Egan. Whatever the personal grievance of having been attacked by the men two months previously, whatever the understandably human nature of revenge, whatever the sense of duty to his job, Brennan, in his role on the bridge, was deciding on British rule and not Irish independence, as were his colleagues in the RIC. So with the reverberation of those gunshots that rang out over Killaloe Bridge, there formed two echoes to that story.

100 years later even his family had inherited only silence from that night. The community at large were heirs to a different understanding of the same story. Having been transferred to O'Brien's Bridge in 1921, Brennan was posted to Gormanstown in January 1922 where the RIC were disbanded. He later emigrated to England and had an address in Benson Street, Liverpool. Where Brennan spent the following decades has not been possible to establish, but at some point he returned to the home place of his wife in Creggs, Co. Roscommon. Tommy Bolton's suggestion that Brennan died in a lunatic asylum reveals that local republicans did not forget his role. However, his register of death shows that Brennan died on 19 April 1953 from carcinoma of the larynx at the age of eighty-one. He had children and grandchildren who loved him.[9]

In October 2019, I spoke with the grandson of John Brennan, who was five years old when his grandfather died. He was aware that John Brennan had been a member of the RIC, with direct memories limited to 'a very tall and austere man' who played the accordion.[10] His mother was Brennan's daughter. Remarkably, only in our discussion did he become aware of his grandfather's role in the story of the Scariff Martyrs. Brennan's central part in one of Clare's most infamous episodes, intensely remembered by a community for 100 years, had been tightly enclosed in silence within his family's memory, a story untold. This was perhaps not unusual. I corresponded also with the granddaughter of Black and Tan, Jack Montague Austin, based in Killaloe on the night of the shootings. Although likely aware of what happened, Austin did not seem to have spoken of his experiences in Ireland and his service records only came to light, sometime after his death.[11]

Col Andrews, who had commanded G Company at the time of the deaths, resigned from the force months later, when financial irregularities became apparent. In January 1923, he was killed at Ex-Officers Automobile Service, his business in London, when an abrasive wheel shattered and hit him in the chest.[12] Faraday, the man who led the company that captured the men, later travelled to Palestine where he continued to represent British imperialism. There, he had to be transferred from Jaffa to Beersheba in February 1934, after he shot a Palestinian dead and on the same day, beat Yacob Ghussein, an Arab youth leader unconscious.[13] He was nevertheless in 1937, awarded the Kings Police Medal for his service in Palestine.[14] He died in February 1986, 'after a long period of pain and suffering'.[15]

In 1922, Black and Tan, V.S. Gwynne was pensioned on a yearly sum of £134. He later married three times and died in Gosport in 1970.[16] Patrick 'Benignus' Cullinan, the Newmarket man who likely had a key role in the gathering of intelligence which led to the capture of the martyrs, spent decades travelling the world as a journalist and writer, last recorded in Jamaica in 1953.[17] The three leading suspects, who undoubtedly were giving information to the crown forces, referred to earlier as Suspects A, B and C, continued to live in the Whitegate area for decades, knowing that their actions, in different ways, led to the capture, torture and murder of three local republicans, as well as their fellow parishioner, Michael Egan.

While the figures central to the deaths of the Scariff Martyrs moved on with their lives, within the community of east Clare, the memory of the men endured. The potency of emotion associated with their story is a defining characteristic of the murders. One of the last people to hear the voices of McMahon, Rodgers, Gildea and Egan was Canon Dan Flannery, who from his house close to Killaloe bridge, heard their cries as they died. Flannery, who himself was close to death, understood the endurance of such moments as previously he had written about the injustice of evictions. Reflecting on the way in which traumatic moments of injustice can be seared into the consciousness, he declared; 'Truly Madame Tussaud's Chamber of Horrors won't be complete till she has an Irish eviction scene, but no tongue can tell, no brush depict, even partially, all the horrors of an Irish eviction'.[18] Canon Flannery died seven months later.

In the case of the Scariff Martyrs, many images have similarly endured and yet are challenging to truly depict. Their capture, their journey on the *SS Shannon*, their beating at the Lakeside Hotel and, most powerfully, their final moments, have been imagined by many both publicly and privately over the following century, and always expressed in palpable sadness. The consistency of feeling for the Scariff Martyrs is illuminating with regard to the cultural meaning of memory associated with the killings. Across multiple interviews their betrayal, the nature of their deaths and subsequent martyrdom was foregrounded in the telling of the story. Additionally, the memory aids associated with the Scariff Martyrs, including the songs and monuments, all focus on their deaths as the beginning and end point of the narrative. Recurrent commemorative activity has maintained a focus on their deaths and largely ignored the surrounding context.

There are undoubtedly aspects to their story which under-line the vicious nature of the war. As IRA men committed to the use of physical force, McMahon, Rodgers and Gildea were involved in the shooting of two policemen who had little chance to defend themselves in a public house and were peripherally involved in the death of a third on a darkened street. Such was the inescapable nature of guerrilla warfare however, and it appears that the three men were prepared to go to lengths they may have previously not imagined, for the cause they fervently believed in. That Rodgers, McMahon and Gildea had an involvement in the killing of three RIC men, was largely unknown to many in the communities of east Clare, as was the execution of three British soldiers who were captured in Scariff three months after the murders in Killaloe.

This book has drawn all available evidence together to narrate and explain the events of November 1920 and situate that experience within the consciousness and memory of the local east Clare community. To understand the endurance of their memory it has been necessary to illuminate their back-ground, contemporary experience, as well as the wide-ranging and consistent efforts to memorialise and remember. While certain aspects have remained hidden, there persists a profound importance to the core aspects of community memory and historical consciousness. To untie the many bonds of memory and history would be to partially disengage a community's connection to its past. Such an approach fails to recognise the nature of the historical experience and its intrinsic connection to emotion, heritage and landscape. A bond was created between the community and the memory, one which elevated the men to near sainthood and allowed a focus on their deaths, their virtue and the rightness of their memory. That emotional inheritance is real and it is important.

Although not rejecting contextual information, it does not require it. The central narrative presenting young men, driven by their desire to achieve independence for their country, done to death in a brutal way, has remained overpowering. To those who fell outside of this narrative, like the families of RIC men killed by the IRA, the emotional inheritance was one taken in silence, finding union only in the personal grief they felt for their loved ones. Yet those loved ones were dead too, no less dead than any other. For two and a half years, the War of Independence was a relentless theatre of experience, played out across the communities of our past. In north-east Clare, attention has primarily been placed on the four martyrs. However, as a direct or indirect result of the increasing violence there in late 1920, thirteen people had died by the end of November. Three soldiers executed in February 1921 were partially connected to the Killaloe killings, while a further tragedy, discussed later, was also an echo of the episode. The seventeen people who died, comprised eight members of the British forces, one alleged civilian spy, five further civilians with no direct republican connection and three IRA Volunteers.

To gain an appreciation of the emotional impact and an insight into the experience of that time, the many years of sitting and listening, questioning and hearing, have been ultimately the most instructive. I began with an admiration for the four men, partly imbibed from the atmosphere I was exposed to in east Clare. After over seventeen years of research, and managing to consciously separate myself from that emotion where necessary, a much deeper understanding of the nuances of that story has resulted. However, the admiration I inherited and embraced has not diminished. The sincerity with which they approached their involvement in the struggle for independence is clear. Equally, their involvement in the cultural revival and in particular the promotion of the Irish language deepens their credibility as revolutionaries. While in captivity, the men repeatedly appealed to the Auxiliaries that Egan was innocent. This final and desperate bid to save the life of Egan, in the closing hours of their own, remains a powerful buffer against charges of recklessness. The innocence of Michael Egan only deepens the sense of pathos, as does his own evident efforts to protect the three Volunteers. Finally, the lack of any arrest or any discernible advantage gained from their interrogation underlines their refusal to give information on their comrades, a mark of honour within republican consciousness across all epochs.

For a century, the story of the Scariff Martyrs has been told. Respectful silence repeatedly descended as the song written just weeks after their deaths echoed through the decades. Regular commemorations drew those with affection or connections to sites of memory, where a collective demonstration of remembering underlined a local determination not to forget. Within the mournful countenance of those bereaved, lived the most heartfelt pain, only truly known to the interior soul of those who bore them.

The type of emotional trauma visited on the families by the deaths on Killaloe bridge, can leave behind wounds with the unique power to hurt each person differently. Such grief is a knife that continues to cut long after the initial effect. Every time the younger sister of 'Brud' McMahon returned to Scariff from her duties as a Catholic nun, she insisted on a vigil to her brother's site of death. When British forces killed him there, Mary McMahon was just fourteen-years-old. From December 1920, until her death in the 1980s, Kathleen

Epilogue

Rodgers (Sr Alphonse Columba) carried with her a little satin bag, garnished with pale blue. The bag, made by a novice at the La Sainte Union Convent in Belgium had within it, a curl of her brother Alphie's hair.[19]

Kathleen's sister Gertie carried a different reminder – a quiet but persistent anxiety, rooted in her own worry that when Alphie and his comrades were 'on the run', she may have innocently told someone of their presence in Williamstown and that this may have resulted in their capture.[20] While her anxiety was likely unfounded, for Gertie it was an intensely real and enduring burden, that she only revealed to her grandson in the wintertime of her life. Such burdens are loaded with a pressing weight, that for some was far too much to bear. On Friday 13 November 1925, just days from the fifth anniversary of the four men's death, in the village of Whitegate a young woman ingested strychnine at the post office where she worked. Within an hour, the thirty-one-year-old mother of two was dead. Nora Corcoran was the oldest sister of Michael Egan. For five long years she had carried a profound agony. Like Gertie, local tradition indicates that Nora too was inflicted with a sense of anxiety that she may have inadvertently given information that led to the capture of her brother and to a death that she could not divest from her consciousness.[21] To stop that perpetual image and to end that inescapable pain, Nora tragically took her own life. Patrick Culloo, the coroner who oversaw an inquest into her death, had five years before looked attentively into the coffin of her brother in Scariff church. The inquest concluded that Nora had died 'from strychnine poisoning, self-administered while mentally effected'.[22] The press recorded how Nora 'had been seriously depressed since her brother was shot'.[23] Weeks later the registrar, Daniel Reidy, who had certified her brother's death, signed his name to confirm Nora's passing, and in so doing silently added a further victim to the story of the Scariff Martyrs.

It is, I feel a duty to include such echoes of the story. Through understanding those reverberations, I believe we can navigate the inverted contours of history and memory, all the way back until we become closer to the pulse of the original experience. It is true that parts of our history will remain forever in the clutch of those beneath the graveyard clay. Nevertheless, by listening deeply and by using the sound of the thunder to lead us back to the lightning, we can discharge perhaps, the true duty of the historian.

In the end, it is the simplicity of their story that is most powerful. Three young men who consciously dedicated themselves to the cause of Irish freedom. For committed men, danger was both everywhere and nowhere. Their youthful enthusiasm was perhaps a barrier against the perils of war-time reality. Michael Egan was an ordinary young man entangled in an extraordinary situation. What should have been a routine and forgettable November Tuesday for Egan, became a forever-remembered episode in the history of his place and country. The type of pain inflicted on the families of the men, and by extension the communities they came from, was not uncommon in Ireland. It was, however, in its own way, unique to the people of east Clare. It is their story and their inheritance. They are heirs to both a beautiful and painful sorrow. Over time that powerful melancholia became transformed into an enduring call to memory, which has fallen for over a century now on the receptive ears of those who remembered.

The connection to those who felt that pain was almost gone when I began my research. Yet the echoes of that trauma lived on in the many tears induced during my interviews and research. On 16 November 2019, I visited two nursing homes in East Clare. At Raheen in Tuamgraney I met with ninety-five-year-old John Minogue, who in the mid-1930s was taught to recite the Scariff Martyrs song by Bridget

Cuneen at Cooleenbridge School. Sitting on his chair in Raheen, over eight decades later, he once more delivered the words with tremendous ferocity. Having finished, he paused and repeated the following line: 'After these will come centuries and we'll easily know their names, for their stored in the annals' roll of history, good people all dear pray.'[24] From there, I travelled to Killaloe where I visited a women who on every 16 November over the previous half century had quietly made her way to the monument on Killaloe Bridge and there hung a wreath. With no one watching, she tightened her coat against the cold November air and walked silently home. I wanted to reassure her that, even though she was now unable, the wreath in memory of the Scariff Martyrs would be there for all to see when dawn broke on 17 November.[25]

ENDNOTES

* Rodgers Collection (RC), Alphie Rodgers to Mrs Nora Rodgers, 23 October 1911; Baby McDermott to Mrs Norah Rodgers, 19 November 1920. 11 February is the Feast day of Our Lady of Lourdes in the Catholic calendar. Alphie was born on 11 February 1893. 'Gertie' referred to in Alphie's letter was his younger sister, who was nine years old at the time.

I Cried after Them

1 Margaret Hoey, Carrigoran, Newmarket-on-Fergus, Co. Clare, 14 November 2008.

Introduction

1 'The Whitegate Shootings', *Irish Times*, 19 November 1920; Brian Graney, 'East Clare's Calvary', *Vexilla Regis, Journal of Maynooth Laymen's Society* (1953), p. 108.
2 Military Archives of Ireland (MAI), MSPC-RO-211, pp. 21–41; Mary Moroney, *A Salute to the Heroes of East Clare* (Ennis, 1976), p. 18.
3 Moroney, *A Salute to the Heroes of East Clare*, p. 18.
4 Joseph McKenna, *Guerrilla Warfare in the Irish War of Independence, 1919–1921* (North Carolina, 2011), p. 235.
5 'McSwiney Funeral', *Irish Times*, 6 November 1920; Bernadette Whelan, *United States Foreign Policy and Ireland* (Dublin, 2006), p. 260.
6 Maire McNamara and Maura Madden (eds), *Beagh: A History* (Beagh History Project, Galway, 1995), p. 114.
7 Meda Ryan, *Tom Barry, IRA Freedom Fighter* (Cork, 2003).
8 Michael Hopkinson, *The Irish War of Independence* (Dublin, 2002), pp. 87–88, pp. 99–100.
9 'Horrible Outrage Near Gort, *Galway Observer*, 6 November 1920, p. 4.
10 'Current Comments', *Young Ireland*, 27 November 1920, p. 1.
11 Hopkinson, *The Irish War of Independence*, pp. 103–105; William Kautt, *The Anglo-Irish War, 1916–1921: A People's War* (Connecticut, 1999), p. 86.
12 Edward Mac Lysaght, *Changing Times: Ireland Since 1898* (Dublin, 1978), p. 97
13 Register of Births in Ireland, District of Scariff, 1897. Daniel Egan worked as a herdsman at Drewsborough House in Tuamgraney for John O'Brien, the grandfather of the author, Edna O'Brien.
14 Interview with Anne Rodgers and Kitty Dillon, Scariff, 20 September 2019.
15 Field notes with John Martin O'Brien, Ballyvannon, Tuamgraney, 15 December 2020.
16 'Remains Buried in Scariff Chapel Yard', *Freeman's Journal*, 25 November 1920, p. 2.
17 In August 1912, Denis McMahon was presented with a ceremonial pipe box by the staff of R. Scott and Co. Ltd.
18 NAI, Census of Ireland, 1911, Sheares Street (North Side) (Cork No. 7 Urban, Cork); RIC Constable Joseph Carbery, Service Number, 43630.

19 Mac Lysaght (1978), p. 97; Interview with William Mac Lysaght, 8 August 2019.

20 'The Killaloe Victims', *Clare Champion,* 4 December 1920, p. 2.

21 Matthew Birmingham, Moyasta, Co. Clare, 5 January 2012.

22 Dr Tom Corbett (remote interview), 31 July 2019.

23 'Remembering the Scariff Martyrs' (East Clare Memorial Committee, Scariff, 2010), p. 12.

24 Register of Births in Ireland, District of Ballinasloe, 1890, https:// civilrecords.irishgenealogy.ie/churchrecords/images/ birth_returns/ births_1890/02415/1900003.pdf (accessed 4 January 2019).

25 Interview with Joe Duane, Kilreekil, Co. Galway, 30 September 2019.

26 Interview with Kathleen Mitchell, Ballinasloe, 5 July 2016.

27 Register of Births in Ireland, District of Ballinasloe, 1899; https:// civilrecords.irishgenealogy.ie/churchrecords/ images/deaths_returns/ deaths_1899/05786/4636205.pdf (accessed 13 January 2019).

28 Martin's surname and that of his family is listed as 'Gay' (a derivative of Gildea and Kildea) on the 1901 Census of Ireland.

29 NAI, Residents of a house 38 in Kilcullen Town (Carnalway, Kildare), 1911.

30 Interview with Fr Manus Rodgers, Silvermines, Co. Tipperary, 17 May 2011.

31 Kathleen Mitchell, 5 July 2016.

32 Correspondence, John Collins to me, 4 April 2020.

33 John S. Kelly Collection, interview with Tommy Bolton, Tuamgraney, Co. Clare, 11 June 1989; Tommy Holland, Whitegate, Co. Clare, 10 September 2010; Anne Rodgers and Kitty Dillon, 20 September 2019 (cassette tape).

34 RC, Kathleen Rodgers, 27 November 1920.

35 Sr Alphonse Columba, 'My Memoires' (Athlone, Undated), p. 1.

36 Irish Jesuit Archive, Mungret College School Register, 1911–1914.

37 Thomas Toomey, *The War of Independence in Limerick, 1912–1921* (Limerick, 2010), p. 496.

38 Bureau of Military History Witness Statement (hereafter BMH WS), James M. Roche, 1225, p. 20.

39 *The Mungret Annual* (June 1921, Vol. V, No. 5), p. 222.

40 Interview with Phil and Kitty McGrath, Dublin, 4 April 2014.

41 IE/MA/CP/5/2/22(i-LI), application for IRA Service Medal for Alphonsus E. Rodgers.

42 Gerald Rodgers made a successful application for Service (1917–21) Medal (MD17588) and is listed in nominal roll for Scariff IRA Company, MA-MSPC-RO-211 (p. 21/41); 'Delia Cleary', *The Mountshannon Review* (Clare, 1996), p. 19.

43 Sr Alphonse Columba, pp. 2–3.

44 *Ibid.*

45 Interview with Paddy Rodgers, Scariff, 10 January 2019.

46 RC, Kathleen Rodgers, 5 December 1920.

47 *Ibid.*, 27 November 1920.

48 Tommy Bolton, 11 June 1989.

49 Margaret Hoey, 14 December 2008.

50 Patrick Madden (ed.), *A History of Gaelic Games in Whitegate and Mount-shannon, 1825–1984* (Clare, 1984), p. 41; Thomas Dillon (ed.), *The Banner, The Claremen and Women's Patriotic, Benevolent and Social Association of New York* (New York, 1963); Gerard Madden, *A History of Tuamgraney and Scariff* (Scariff, 2000), p. 96; Seán Spellissy, *A History of County Clare* (Dublin, 2003), p. 65; Seán Kierse, *The Killaloe Anthology* (Killaloe, 2001), pp. 201–202; Seán Kierse, *History of Smith O'Briens GAA Club*, pp. 151–152; Griffin, Kevin M. and Griffin, Kevin A., *The Renihan Diaries, c. 1882–1925* (Ballina, 2005); MacLysaght (1978), pp. 109–110; Edward MacLysaght, *East Clare 1916–1921* (Ennis, 1954), p. 67; Moroney (1976); Henry W Nevinson, *Changes and Chances* (London, 1923), p. 141; Seán Hogan, *The Black and Tans in North Tipperary* (Tipperary, 2013), p. 287.
51 Graney, 'East Clare's Calvary', p. 105; The contribution made by Henry O'Mara in February 1957, comprises an almost identical account written by Graney in 1953, in *Vegilla Regis*; see NAI, BMH Henry O'Mara, WS 1653.
52 *Ibid.*
53 Romer C. Grey, *The Auxiliary Police* (London, 1920), p. 4.
54 F. P. Crozier, *Ireland Forever* (London, 1932), p. 196.
55 National Archives of the United Kingdom (NAUK), 'British Court of Inquiry in Lieu of Inquest in case of Martin Kildea, Alfred Rodgers, Michael McMahon and John Egan', WO 35/153A.
56 'Four Shot in Killaloe', *Irish Independent*, 19 November 1920.
57 Frank Connolly, *The Christy Moore Songbook* (Kerry, 1984), p. 54.

1 'We should take off our hats'

1 'Great Demonstration in Scariff', *Clare Champion*, 26 November 1921, Mike 'the Hawk' Daly was noted in GAA circles as a hurling referee, who maintained a firm republican position throughout his life, Interview with Pat McNamara, Killaloe, 4 November 2019.
2 Seán Kierse Collection, Recording with Mike Daly, Killaloe, Co. Clare, 5 January 1972 (transcript).
3 'Echo of Killaloe Tragedy', *Clare Champion*, 30 September 1922, p. 5.
4 The earliest republican monument was erected in June 1923 in the village of Murroe, Co. Limerick.
5 Correspondence, Seán Kierse, 5 November, 2010; The inscription on the Killaloe Bridge monument, written in old Irish script is translated as follows: 'In Loving Memory of the Valiant Men, Michael McMahon, Martin Gildea, Alphonsus Rodgers, Michael Egan, four soldiers of the Irish Republican Army, Killed by The Emissaries of England on this bridge, at the Midnight Hour, the 16th of November 1920. May God have mercy on their souls.'
6 Cuimhneamh an Chláir (CAC); interview with Jack Quigley, Ballina, Co. Tipperary, 14 March 2012.
7 'Anniversary of Killaloe Tragedy', *Clare Champion*, 29 November 1924, p. 1; 'Killaloe Bridge Tragedy', *Limerick Leader*, 21 November 1921, p. 2.
8 Michael Daly travelled on *The Adriatic* from Cobh in July 1923 to New

York, 'Emigrants from Killaloe Parish through Ellis Island', http://www. clarelibrary.ie/eolas/coclare/genealogy/don_tran/emigration/killaloe_ parish_through_ellisisland_emigrants.htm (accessed 2 May 2018).

9 Interview with Maeve Hayes, Killaloe, 10 November 2017.

10 Carol McNamara to me, 31 March 2020, Pádraig Ó Cadhla was the first man to translate *Alice in Wonderland* into Irish.

11 University College Dublin (UCD), National Folklore Collection School's Folklore Scheme (NFCS), 591: 226, Collector: Mícheál Ó Duanáin, Tuamgraney National School, Co. Clare; in Tuamgraney, nineteen copybooks referred to the Scariff Martyrs, while in the two national schools closest to Scariff town, the incident was not mentioned.

12 UCD, NFCS, MS 591, 229, Collector: Brigid Mac Mahon, Tuamgraney National School.

13 *Ibid.*, MS 591: 232, Collector: James G. Minogue.

14 CAC, ; interview with Fr Jim Minogue, Milford Hospice, Limerick, 31 March 2014.

15 Dáil Éireann Parliamentary Debates, 4 February 1942, http://historical -debates.oireachtas.ie/D/0085/D.0085. 194202040033.html (accessed 2 January 2010).

16 Donal Ó Drisceoil, 'Moral Neutrality' censorship in Emergency Ireland', *History Ireland*, Volume 4, Issue 2 (Summer 1996); 'Shootings Recalled', *Clare Champion*, 22 November 1941, p. 5.

17 Seosamh Ó Longaigh, 'Emergency Law in Action, 1939–1945'; see Uinseann Mac Eoin, Uinseann, *The IRA in the Twilight Years, 1923–1948* (Dublin, 1997); in 1939, the IRA declared war on Britain. As a result, the Irish State interned republicans in the Curragh. Among the camp authorities was Capt. Jerry McNamara who in 1920 was a member of the Scariff IRA Company. He was accused of being 'the bastard that ordered Barney Casey's execution', see Uinseann Mac Eoin Collection, UMCE-S-T-18, Palkie Joe Dolan.

18 'Shootings Recalled', *Clare Champion*, 22 November 1941.

19 Ian McCabe, *A Diplomatic History of Ireland, 1948–49: The Republic, the Commonwealth and NATO* (Dublin, 1991), pp. 22–24.

20 Correspondence, John Fahey, Dublin, to me, 13 June 2019.

21 Maeve Hayes, 28 June 2011.

22 'Great Demonstration in Scariff', *Clare Champion*, 26 November 1921.

23 'Anniversary Mass', *Irish Independent*, 25 November 1922.

24 'Scariff', *Clare Champion*, 27 January 1945, p. 1.

25 'East Clare Memorial', *Irish Independent*, 10 March 1945, p. 5.

26 'Sunday's Historic Event', *Clare Champion*, 17 November 1945, p. 5.

27 Interview with Kathleen Mitchell, Loughrea, Co. Galway, 6 July 2016.

28 The inscription on the monument in Scariff, written in 'Old Irish' includes the following imploration: 'Be loyal to Ireland as were these great men. Erected by Gaels who did not forget their effort and the cruel death they suffered and so that this monument will be a guiding star to our children and our children's children.'

29 'List of Subscriptions', *Clare Champion*, 29 December 1945, p. 2.

30 'Scariff', *Clare Champion*, 15 November 1947.

31 'Tuamgraney', *Clare Champion*, 31 March 1951.

32 Anne Dolan, *Commemorating the Irish Civil War* (Cambridge, 2003) p. 127.

33 'National Monument Dedicated', *Clare Champion*, 24 April 1954, p. 1.

34 'They died on the bridge at Killaloe fifty years ago', *Clare Champion*, 14 November 1970.

35 'East Clare Remembers its four martyrs', *Clare Champion*, 28 November 1970, p. 7.

36 'Mass for Local Martyrs', *Clare Champion*, 17 November 1995.

37 Interview with Tom Lynch, Whitegate, Co. Clare, 11 May 2011.

38 'Killaloe Notes', *Nenagh Guardian*, 19 February 1972, p. 8; a fourteenth victim, John Johnston, died in June 1972.

39 Interview with May Ryan, Ballyvannon, Tuamgraney, 14 January 2013.

40 'Killaloe', *Clare Champion*, 22 November 1941, 'They died on the bridge at Killaloe fifty years ago', *Clare Champion*, 14 November 1970, p. 10; 'Scariff's Tributes to her four martyrs', *Clare Champion*, 21 November 1970, p. 1; 'Mass for Local Martyrs', *Clare Champion*, 17 November, 1995; 'Lecture in Killaloe', *Clare Champion*, 23 April 1938, p. 6.

41 'Scariff Martyrs remembers in private ceremonies', *Clare Echo*, 19 November 2020; the commemorations were addressed by Cllr Pat Hayes, Shane Walsh and Tomás Mac Conmara. In Scariff, Pat O'Neill sang 'the Scariff Martyrs' while at Killaloe, 'The Four Who Fell' was sung by Cailíní Lua. Jack Hogan, the grandfather of one of the bandmembers, Tara Brady, was a member of The Shannon Folk Four, who popularised the song in the 1960s.

42 Correspondence, Dr Helen O'Shea to me, 4 June 2015.

43 Michael O'Gorman, 22 October 2012

44 Interview with Joe Fitzgerald, Corigano, Bodyke, Co. Clare, 30 October 2018 (with Jimmy Walsh in attendance).

45 Connolly (1984), p. 54.

46 Correspondence, Christy Moore to me, 13 May 2020; Mrs Murphy was born Margaret Canny in Tuamgraney and was twenty-four at the time of the funerals.

47 CAC; interview with John Minogue, Gleandree, Feakle, 6 May 2011 (CD).

48 UCD, NFSC, The Schools' Collection, Rody O'Gorman, Woodford National School, Galway, Volume 0050, p. 384.

49 Margaret Hickey, Irish Days, *Oral Histories of the Twentieth Century*, (England, 2001), p. 92

50 Correspondence, Cyril O'Donoghue to me, 6 July 2013.

51 Tommy Holland, 10 September 2010; Michael O'Gorman, 22 October 2012; CACA, Seán Crowe, 24 October 2010; Tom Lynch, 11 May 2011.

52 Interview with Anna Mae McNamara, Ballymalone, Tuamgraney, 14 April 2013. Note: Mrs McNamara is my mother.

53 CAC; interview with JP Guinnane and Paddy Clancy, Kilkishen, 3 November 2011.

54 Interview with Dolly Lynch, Kilkishen, 16 November 2010.

55 Tom Lynch, 11 May 2011.

56 Seamus Mac Mathúna recorded Robbie McMahon singing the song in the 1950s while in June 1974, folklore collector Tom Munnelly recorded Ned Shaughnessy from Kilkishen, NFC, UCD, 'The Four Martyrs of Killaloe', 306/A/2; the singer Seán Donnellan also was noted for his rendition of the song, see *Songs My Father Sang* (CD, 2004).

57 Correspondence, Michael McNamara, Ogonnelloe to me, 24 August 2019.

58 RC, 'D.P. O'Farrell to Mrs Rodgers, 8 March 1922.

59 John McLaughlin, *One Green Hill. Journeys through Irish Songs* (Belfast, 2003), p. 92.

60 Jack Noonan, *A Short Collection of Poems* (Limerick, 1984), p. 8; 'Killaloe', *Limerick Leader*, 21 November 1998, p. 23.

61 Joe Noonan, *Songs and Recitations* (Clare, 1990), pp. 120–121; Four further poems have been composed including; 'From Williamstown to Killaloe' written by Seán Crowe, see Seán Crowe, *A Peaceful Place, Poetry* (Clare, 2010), p. 86; 'Heroes All', by Mary McCarthy from Killaloe, as well as 'They Will Never Be Forgotten' and 'The Plaque on the Bridge of Killaloe', by Pat Conroy from Ballina in Co. Tipperary.

62 Correspondence, Noreen McGrath O'Connor to me, 14 November 2020; the poem is published in Noonan, *Songs and Recitations*, pp. 120-121.

63 RC, letter from J. Stanley Photographer to Rodgers Family, 30 August 1921.

64 Interview with Fr Manus Rodgers, Silvermines, Co. Tipperary, 17 May 2011 (handwritten notes).

65 Tom Lynch, 11 May 2011.

66 Michael O'Gorman, 22 October 2012.

67 CAC; interview with Kathleen Nash, Roscrea, Co. Tipperary, 11 October 2009.

68 Seán Crowe, 24 October 2010.

69 Interview with Flan O'Brien, Ballymalone, Tuamgraney, 22 October 2008.

70 UCD, NFSC, Josie Moloney, Clonlara National School, Volume 0585, p. 132

71 Correspondence, Mary McGrath, 19 June 2013.

72 Patricia Sheehan Collection, Morgie O'Connell, Cranny, 22 July 2019 (digital audio).

2 'For generations there had been a demand'

1 Niall Ó Ciosáin, 'Approaching a Folklore Archive: The Irish Folklore Commission and the Memory of the Great Famine, *Folklore 115* (Dublin, 2004), p. 225.

2 Jimmy Slattery, BMH WS 445.

3 Feakle Graveyard, grave of Michael Slattery.

4 National Library of Ireland, Inchiquin Papers, Collection 143, ms, 45, 436/5, 28 November 1869; see Caroline McGuire, *Peasants into Patriots Instruments of Radical Politicisation in Clare 1800–1907* (PhD Thesis, Mary Immaculate College, 2011).

5 NAI, CO904/182/Reel 110, 1872–1914: Armed meetings, agrarianism – reports, returns of legal advisors (15 April 1874).

6 The following Scariff men were noted as members of the IRB in 1890:

Michael Collins, Martin Crotty, Michael McNamara, Michael Minogue, John Moloney, Matthew O'Brien, Edward O'Farrell, Francis O'Farrell, Martin Scanlon, and James Whealan.

7 'Death Register of John Moloney', https://civilrecords.irishgenealogy.ie/churchrecords/images/deaths_returns/deaths_1881 /06436/4849279.pdf (accessed 12 May 2019).

8 'Riot at Bodyke', *Yorkshire Post*, 3 June 1881, p. 5; 'The Fatal Affray at Bodyke', *Dublin Weekly Nation,* 9 July 1881, p. 3.

9 The monument can be seen at Kilnoe graveyard, Bodyke.

10 Jimmy Walsh, 5 May 2012.

11 Tommy Bolton, 11 June 1989.

12 *Ibid.*

13 Civil Records, Death Register of John Garvey, 14 March 1888; Correspondence, Pauleen Cass to me, 8 February 2021; National Archive of Australia, Service Records of Michael Keane, Series B884, N69399.

14 'Anarchy in Clare', *Motherwell Times*, 2 September 1893, p. 3.

15 MA-MSPC-RO-207, 'Caherhurley IRA Company'.

16 'The Battle of Bodyke', *Belfast Morning News*, 4 June 1881, p. 4

17 'Mrs Margaret Turner', *Clare Champion*, 3 February 1951, p. 5.

18 John S. Kelly, *The Bodyke Evictions* (Clare, 1987).

19 Henry Norman, Bodyke, *A Chapter in the History of Irish Landlordism* (London, 1887), pp. 59–61.

20 *Ibid.*

21 Jim O'Driscoll, Wicklow to me, 17 May 2020; Brid Durack, Wexford (remote interview), 9 February 2021.

22 Durack/McNamara Family Collection, Barntown, Wexford.

23 Sheedy, Kieran, *Feakle* (Clare, 1990), p. 106.

24 MAI, Seán Clancy Collection; interview with Lt Col Seán Clancy, Dublin, 24 June 2002.

25 'County Clare Hurling Championship', *Celtic Times*, 11 June 1887, p. 5.

26 John Minogue, 6 May 2011.

27 Kathleen Nash, 14 October 2009.

28 Tom Lynch, 11 May 2011.

29 Daniel McCarthy, *Ireland's Banner County* (Clare, 2002), pp. 88–109.

30 Thomas 'Tomo' Tuohy, BMH WS 983, p. 3; MAI, IRA Brigade Reports, (A22), East Clare IRA Brigade, Account of Pat 'Thade' McGrath, p. 18.

31 Pádraig Óg Ó Ruairc (ed), *The Men Will Talk To Me, Clare, Interviews by Ernie O'Malley* (Cork, 2016), p. 162.

32 'Count Plunkett', *Clare Champion,* 10 February 1917, p. 2.

33 John or Seán 'Jack' Brady was a well-known Fianna Fáil county councillor, and holds the record as Clare County Council's longest serving chairman. He was also a member of Seanad Éireann from 1961 to 1965.

34 'Tomgraney', *Clare Champion*, 5 May 1917, p. 1.

35 Joseph Noonan, BMH WS 1,287, p. 1.

36 MAI, MSPC, Pension application of Percy Lucas, 49SP689, p. 44.

37 'Sinn Féin Founder', *Clare Champion*, 14 November 1936, p. 5.

38 Tomás Mac Conmara, *Days of Hunger, The Clare Volunteers and the Mountjoy*

Hunger Strike of 1917 (Clare, 2017).

39 National Archives of Ireland (NAI), Colonial Office Records (CO), Police Reports, 1914–21, Inspector Generals and County Inspectors monthly confidential reports, 'County Inspector for Clare, Report for the month of November 1917'.

40 William MacLysaght, 8 August 2019.

41 Fr Manus Rodgers, 17 May 2011.

42 'Big Cattle Drives', *Clare Champion,* 9 February 1918, p. 1

43 'Prisoners on hunger strike', *Clare Champion,* 9 February 1918, p. 1.

44 Paddy Gleeson, O'Callaghan's Mills, 15 May 2004.

45 'Court Rushed at Ennis', *Clare Champion,* 16 February 1918, p. 1.

46 Paddy Gleeson, 15 May 2004.

47 'Cattle Drives in East Clare', *Clare Champion,* 2 February 1918, p. 2; 9 February 1918, p. 1.

48 *Ibid.*

49 *Ibid.*

50 NAI, Police Reports, Report of County Inspector for Clare to RIC Office, 'Cattle Drives in Clare', 26 January 1918.

51 Michael Gleeson, WS 1,288, pp. 6–7; Thomas McNamara, WS 1,077, pp. 3–4.

52 'Scariff Riots', *Irish Times,* 29 March 1918; Dr FC Sampson was given £893 17/9; see 'Wanton Damage in Scariff', *Irish Times,* 13 July 1918.

53 'To the Irish Volunteers, County Clare', *Clare Champion,* 9 February 1918, p. 2.

54 Seán Murnane, BMH WS 1,048, p. 7.

55 J. J. Lee, Ireland, *1912–1985, Politics and Society* (Cambridge, 1989), p. 39.

56 'East Clare Quiet Yesterday', *Yorkshire Post,* 2 March 1918, p. 6.

57 'The Green Sphinx', *Aberdeen Evening Express,* 6 March 1918, p. 1.

58 'Forbidden Movement's, *Weekly Freeman's Journal,* 23 March 1918, p. 6.

59 NAI (CO 905), Parts 1–7, Police Reports, 1914–1921, Reel 65, Box 104–5 (18085 Secret), RIC County Inspector's Report for Clare for the month of January 1918.

60 NAI, RIC Inspector General, Report for the month of February 1918, 18567/S, p. 96.

61 'Future of Ireland', *Irish Independent,* 2 February 1918, p.

62 NAI, Crime Special Branch, Republican Speeches, 1918–1919.

63 Joseph Noonan, BMH WS 1,287, pp. 2–3.

64 NAI, CSO, State of the County Papers (c. 1820) SOC 2183/14; The Ribbonmen were a Catholic secret society, who in response to the conditions of their co-religionists, violently confronted landlords and their agents in the early 1800s.

65 Charles O'Callaghan from Mountshannon was reputedly beaten to death in Scariff, having vocally declared his loyalty to 'organism' in 1824; see Molua, *Organ of the Association of St Gregory* (Dublin, 1941), p. 43; An alternative tradition suggests that he was killed with rocks close to Whitegate to prevent him from executing evictions on tenants, Tommy Holland, 17 October 2019.

66 NFCS, Volume 0036, p. 0041, Baile Meadhonach, Collector Eileen Dolan.

67 'Politics and Society in East Galway, 1914–21', Conor McNamara in St Patrick's College, Drumcondra, December 2008.

68 'Bomb thrown at a Military Officer's Residence', *The Scotsman,* 14 March 1918, p. 4.

69 'Lecture in Scariff', *Clare Champion*, 23 March 1918, p. 2.

70 *Ibid.*

71 *Freeman's Journal*, 19 April 1918, p. 4.

72 Ger Browne, *Clare Men and Women in the Great War 1914–1918*, http://www.clarelibrary.ie/eolas/coclare/history/clare_men_women_great_war_2.pdf (accessed, 12 January 2019).

73 Maurice Manning, *James Dillon, A Biography* (Dublin 1999), p. 23.

74 Tom McGillacuddy, Tom (ed.), *The Crooked Ash, The History of Scariff GAA* (Nenagh, 1987), pp. 29–32.

75 'Clare Orders Cancelled', *Irish Independent,* 4 July 1918, p. 2.

3 'Suffer, endure and fight'

1 'Stirring Period Recalled', *Clare Champion*, 14 November 1936, p. 1; Brennan was then speaking as Chief of Staff of the Irish Army, a position he held from 1931 to 1940.

2 MacLysaght (1954), p. 12.

3 *Ibid.*, p. 1.

4 McLaughlin (2003), p. 24.

5 'Fight with Raider', *Pall Mall Gazette*, 6 January 1920, p. 2.

6 The letter is printed in full in Madden, *A History of Tuamgraney and Scariff*, (2000), pp. 176–8.

7 *Ibid.*

8 Patrick Buckland, *Irish Unionism*, Volume 1 (Dublin, 1973), p. 427.

9 Michael Brennan, *The War in Clare* (Dublin, 1980), p. 80.

10 'Clare Assizes', *Clare Champion*, 5 March 1921, p. 3.

11 *Ibid.*

12 Albert Coyle (transcriber), *Evidence on Conditions in Ireland: Affidavits and Exhibits Presented Before the American Commission on Conditions in Ireland* (Washington, 1921), pp. 374-376.

13 Michael O'Gorman, 22 October 2012.

14 Margaret Hoey, 14 December 2008.

15 Hopkinson (2002), pp. 25–7.

16 'Scariff Guardians', *Clare Champion*, 25 January 1919, p. 5.

17 In Killaloe, Harrington had a reputation for anti-republicanism. In 1917 he assaulted a republican following the East Clare by-election, see 'Convicted Policeman', *Clare Champion*, 10 November 1917, p. 1.

18 MAI, MAPC, application of Patrick Rice to the Committee of Enquiry into Resignations and Dismissals from the RIC.

19 MAI, Brigade Activity Reports (A22), East Clare Brigade, 1st Western Division.

20 Michael Brennan, BMH WS 1068, p. 34.

21 Joseph Clancy, BMH WS 1370, p. 3.

22 Richard Abbott, *Police Casualties in Ireland, 1919–1922* (Cork 2019), p. 33.

23 Michael Brennan, BMH WS 1068, p. 37.

24 Thomas McNamara, BMH WS 1077, p. 5; Tony Muggivan, 8 August 2019.

25 Thomas McNamara, BMH WS 1077, p. 5.

26 Kenneth Griffith and Timothy O'Grady, *Curious Journey: An Oral History of Ireland's Unfinished Revolution* (London, 1982), p. 132

27 Hopkinson (2002), pp. 31–2

28 Desmond Ryan, *Seán Treacy and The Third Tipperary Brigade* (Tralee, 1945), p. 125.

29 'Raid on Barracks', *Clare Champion*, 1 November 1919, p. 1.

30 John 'Bishop' Ryan, BMH WS 1136, p. 4.

31 *Ibid.*

32 'Raid on Barracks', *Clare Champion*, 1 November 1919, p. 1.

33 MAI, BMH, Seán Murnane, WS, 1048, p. 9; *Irish Independent,* 9 August 1919, p. 5.

34 Abbott (2019), p. 165.

35 Hopkinson (2002), p. 129.

36 Clare Museum (CE 2000.195), 'IRA Proclamation 1919'.

37 *Ibid.*

38 'Police Hut raided in Scariff', *Irish Times*, 9 August 1919.

39 Register of Births: https://civilrecords.irishgenealogy.ie/churchrecords/images/birth_returns/births_1893/02300/1862824.pdf.

40 Register of Birth, 'Joseph Noonan', https://civilrecords.irishgenealogy.ie/churchrecords/images/birth_returns/births_1895/   02201/1831894.pdf (accessed 3 October 2019).

41 Madden (2000), p. 176.

42 O'Meara Family Collection, recording with Paddy O'Meara, March 1976 (recorded by Marie O'Meara – cassette tape), Denis Flannery's register of birth confirms that he was born on 7 August 1919.

43 Michael Brennan, BMH WS 1068, p. 35.

44 MAI, MSPC, application of Annie O'Driscoll (nee O'Mara), MSP 34REF59967, pp. 12, 16, 37–39.

45 'Meetings, Fairs, Markets, Prohibited', *Freeman's Journal*, 16 August 1919, p. 2.

46 'Irish Constables Fired on', *Sunderland Daily Echo*, 1 October 1919, p. 6.

47 MAI, Pension application of Bridget Slattery, MSP34REF9952, pp. 10 –11.

48 Kierse Collection, Mike Daly, 5 January 1972.

49 Ryan (2003), p. 15.

50 W. E. Vaughan (ed.), *A New History of Ireland: Ireland Under the Union, 1870–1921* (Oxford, 2010), p. 243.

51 *Ibid.*

52 Kieran Sheedy, *The Clare Elections* (Dublin, 1993), p. 626.

53 'Ballot Boxes Burned', *Munster News*, 9 June 1920, p. 3.

54 'Sinn Féin arrests, *Irish Times*, 7 February 1920.

55 '1917–1920' James Foran Private Collection; Mac Curtain was murdered by the RIC on 20 March 1920 at his home in Cork City.

56 'Barrack Burning', *Clare Champion*, 23 October 1920, p. 5.

57 Michael Gleeson, BMH WS 1288, p. 8.
58 Interview with James O'Brien, Scariff, 27 March 2012.
59 Thomas McNamara, BMH WS 1077, p. 7.
60 MAI, East Clare IRA Brigade, statement of activities, http://mspcsearch. militaryarchives.ie/docs/files/PDF_Membership/7/A22%20East%20 Clare%20Brigade.pdf (accessed 12 October 2019).
61 Joseph Clancy, BMH WS 1370, pp. 6–7.
62 IE/MA/CP/5/2/22 (XXII), IRA HQ, 'Intelligence', to O/C, East Clare Brigade, 19 April 1921.
63 Correspondence, Joe Brady, Kilmurry, Sixmilebridge, Co. Clare, to me, 27 January 2020.
64 Michael O'Gorman, 22 October 2012.
65 *Ibid.*
66 *Ibid.*
67 Interview with Paddy Murray, Derrycon, Whitegate, Co. Clare, 10 January 2019.
68 James O'Brien, 27 March 2012.
69 Interview with Mary Kate O'Looney (Mason), Lahinch, Co. Clare, April 1985 (interviewed by Fintan McMahon – CD).
70 *Ibid.*
71 My fieldwork.
72 John Minogue, 6 May 2011.
73 Tony Muggivan, 8 August 2019.
74 *Ibid.*, 10 January 2019.
75 MAI, BMH, Seán Moroney, WS 1462, p. 8; Michael V. O'Donoghue, WS 1462, p. 8.
76 MAI, BMH, Liam Haugh, WS 474, p. 35.
77 James Foran Private Collection, '1917 – 1920'.
78 'Football Semi-Final', *Limerick Leader*, 20 August 1920, p. 2.
79 On Bloody Sunday, 21 November 1920 a group of IRA Volunteers shot dead thirteen British intelligence agents (the Cairo Gang) across Dublin City. That afternoon, British forces fired into the crowd at Croke Park, killing or fatally wounding fourteen civilians.
80 'Amazing Daylight Exploit', *Clare Champion*, 26 June 1920, p. 1.
81 'Daring Crime in County Cork', *Irish Times*, 28 June 1920, p. 5; Aideen Carroll, Seán Moylan, *Rebel Leader* (Cork, 2010), p. 53; Brennan (1980), pp. 54–6.
82 Correspondence, Ruth Wheeler to me, 19 November 2011.
83 Galvin Collection, Summary of Norah Moloney's Activities; Correspon dence, Tom O'Brien, Ogonnelloe, to me, 19 May 2020
84 MAI, Brigade Activity Reports (A22), East Clare Brigade.
85 Joseph Noonan, BMH WS 1287, p. 11.
86 Galvin Collection, Letter from Helena Tuohy to Kathleen Foley, 2 May 1939.
87 *Ibid.*, letter from Mary Ryan to Kathleen Foley, 18 April 1940.
88 *Ibid.*
89 MSP34REF47693, application of Mary Moroney, Kealderra, O'Callaghan's

Mills, Co. Clare.

90 MAI, MSPC, Annie O'Driscoll, MSP34REF59967, Testimony of Rev. John Kennedy, 20 July 1942.

91 NFCS, MS 591, 404–405, Peggy Kiely, Killaloe (B) National School. County Clare; The Ailbhaun, is an elevated walkway adjacent to Killaloe town which overlooks Lough Derg.

92 Kierse Collection, Mike Daly, 5 January 1972,

93 MAI, IE/MA/CP/5/2/22, IRA HQ, 'Intelligence', to O/C, East Clare Brigade, 23 February 1921.

94 Kierse Collection, Mike Daly, 5 January 1972. In January 1921, just weeks after the Killaloe shootings, four young Killaloe men, Francis Noonan, Patrick Keshan, as well as brothers William and Joseph Malone, all joined G Company of the Auxiliaries; see Ger Browne, Killaloe – Ballina and The Great War, https://www.clarelibrary.ie/eolas/coclare/history/clare_men_women_great_war_32.pdf (accessed 21 February 2021).

95 *Ibid.*

96 IE/MA/CP/5/2/22, IRA HQ, 'Intelligence', to O/C, East Clare Brigade, 21 March, 1921; in 1925, the charge that he was 'popular with the Black and Tans' was made against Harry Le Froy, as part of a court case relating to unpaid rates, see 'Dark and Evil Days', *Saturday Record,* 28 November 1925, p. 3.

97 MAI, MPSC, application of Bella Lucas, Derrycastle, Ballina, County Tipperary, MSP34REF10997.

98 MAI, Brigade Activity Reports, (A22) East Clare Brigade.

99 'Arrests in Provinces', *Freeman's Journal*, 19 February 1921, p. 5.

100 'Obituary', *Limerick Leader*, 01 August 1921, p. 2.

101 MAI, UMCE-S-A-26, Interview with Dan Gleeson, 1978.

102 David Bonner, *Executive Measures, Terrorism and National Security: Have the Rules of the Game Changed?* (Ashegate, 2007), pp. 76–77.

4 'He got a slash hook and wanted to go out'

1 Michael Fitzgerald died on 17 October, sixty-seven days into his hunger strike while MacSwiney and Murphy died after seventy-six and seventy-four days respectively, see Dave Hannigan, Terence MacSwiney, The Hunger Strike that Rocked an Empire (Dublin, 2012).

2 NAUK, Court of Inquiry, WO 35/153A.

3 'John J. Fitzgerald 1898–1920', http://www.bloodysunday.co.uk/murdered-men/fitzgerald.html (accessed 28 September 2019).

4 *Ibid.*

5 Michael O'Gorman, 22 October 2012.

6 Paddy Rodgers, 10 January 2019.

7 Ó Ruairc (2016), p. 150; Fr Manus Rodgers, 17 May 2011.

8 Correspondence, Máire Lowe to me, 9 September 2019.

9 Tommy Bolton, 11 June 1989.

10 Tony Muggivan, 10 January 2019.

11 MAI, 24SP8528, application of Peter Higgins, Newmarket-on-Fergus, Co. Clare.

12 *Ibid.*, BMH Michael Brennan, WS 1068, p. 50; Tomas Ó Maoileóin, BMH WS 845, Appendix 3.

13 *Ibid.*, BMH, Michael Gleeson, WS 1288, p. 10.

14 MAI, MSP34REF474, application of Michael Lenihan, Bodyke, Clare, p. 9.

15 *Ibid.*, pp. 8–9.

16 Seán Murnane, WS 1048, pp. 11–12; MSP34REF474, Michael Lenihan, pp. 8-9.

17 MAI, Brigade Activity Reports, (A22) East Clare Brigade.

18 Timothy Tuohy, BMH WS 983, pp. 12–13.

19 Michael O'Gorman, 22 October 2012.

20 Galvin Collection, Helena Tuohy to Kathleen Foley, 2 May 1939.

21 *Ibid.*, Mary Ryan to Kathleen Foley, 18 April 1940

22 Ó Ruairc (2016), p. 69.

23 MAI, Bridget Slattery, MSP34REF9952.

24 Field Recording with Paddy Gleeson, Scariff, Co. Clare, 12 April 2009.

25 Joseph Noonan, BMH WS 1,287, pp. 3–4.

26 Seán Murnane, BMH WS 1048, pp. 11–12.

27 Mick O'Dea, BMH WS 1152, p. 10.

28 Michael O'Gorman, 22 October 2012.

29 Michael Gleeson, BMH WS 1288, pp. 8–10.

30 Seán Murnane, BMH WS 1048, pp. 12.

31 Michael O'Gorman, 22 October 2012.

32 Brennan (1980), p. 57.

33 'Scariff Barrack Attack', *Clare Champion*, 29 January 1921, p. 1; 'Attack on Scariff Police Barracks', *Saturday Record*, 25 September 1920, p. 2; Sullivan and Broderick were later treated by Dr Patrick Holmes.

34 'Murder Most Foul', *Daily Herald*, 20 November 1920, p.1.

35 Seán Moroney, BMH WS 1462, p. 3.

36 Joseph Noonan, BMH WS 1287, pp. 3–4.

37 In Brennan's statement he claims that he tried to burn the barrack while Seán Moroney and others claim they were refused permission to burn it.

38 Joseph Clancy, BMH WS 1370, pp. 7–8.

39 Timothy Tuohy, BMH WS 983, pp. 14.

40 Joseph Noonan, BMH WS 1287, pp. 3–4.

41 Kathleen Nash, 11 October 2009; While Kathleen suggests the IRA 'blew up' the barracks, she was probably hearing multiple gunshots over a sustained period.

42 Tony Muggivan, 10 January 2019.

43 Michael O'Gorman 22 October 2012.

44 'Unsuccessful Attack on Scariff Barracks', *Limerick Chronicle*, 21 September 1920, p. 3.

45 Tomás Malone, BMH WS 845, p. 26.

46 Michael Gleeson, BMH WS 1288, p. 11.

47 Brennan, *The War of in Clare*, pp. 38–9.

48 Michael O'Gorman, 22 October 2012.

49 'Black and Tan Raids', *Daily Herald*, 27 September 1920, p. 1.

50 Michael Brennan, BMH WS 1068, pp. 60–1; Joseph Noonan, WS 1287,

pp. 5–6

51 Paddy Gleeson, 12 April 2009.

52 Henry O'Mara, BMH WS 1653, p. 6.

53 'Barrack Burning', *Clare Champion*, 23 October 1920, p. 5.

54 'The Belfast Pogrom', *Clare Champion*, 23 September 1920, p. 3; The Belfast Boycott was introduced in mid-1920 by Dáil Éireann and targeted Belfast banks and businesses, in response to increasing attacks on Catholics in the north of Ireland, led by senior police figures, see See Alan Parkinson, *Belfast's unholy war* (Dublin, 2004).

55 Interview with Arthur O'Donnell, Cahir, Co. Tipperary, 6 November 2019.

56 Paddy Rodgers, 10 January 2019.

57 Interview with Caimin O'Halloran, Tuamgraney (remote), 06 February 2021.

58 'Raids in Scariff', *Dublin Evening Telegraph*, 24 September 1920, p. 1

59 Thomas McNamara, WS 1077, pp. 11–12.

60 Correspondence, Gina Sparling to me, 25 April 2020.

61 Letter, Kathleen Rodgers, 20 September 1920.

62 *Ibid.*, 3 April 1920.

5 'The boys began to fire'

1 'Served in Clare', *Clare Champion*, 23 September 1920, p. 3.

2 'Clare Policeman Resigns', *Clare Champion*, 23 September 1920, p. 3.

3 Royal Irish Constabulary Service Records 1816–1922 (HO 184) (www.findmypast.ie)

4 'Royal Irish Constabulary 1867–1922', http://www.policerollofhonour.org.uk/forces/ireland_to_1922/ric/ric_roll.htm (accessed 21 June 2018).

5 In 1921, crown forces used a service room in Scariff Market House to interrogate suspects in the absence of a barracks.

6 CAC, interview with Mae Tuohy, Feakle, Co. Clare, 13 April 2011.

7 Seosamh Mac Mathúna, *Kilfarboy, A History of a West Clare Parish* (Clare, 1978), p. 87.

8 'West Clare Tragedies', *Clare Champion*, 5 February 1921, p. 5.

9 *Ibid.*

10 NAI, Census of Ireland, 1911.

11 'Ennistymon and Lahinch', Clare Champion, 2 October 1920, p. 3; Correspondence, Joe Sammon, Galway, to me, 4 October 2020.

12 'West Clare Burnings', *Clare Champion*, 5 February 1921, p. 3.

13 *Ibid.*

14 NAI, Inspector General's Report for October 1920, TNA: PRO CO 904/113.

15 'Scariff Board of Guardians', *Clare Champion*, 23 September 1920, p. 3.

16 Timothy Tuohy, BMH WS 983, p. 15.

17 RC, 'Permission to Travel', note signed by Lt M.W. Spicer, 25 September 1920.

18 Seán Crowe, 26 September 2011.

19 *Ibid.*

20 Joseph Noonan, BMH WS 1287, p. 7.

21 *Ibid.*
22 Michael Brennan, BMH WS 1068, p. 62.
23 Seán Crowe, 26 September 2011.
24 Joseph Noonan, WS 1287, p. 7.
25 'Two Policemen Shot', *Limerick Chronicle*, 28 September 1920, p. 3; 'Police shootings', *Clare Champion*, 12 February 1921, p. 1; 'Broadford Sergeant Shot Dead', *Saturday Record*, 2 October 1920, p. 2.
26 *Ibid.*
27 *Ibid.*
28 Joseph Clancy, WS 1370, p. 9.
29 Seán Crowe, 26 September 2011.
30 *Ibid.*
31 'East Clare Tragedy', *Limerick Leader*, 27 September, p. 2.
32 'East Clare Village Evacuated', *Saturday Record*, 2 October 1920, p. 3.
33 'Two Policemen Shot', *Limerick Chronicle*, 28 September 1920, p. 3.
34 'Constable Shot Dead in Broadford', *Clare Champion*, 2 October 1920, p. 5
35 NAUK, CO 904/142 Summary of Police Reports September 1920, HO 184/32.
36 'Broadford Sergeant Shot Dead', *Saturday Record*, 2 October 1920.
37 Abbott (2019), p. 126.
38 'Police shootings', *Clare Champion*, 12 February 1921, p. 1.
39 *Ibid.*
40 'Sergeant Martin Turnbull' RIC Service Records 1816–1922 (HO 184).
41 'James Hogan, revolutionary, historian, political scientist (1898–1963)', *History Ireland*, Issue 1 (Spring 1999, Volume 7); Hogan's uncle PJ Hogan was one of the men who travelled to Killaloe for the bodies of the Scariff Martyrs.
42 Joseph Noonan, BMH WS 1287, p. 7.
43 There is further irony in the fact that Martin Gildea's cousin Thomas Kelly was a member of the RIC from New Inn; see Michael Healy, BMH WS 1064, pp. 4–5. Another cousin, Patrick Gildea was also a member of the RIC in Kerry.
44 'Shot Leaving a Hotel', *Freeman's Journal*, 1 October 1920, p. 3.
45 'Ennistymon and Lahinch', *Clare Champion*, 2 October 1920, p. 3
46 'Police Attacked in O'Brien's Bridge', *Limerick Chronicle*, 30 September 1920, p. 3; 'The O'Brien's Bridge Shootings', *Irish Times*, 2 October 1920, p. 6.
47 'Shot Leaving a Hotel', *Freeman's Journal*, 1 October 1920, p. 3; David Duirnin, *The Irish Medical Profession and The First World War* (Dublin, 2019), p. 51.
48 'Shot Leaving a Hotel', *Freeman's Journal*, 1 October, 1920, p. 3; in some reports, it was claimed that the IRA fired through the window; see 'Fired at through public house window', *Clonmel Chronicle*, 2 October 1920, p. 3.
49 'Shot Dead', *Limerick Leader*, 1 October 1920, p. 2.
50 Ó Ruairc (2016), pp. 139–40.
51 MAI, BMH, John 'Bishop' Ryan, WS 1136, p. 5; Correspondence, Tom O'Brien, to me, 19 May 2020.

52 MAI, BMH, John 'Bishop' Ryan, WS 1136, p. 5; interview with Mick Ryan, Sallybank, Clonlara, Co. Clare, 10 December 2013.

53 John 'Bishop' Ryan, BMH WS 1136, pp. 5–6.

54 *Ibid.*, p. 6.

55 RIC Service Records 1816–1922 (HO 184).

56 Kierse Collection, Recording with Denis Cusack of Ballyea, Boher, Ballina, February 1974 (transcript).

57 Michael Brennan, BMH WS 1068, p. 63.

58 John 'Bishop' Ryan, BMH WS 1136, p. 5.

59 'Shot Dead', *Limerick Leader*, 1 October 1920, p. 2.

60 Michael Brennan, BMH WS 1068, p. 63.

61 'Shot Dead', *Limerick Leader*, 1 October 1920, p. 2.

62 'Alarm in O'Brien's Bridge', *Limerick Chronicle*, 5 November 1920, p. 2.

63 John 'Bishop' Ryan, BMH WS 1136, p. 6.

64 'New Measures', *An tÓglách*, 1 October 1920, p. 1.

65 'Editorial', *Clare Champion*, 23 October 1920, p. 3.

66 NAI, The British in Ireland (CO904), Police Reports, Box 148.

67 'Burned by armed men', *Limerick Chronicle*, 9 October 1920, p. 2.

68 Paddy Gleeson, 15 May 2004.

69 *Ibid.*

70 The townland was incorrectly spelled Kielty in press reports.

71 'Of Enormous Importance', *Clare Champion*, 29 January 1921, p. 1.

72 Ó Ruairc (2016), pp. 164–165.

73 Paddy Gleeson, 12 April 2009.

74 *Ibid.*, 15 May 2004.

75 'Of Enormous Importance', *Clare Champion*, 29 January 1921, p. 1.

6 *'Praying hard that their houses wouldn't be burned'*

1 RIC Service Records 1816–1922 (HO 184).

2 Interview with Nuala Hogan, Newmarket-on-Fergus, 2 June 2011.

3 Tomo Tuohy, BMH WS 983, p. 15.

4 *Ibid.*; Later that night Moloney, along with another postman Michael Keating, were shot at and badly beaten by British forces while his house was set on fire; 'Feakle Burnings', *Clare Champion*, 5 February 1921, p. 5.

5 Timothy 'Tomo' Tuohy, BMH WS 983, pp. 17–19.

6 Coyle, *Evidence on Conditions in Ireland*, p. 373.

7 *Ibid.*: Seán Moroney implied that it was he and Pat Houlihan who fired the fatal shots, from within the post office building; see Seán Moroney, BMH WS 1462, p. 5.

8 'Feakle Tragedy', *Clare Champion*, 9 October 1920, p. 3; 'The Feakle Ambush', *Saturday Record*, 16 October 1920, p. 3.

9 'Police shootings', *Clare Champion*, 12 February 1921, p. 1.

10 According to the Census of Ireland in 1911, both men were living in Corlea in Feakle, Stanley in Knockbeha and Sammon in Pollatrumpa.

11 TJ McGuinness, Feakle, to me, 11 October 2020.

12 Ó Ruairc (2016), p. 163.

13 'Editorial', *Clare Champion*, 16 October 1920, p. 5.

14 'A Night of Terror', *Freeman's Journal*, 23 October 1920, p. 2.

15 'The Fate of Feakle', *Munster News*, 13 October 1920, p. 3.

16 CAC, Interview with Conor Tuohy, Feakle, 12 October 2012; Francis Doherty did not have children when he was killed.

17 Mae Tuohy, 13 April 2011.

18 Timothy 'Tomo' Tuohy, BMH WS 983, p. 20–21; 'Feakle Burnings', *Clare Champion*, 5 February 1921, p. 3.

19 Correspondence, Fr Martin Bugler, 19 February 2014.

20 'Flight from Burning Homes', *Wicklow People*, 16 October 1920, p. 5.

21 NAI, RIC County Inspector's Report for October 1920, TNA, PRO, CO 904/110.

22 Thomas Tuohy, BMH WS 983, p. 16.

23 'Destruction of Houses, House of Commons Debate, 2 June 1921.

24 NAI, RIC County Inspector's Report for October 1920, TNA, PRO, CO 904/110.

25 'Reprisals in Feakle', *Saturday Record*, 16 October 1920, p. 3; Annie Houlihan, a member of Feakle Cumann na mBan, claimed in 1938, that the organisation ceased to function in Feakle following the attack on the RIC, Mary Galvin Collection, Annie Houlihan to Mrs Nan Foley, 15 July, 1938.

26 Nuala Hogan, 2 June 2011; Dr J.J. Stuart (1904–1980) was a native of Ogonnelloe, and president of the GAA from 1958 to 1961.

27 'Sgt John McFadden killed in Co. Clare 1921', https://irishconstabulary. com/sgt-john-mcfadden-killed-in-co-clare-1921-t1306.html (accessed 12 May 2018).

28 'The Feakle Ambush', *Saturday Record*, 16 October 1920, p. 3.

29 Seán Moroney, BMH WS 1462, p. 11.

30 Brennan (2002), p. 61.

31 Tomás Mac Conmara, 'Cross-county action reached deep into the fabric of Clare life', in *Clare Champion* (Living), 23 April 2021, p. 4.

32 'Astounding Story', *Freeman's Journal*, 15 October 1920.

33 *Ibid.*

34 *Ibid.*

35 'Death of East Clare Patriot', *Clare Champion*, 24 October 1963, p. 5.

36 Seán Nugent, Clonusker, Scariff, 22 April 2010 (handwritten notes).

37 'The Feakle Ambush', *Clare Champion*, 30 October 1920, p. 5.

38 Tomo Tuohy, BMH WS 983, p. 20; Michael 'Marshall' McMahon, 10 January 2011.

39 MAI, MSP34REF47693, application of Mary Moroney, Kealderra, O'Callaghan's Mills, Co. Clare, p. 27, 50.

40 'A Sad Case', *Clare Champion*, 29 January 1921, p. 1.

41 Conor Tuohy, 12 October 2012.

42 CAC, Seán Nugent, Clonusker, Scariff, 22 April 2010.

43 Correspondence, Fr Martin Bugler, 19 February 2014.

44 Conor Tuohy, 12 October 2012.

45 NAI, CO, Inspector General's Report for October 1920, TNA: PRO CO 904/113.

46 Timothy Tuohy, BMH WS 983, pp. 20–2.

47 Interview with Timothy, 'Brod' Minogue, Mountshannon, Co. Clare, 13 December 2011; 'Priest's Servant Kidnapped', *Londonderry Sentinel*, 30 October 1920, p. 6.

48 'Woman Kidnapped in Clare', *Belfast Newsletter*, 26 October 1920, p. 5.

49 'McSwiney Funeral', *Irish Times*, 6 November 1920.

50 Timothy 'Tomo' Tuohy, BMH WS 983, p. 22; The Volunteers involved were Joe and Jack Tuohy from Dromore, Thomas Tuohy from Gurraun (later lived in Whitegate) and Tomo Tuohy, Kildavin, O/C of the Feakle Company; see MAI, application of Thomas Tuohy, MSP34REF10118.

51 NAI, RIC Clare County Inspector's Report for October 1920, TNA, PRO, CO 904/110.

52 'A Sad Case', *Clare Champion*, 29 January 1921, p. 1.

53 *Ibid.*

54 Tomo Tuohy, BMH WS 983, p. 22.

55 Paddy Gleeson, Kealderra, O'Callaghan's Mills, 15 May 2004.

56 Mae Tuohy, 13 April 2011.

57 Handwritten notes from interview with Mae Tuohy, 13 April 2011.

58 Correspondence, Liam Counihan, USA to me, 23 April 2013

59 Liam Counihan, 7 June 2013.

60 *Ibid*, 25 April 2013.

61 *Ibid.*

62 NAI, 1911 Census of Ireland, Feakle Parish, Ayle townland.

63 'Clare Process Server Shot Dead', *Limerick Chronicle*, 30 October 1920, p. 2; 'Kidnapped and Murdered', *Irish Times*, 29 October 1920, p. 5.

64 Clare Museum (CE: 200.195), 'East Clare IRA Proclamation'.

65 'A Sad Case', *Clare Champion*, 29 January 1921, p. 1.

66 Tomo Tuohy, BMH WS 983, pp. 21–22.

67 *Ibid.*

68 Ó Ruairc (2016), p. 162.

69 NAI, RIC Clare County Inspector's Monthly Report for October 1920 TNA, PRO, CO 904/110

70 *Ibid.*

71 Ó Ruairc (2016), p. 162.

72 William Delany, *The Green and the Red: Revolutionary Republicanism and Socialism in Irish Socialism in Irish History: 1848–1923* (New York, 2001), p. 472.

73 Correspondence, Rosemary McCarthy O'Neill to me, 12 March 2020. For Register of Death for James Treacy, see Civil Records (civilrecords.irish genealogy.ie/churchrecords) James Treacy, 28 October 1920.

74 Seán Crowe, 24, October 2010.

75 'Attacks on Police', *Limerick Chronicle*, 5 November 1920, p. 2.

76 'Kevin Barry Executed', *Limerick Chronicle*, 5 November 1920, p. 2.

77 NAI, Inspector General's Report for October 1920 TNA: PRO CO 904/113.

78 RIC Service Records 1816–1922 (HO 184).

79 Kierse Collection, recording with Tim Ryan-Hannon, O'Brien's Bridge, 3 July 1983 (transcript).

7 'Sold and traced'

1 CAC, Interview with Patrick Skeehan, Bridgetown, Co. Clare, 15 October 2010 (interviewed by Ruth Minogue).

2 Ó Ruairc (2016), p. 151.

3 Con Hogan, Tulla, 14 March 2010

4 Tommy Holland, 17 October 2019; The building had been owned by Charles O'Callaghan, who was killed in 1824 (see p. 249, endnote 6).

5 Ryan, Michelle, 'The Sporting Lodge, Williamstown, Whitegate: Architecture, Objects and History'. Unpublished Master's Thesis.

6 Waterways Ireland Archive, interview with Tommy Holland, 22 January 2016.

7 Thomas McNamara, WS 1077, pp. 13–14.

8 Ned Broy, WS 1280, p. 33.

9 Correspondence, PJ Reidy to me, 21 October 2019.

10 'Capt. Patrick Benignus Cullinan MC, Leinster Regt', http://theauxiliaries. com/men-alphabetical/men-c/cullinan-pb/cullinan.html (accessed 14 January 2019).

11 NAUK, *Survey of SS Shannon* by Charles J. Coffey, consulting engineer, 16 December 1921, PRO, Kew, HO 351 111.

12 Joseph Clancy, BMH WS 1370, p. 10.

13 Ó Ruairc (2016), p. 15.

14 *Ibid.*

15 Tommy Bolton, 11 June 1989; Tommy was referring to Denham Sparling, whose father George, a merchant from Scariff, died in April 1909, see https://civilrecords.irishgenealogy.ie/churchrecords/images/deaths_ returns/deaths_1909/05457/4527270.pdf.

16 Paddy O'Meara, March 1975.

17 Caimin O'Halloran, 6 February 2021.

18 Tommy Holland, 23 May 2018.

19 Kathleen Mitchell, 5 July 2016.

20 *Ibid.*; Martin Gildea's father died on 7 April 1930.

21 Peter Howley, BMH WS 1379, pp. 21, 31.

22 Interview with Joe Duane, Kilreekil, Co. Galway, 30 September 2019.

23 *Ibid.*

24 Hickey, *Irish Days,* p. 92.

25 Sonny was referring to Michael Hogan, a thirty-five-year-old publican and shopkeeper from Gorteeny.

26 Interview with Anthony 'Sonny' Hackett, 4 November 1996 (interviewed by John Joe Conwell and video by Tom Burke); later, Anthony implies that the men may have been Jim Tuohy, Seán O'Halloran and Peter Flannery. However, the latter were recorded in the Sixmilebridge/Cratloe area during the time referred to by Sonny. Given the timing, his references to the Scariff Martyrs, as well as the knowledge that the three Volunteers travelled through Gorteeny, it is certain the men he helped in November 1920 were McMahon, Rodgers and Gildea.

27 Interview with Dermot Moran, Woodford, Co. Galway, 12 February 2011 (handwritten notes).

28 Anne Rodgers and Kitty Dillon, 23 September 2019.

29 *Ibid.*

30 My fieldwork.

31 Tommy Holland, 10 September 2010.

32 MAI, MPSC, application of Bella Lucas, MSP34REF10997.

33 *Ibid.*

34 There were IRA dugouts in Mountshannon in the townlands of Sillernane, Bohatch, Derrycon and Middleline; see Tom McNamara, BMH WS 1077, pp. 11–12.

8 *'Without clergy, judge or jury'*

1 Grey (1920), p. 2.

2 RIC Service Records 1816–1922 (HO 184).

3 'Killaloe Compensation Claims, Dáil Éireann Debate, 16 July 1935. On the night of 12 August 1922, the Lakeside Hotel was burned to the ground by republicans.

4 Peter Cottrell, *The Anglo-Irish War: The Troubles of 1913–1922* (Oxford, 2006), p. 57.

5 F.P. Crozier, *Ireland Forever* (London, 1992), p. 95.

6 Kierse (2001), pp. 151–2.

7 Ó Ruairc (2009), p. 187.

8 Grey (1920), p. 4.

9 Mark Custance, Shiner & Co, *From the Western Front to Bristol Millionaire* (Bristol, 2001), p.170

10 Grey (1920), pp. 3–4.

11 Kierse Collection, Recording with John O'Byrne, Killaloe, Co. Clare, 31 January 1978 (transcript).

12 MAI, IE/MA/CP/5/2/22 (XXII), IRA HQ, 'Intelligence', to O/C, East Clare Brigade, 19 April 1921.

13 Paddy O'Meara, March 1975, on the recording Paddy revealed that 'I slept with 'em the night before they were taken out of it',.

14 Ryan, 'The Sporting Lodge', p. 69.

15 In July 1916, Joe McEvoy's eighteen-year-old son Michael was killed in Mesopotamia during the First World War with the British Army; see Ger Browne, Clare Men & Women During WW1 http://www.clarelibrary.ie/eolas/coclare/history/clare_men_women_great_war_2.pdf (accessed, 12 August 2018).

16 Graney, 'East Clare's Calvary', p. 105.

17 In 1897, when the Duke of York (later King George V) travelled with a royal party up the River Shannon, several sites along that route were named in honour of the visit including the quay at Killaloe.

18 Kierse Collection, Mike Daly, 5 January 1972.

19 Graney, 'East Clare's Calvary', p. 105.

20 Tony Muggivan, 10 January 2019

21 Graney, p. 105.

22 NAUK, 'British Court of Inquiry', WO 35/153A.

23 'An Extraordinary Case', *Clare Champion*, 8 January 1921, p. 3.

24 Williamstown House had an enclosed yard with servant's apartments, a coach house, fowl house, hay loft, a turf shed and toilets; 'Sale Notice for Williamstown Lodge', *Irish Times*, 31 May 1906, p. 12.

25 NAUK, 'British Court of Inquiry, WO 35/153A.

26 *Ibid.*

27 'An Extraordinary Case', *Clare Champion*, 8 January 1921, p. 3.

28 'The Whitegate Shootings', *Irish Times*, 19 November 1920, p. 5.

29 Scallops were sally or willow rods used as part of the thatching process to fix the straw onto a layer of 'scraw' (usually sod peat or heather) which was layered under the thatch. The scallops helped to stabilise and protect the thatch from high winds.

30 Interview with Michael 'Hookey Farrell, Whitegate, Co. Clare, 26 April 2011.

31 Graney, p. 105.

32 Tommy Holland, 10 September 2010.

33 *Ibid.*

34 Graney, pp. 105–6.

35 *Ibid.*

36 Seán Crowe, 24 October 2010.

37 Graney, p. 105.

38 In the 1930s, a large collection of Bronze Age axe heads was discovered on the bed of Lough Derg, close to BeálBorú; see Clare Museum, CE. 1974:29.

39 *Ibid.*

40 Kierse Collection, Mike Daly, 5 January 1972.

41 *Ibid.*

42 Graney, p. 106.

43 *Ibid.*

44 *Ibid.*, p. 106.

45 Lorcan Collins, *Ireland's War of Independence, 1919-1921: The IRA's Guerrilla Campaign* (Dublin, 2019), p. 93.

46 Crozier, *Ireland Forever*, p. 201.

47 Mike Daly, 5 January 1972.

48 Eunan O'Halpin, *Kevin Barry: An Irish Rebel in Life and Death* (Dublin, 2020), pp. 65-68.

49 *Irish Bulletin*, 19 November 1920; 'Current Comments', *Young Ireland*, 27 November 1920

50 'Murder of Fr Griffin', *Galway Observer*, 27 November 1920; D. M., Leeson, *The Black and Tans: British Police and Auxiliaries in the Irish War of Independence, 1920 –1921* (Oxford, 2012), p. 52.

51 Graney, pp. 106–7.

52 *Ibid.*, p. 105.

53 'Sequel to Midnight Shots and Cries at Killaloe', *Saturday Record*, 27 November 1920, p. 3.

54 Maeve Hayes, 28 June 2011.

55 *Ibid.*

56 John Fahey to me, 22 October 2019.

57 Clare County Library, Killaloe Folklore Collection, interview with Jerry Gough, Killaloe, c. 1990.

58 *Ibid.*, p. 106.

59 Jerry Gough, c. 1990.

60 Mary Faul, Killaloe, 28 November 2019 (handwritten notes).

61 *Ibid.*

62 Graney, p. 109.

63 CAC, Tom Cooney, 11 December 2011.

64 Graney, p. 110.

65 Arthur O'Donnell, 7 November 2019.

66 MacMahon Family Collection, Queen Alexandra's Imperial Military Nursing Service Administrative Papers of Johanna Scott, 30 October 1914 to 23 March 1919.

67 Correspondence, Niall McMahon, Máire Lowe and Niamh O'Hanlon to me, 20–30 July 2019.

68 'Ghastly Sights', *Freeman's Journal*, 19 November 1920, p. 6; 'Clare Tragedy', *Limerick Chronicle*, 18 November 1920, p. 3.

69 Graney, p. 112.

70 Maura Gleeson, Killaloe, 14 October 2019 (remote correspondence).

9 'If you were at their funeral'

1 Sequel to Midnight Shots and Cries at Killaloe', *Saturday Record*, 27 November 1920, p. 1.

2 John Fahey to me, 22 October 2019.

3 'The Clare Tragedy', *Nenagh Guardian*, 20 November 1920, p. 5.

4 Graney, p.110.

5 'The Clare Tragedy', *Nenagh Guardian*, 20 November 1920, p. 5.

6 Michael O'Gorman, 22 October 2012

7 Leeson, (2012), p. 189.

8 'A Besieged Village', *Nenagh Guardian*, 20 November 1920, p. 3.

9 MAI, BMH, Leo Buckley, pp. 6-7; Freeman's Journal, 22 November 1920.

10 Caimin O'Halloran, 6 February 2021.

11 'An Extraordinary Case', *Clare Champion*, 8 January 1921, p. 3.

12 'The Clare Tragedy', *Nenagh Guardian*, 20 November 1920, p. 5.

13 Tony Muggivan, 8 August 2019.

14 Correspondence, Pat Flynn, Feakle to me, 11 October 2020.

15 Ó Ruairc (2016), p. 152; in the book, the placename Kincora, which lies just north of Killaloe, has been incorrectly misinterpreted as 'Kinvara'.

16 Con Hogan, 14 March 2010

17 Kathleen Mitchell, 5 July 2016; according to John Martin O'Brien, his uncle Thomas Hill from Ballymalone in Tuamgraney was asked to sit in one of the carriages on the way to Scariff Town and he, with his brother, Michael were involved in guarding the bodies at Scariff church; Brian Graney had written of 'four afflicted mothers' in the church. However, Nora Gildea had been dead for many years at that point.

18 Ó Ruairc (2016), p. 153.

19 'Official Statement', *Limerick Chronicle*, 21 November 1920, p. 3; 'Tragedy

Near Cratloe', *Saturday Record*, 27 November 1920, p. 1.

20 Correspondence, Rosemary McCarthy O'Neill to me, 12 March 2020.

21 Michael O'Gorman, 22 October 2012.

22 Correspondence, Stiofán Ó Comhraí to me, 13 August 2019.

23 Brian Heffernan, *Freedom and the Fifth Commandment: Catholic Priests and Political Violence in Ireland, 1919–21* (Manchester, 2016), p. 193.

24 For the best account of Peadar Clancy, see Cormac Ó Comhraí, Stiofán Ó Comhraí, Peadar Clancy: Easter Rising Hero, Bloody Sunday Martyr (Galway, 2016).

25 Paddy Gleeson, 12 April 2009.

26 *Ibid.*

27 Michael O'Gorman, 22 October 2012.

28 CAC, John Michael Tobin, 25 August 2010.

29 'John J Fitzgerald 1898–1920', http://www.bloodysunday.co.uk/murdered -men/fitzgerald.html (accessed 28 September 2019)

30 'Remains Buried in Scariff Chapel Yard', *Freeman's Journal*, 25 November 1920, p. 2.

31 Anna Mae McNamara, 29 September 2008..

32 John Michael Tobin, 25 August 2010.

33 Kathleen Nash, 5 October 2009.

34 Kathleen Mitchell, 5 July 2016.

35 'Clare Church Searched', *Irish Independent*, 18 November 1920.

36 Margaret Hoey, 14 November 2008.

37 'Clare Church Searched', *Irish Independent*, 18 November 1920.

38 Con Hogan, Tulla, 14 March 2010.

39 'Murder Most Foul', *Daily Herald*, 20 November 1920, p. 1.

40 Kathleen Mitchell, 5 July 2016.

41 Conor Tuohy, 12 October 2012.

42 *Ibid.*

43 'Remains Buried in Scariff Chapel Yard', *Freeman's Journal*, 25 November 1920, p. 2.

44 John Michael Tobin, 25 August 2010.

45 MAI, MSP34REF48649, application of Annie McNamara, p. 39.

46 *Ibid.*

47 'Clare Church Searched', *Irish Independent*, 18 November 1920

48 Margaret Hoey, 14 November 2008

49 MacLysaght (1978), pp. 98, 109–10.

50 *Ibid.*, p. 98.

51 Hopkinson (2002), p. 91; Iosold Ní Dheirg, *The Story of Michael Collins* (Cork, 2011), p. 74.

52 MacLysaght (1978), p. 98.

53 MAI, MSPC, application of Margaret Clune, DP24871.

54 'Late Mr. T.C. Clune', House of Commons, Written Answers, 29 November 1920, HC Deb 29 November 1920 https://api.parliament. uk/historic-hansard/written-answers/1920/nov/29/late-mr-t-c-clune (accessed 12 May 2015).

55 William MacLysaght, 8 August 2019.

56 Anne Mae McNamara, 12 October 2019. The alter Annie Brady's commemorative railing enclosed was built in the late 1800s by James Pearse, the father of Irish revolutionary, Pádraig Pearse. The railing was removed in the 1970s.

57 'Killaloe Tragedy', *Clare Champion*, 27 November 1920, p. 1.

58 *Ibid.*

59 Rodger's Collection, letter from J. S. Rodgers to Mrs Rodgers, 4 December 1920.

60 Michael O'Gorman, 22 October 2012

61 Margaret Hoey, 14 November 2008.

62 RC, Kathleen Rodgers, 05 December 1920.

63 Rodger's Collection, letter from J.S. Rogers to Mrs Rodgers, 4 December 1920.

64 *Ibid.*, 'unknown' to Mrs Rodgers, 21 November 1920.

65 *Ibid.*, John Murphy to Mrs Rodgers, 19 November 1920.

66 *Ibid.*, Micheál Gunning to Mrs Rodgers, date unknown.

67 Brendan Niall, *The Riddle of Father Hackett: A Life in Ireland and Australia* (Australia, 2009), p. 122.

68 RC, John Fahy to Mrs Hynes, 3 December 1920.

69 *Ibid.*, Unknown, St Louis's Convent, Kiltimagh, 19 November 1920.

70 MacLysaght (1978), p. 96.

71 Henry W. Nevinson, Changes and Chance (London, 1923), p. 212.

10 'The day will come'

1 Fitzpatrick, David, *Politics and Irish Life, 1913–21: Provincial Experiences of War and Revolution* (Dublin, 1977), p. 26.

2 David Fitzpatrick quoted without questioning, the apparent positive effect of the Auxiliaries on Killaloe without acknowledging the shooting of the Scariff Martyrs in his much lauded publication on Clare, see Fitzpatrick, *Politics and Irish Life*, p. 26; equally, Leeson detailed the damage caused to the *SS Shannon* but failed to mention its use in the capture of the Scariff Martyrs and omits reference to the incident entirely; see Leeson, *The Black and Tans*, pp. 127–8.

3 Correspondence, John Fahey to me, 22 October 2019.

4 MAI, IE/MA/CP/5/2/22, IRA HQ, 'Intelligence', to O/C, East Clare Brigade, 23 February 1921.

5 Interview with Pat O'Halloran and Con Hogan, Tulla, 8 November 2008.

6 'Monument to be Erected', *Irish Independent*, 24 November 1920, p. 5.

7 *Irish Bulletin*, A full reprint of the official newspaper of Dáil Éireann giving news and war reports, Volume 4, Part One (3rd January 1921–16th March 1921), pp. 1718–1718.

8 Kierse Collection, Mike Daly, 5 January 1972.

9 'Lady Died from Fright', *Evening Echo*, 8 December 1920, p. 4; 'Died from Fright', Freeman's Journal, 8 December 1920, p.5; 'Ellen Kennedy, Death Register', https://civilrecords.irishgenealogy.ie/churchrecords/images/deaths_returns/deaths_1920/05109/4404263.pdf (accessed 28 November 2019); Correspondence, Frieda Gleeson to me, 1 March 2020.

10 NAUK, WO 35/159N/30; 'Clare Asylum Searched, an Inmate Shot Dead', *Irish Times*, 30 November 1920, p. 5; 'Other Horrors', *Drogheda Independent*, 4 December 1920, p. 5.

11 'Incidents in the Provinces', *Irish Times*, 22 December 1920, p. 6.

12 'Two Killaloe Priests on Trial', *Clare Champion*, 22 January 1921, p. 1.

13 'Glenwood Ambush', *Sixmilebridge Parish Magazine* (1992), pp. 82–83.

14 Margaret Hoey (video), Carrigoran Nursing Home, Newmarket, 12 January 2009.

15 NAI, R.I.C. County Inspectors report Clare February 1921 (C/O 903 – 904); Williams had a son born in May 1919, while Walker had a young daughter. Although it has been suggested one of the men was as young as seventeen, the youngest, Walker, was twenty-four years old.

16 CAC, Interview with Fr Martin Bugler, Scariff, 21 September 2010.

17 Seán Moroney, BMH WS 1462, p. 12.

18 Seán Nugent, 22 April 2010.

19 Galvin Collection, letter from Helena Tuohy to Kathleen Foley, 2 May 1939.

20 'A Sunday in Scariff', *Freeman's Journal*, 23 May 1921, p. 4.

21 Stiofán Ó Comhraí to me, 13 August 2019.

22 'Police Operations, Scariff', House of Commons Debate, 2 June 1921; Mosley went on to lead the British Union of Fascists. He was portrayed in the British crime drama series, *Peaky Blinders* in 2019.

23 'To Collect Men Leaving Church', *Freeman's Journal*, 16 May 1921, p. 5.

24 'A Sunday in Scariff', *Freeman's Journal*, 23 May 1921, p. 4.

25 'Trip through the Century with Dr Mac Lysaght', *Clare Champion Souvenir Supplement 1903–1978*, p. 20.

26 Tommy Bolton, 11 June 1989.

27 Interview with Palkie McNamara, Killaloe, 12 July 2004.

28 'Great Destruction of Property', *Irish Times*, 16 June 1921, p. 5.

29 NAUK, 'Court of Inquiry in Lieu of Inquest – Civilian James Grogan, Core, Feakle, Co. Clare' (WO 35/151A).

30 'Feakle Man Shot', *Clare Champion*, 9 July 1921, p. 3.

31 Leslie Shiner claimed that local women from Killaloe, who 'were doing a roaring trade' were drafted in as prostitutes, see Custance, Shiner & Co, p. 187.

32 The term 'bodysnatchers' is usually reserved for people who interfere with corpses to steal valuables or to sell bodies for profit. The name which seems to have been self-titled, was likely connected to their role in the capture and death of the Scariff Martyrs.

33 NFSC, Volume 0585, p. 256, Broadford National School.

34 *Sunday Business Post*, 29 February 2004, p. 4.

35 Peter Standford, *Judas: The Most Hated Name in History* (London, 2015), p. 132.

36 Kathleen Mitchell, 5 July 2016.

37 Noonan, *Songs and Recitations*, pp. 116–17.

38 Rodger's Collection, 'The Scariff Martyrs', D.P. O'Farrell to Mrs Rodgers, 8 March 1922.

39 Ó Ruairc, Pádraig Óg, 'Spies and informers beware!': IRA executions of alleged civilian spies during the War of Independence 1919 –1921, *History Ireland*, Issue 2 (May/June 2017), Revolutionary Period 1912–1923, Vol. 25.

40 MacLysaght (1978), p. 14.

41 Patrick Reidy, BMH WS 1112, p. 4.

42 Brennan (1980), p. 53.

43 UCD Archives, Mulcahy Papers, P7/A/17, O/C East Clare to IRA GHQ, April 1921

44 MAI, MSP34REF59959, application of Bridget Lynch (evidence given to interviewing officer on 22 July 1942).

45 MAI, UMCE-S-A-26, interview with Dan Gleeson, 1978.

46 Margaret Hoey (Video), Carrigoran Nursing Home, Newmarket, 12 January 2009.

47 Seán Nugent, 22 April 2010; Michael O'Gorman, 22 October 2012.

48 Seán Crowe, 24, October 2010

49 'Incidents in the Provinces', *Irish Times*, 22 December 1920, p. 6.

50 'UK refuses to release 100-year-old details of its Irish spies', *Irish Independent*, 7 September 2019.

51 NAUK, Fieldwork research, Intelligence Notes, CO 903, WO 35, expenditure of RIC (T 192)

52 Seán Crowe, 24 October 2010.

53 Name withheld at request of interviewee.

54 Paddy Murray, 10 January 2019.

55 IE/MA/CP/5/2/22, IRA HQ, 'Intelligence', to O/C, East Clare Brigade, 28 February 1921.

56 Michael O'Gorman, 22 October 2012.

57 NAUK, 'British Court of Inquiry, WO 35/153A

58 Ned Broy, BMH WS 1280, p. 1.

59 McLaughlin (2003), p. 92; 'Engagements', *Irish Society* (Dublin), 16 October 1920, p. 3.

60 Ó Ruairc (2016), pp. 139–141. Emma McKeogh was a daughter of Patrick Rohan, a grocer in Scariff Town.

61 Brennan (1980), p. 74.

62 *Ibid.*

63 Pádraig Óg Ó Ruairc, 'Spies and informers beware!': IRA executions of alleged civilian spies during the War of Independence 1919 –1921, *History Ireland*, Issue 2 (May/June 2017), Revolutionary Period 1912–1923, Vol. 25.

64 NAUK, Irish Distress Committee and Irish Grants Committee (CO 762, 198/19), claim by Amelia Blennerhassett.

65 *Ibid.*

66 Thomas McNamara, BMH WS 1077, p. 15.

67 *Ibid.*, pp. 12–14; Pat Duggan was a critical source of intelligence for IRA, having managed to find himself 'absolutely in the enemy's confidence', see MAI, MSPC, application of Patrick Duggan, W24SP12781.

68 NAI, BMH, Thomas McNamara, WS. 1077, p. 8.

69 IE/MA/CP/5/2/22, HQ, East Clare Brigade, to IRA HQ, Dublin, 14 March 1921.

70 IE/MA/CP/5/2/22, IRA HQ, 'Intelligence', to O/C, East Clare Brigade, 23 February 1921.
71 MAI, MSP34REF20326, application of Mary A. Ryan, Newport, Tipperary, p. 23, 26.
72 Reference of Charlie Turner in MAI, MSP34REF48886, application of Patrick McInerney, (1RB4601), p. 11
73 NAI, Court-martial case registers, June 1916-1921 (WO 35/132-137, and WO 35/139), specific file number withheld.
74 Tommy Holland, 10 September 2010.
75 UCD Archives, RMP, 'Limerick Curfew Murders', P7/A/17.

11 'Murder is murder'

1 Bonner (2007), pp. 76–77.
2 NAUK, 'British Court of Inquiry, WO 35/153A.
3 'An Extraordinary Case', *Clare Champion*, 8 January 1921, p. 3.
4 'John Francis Eastwood', http://www.thepeerage.com/p22906.htm#i229056 (accessed 7 August 2019).
5 The papers of Lt Lees were donated to King's College London in 1987. Although it contains correspondence from his period in Limerick, my inspection of the material in London found no reference to the Killaloe killings (my fieldwork at King's College London, 24 July 2014).
6 Ó Ruairc (2009), pp. 242–3.
7 'Feakle Man Shot', *Clare Champion*, 9 July 1921.
8 NAUK, 'Court of Inquiry in Lieu of Inquest – Civilian James Grogan, Core, Feakle, Co. Clare' (WO 35/151A)
9 Paul O'Brien, *Havoc: The Auxiliaries in Ireland's War of Independence* (Cork, 2017), pp. 80, 84.
10 Paul McMahon, *British Spies and Irish Rebels: British Intelligence and Ireland, 1916–1945* (London, 2008), p. 29.
11 Ó Ruairc (2009), p. 189.
12 NAUK, 'British Court of Inquiry', WO 35/153A.
13 *Ibid.*
14 'Sergeant John Brennan', RIC Service Records 1816–1922 (HO 184).
15 NAUK, 'British Court of Inquiry', WO 35/153A.
16 Graney, 'East Clare's Calvary', pp. 106–8.
17 Carroll, *Seán Moylan*, p. 98.
18 T. Ryle Dwyer, *Michael Collins, The Man Who Won the War* (Cork, 1990), p. 92.
19 Graney, p. 106.
20 *Ibid.*
21 Correspondence, Kevin Ford, New Zealand to me, 10 December 2020.
22 'Injuries Result in Death', *The Evening Post (NZ)*, 09 October 1926, p. 14.
23 CAC, Michael 'Hookey Farrell, 26 April 2011.
24 Graney, 'East Clare's Calvary', pp. 106–7.
25 Michael O'Gorman, 22 October 2012.
26 'Attempt to Escape from Custody', *Irish Times*, 18 November 1920, p. 5; 'Four Men Killed in County Clare', *Irish Independent*, 18 November 1920.

27 'Sensational Report', *Clare Champion*, 20 November 1920, p. 3; 'Tragic Occurrence in Whitegate', *Saturday Record*, 20 November 1920, p. 4; 'Sequel to Midnight Shots and Cries at Killaloe', *Saturday Record*, 27 November 1920, p. 1

28 'Attempt to Escape from Custody', *Irish Times*, 18 November 1920, p. 5.

29 Thomas D. Rossing, Paul A. Wheeler, F. Richard Moore, *The Science of Sound* (San Francisco, 2002).

30 Monthly weather report of the Meteorological office of the United Kingdom, November 1920, http://www.metoffice.gov. uk/media/pdf/h/r/Nov1920.pdf (accessed 8 August 1920).

31 Graney, p. 108.

32 *Ibid.*

33 'Murder Most Foul', *Daily Herald*, 20 November 1920, p. 1.

34 *Ibid.*, p. 109.

35 *Freeman's Journal*, 19 November 1920.

36 Jack Hogan, Killaloe to me, 29 January 2021.

37 Grey (1920), p. 2.

38 *Ibid.*

39 Graney, p. 109.

40 Paddy Rodgers, 10 January 2019.

41 Graney, p. 108.

42 NAUK, 'British Court of Inquiry', WO 35/153A.

43 *Irish Bulletin*, 18 November 1920, p. 7.

44 'County Clare Tragedy', *Dublin Evening Telegraph*, 17 November 1920; 'Right to Shoot to Kill, *Leeds Mercury*, 19 November 1920, p. 1.

45 'Midnight Clare Horror', Freeman's Journal, 18 November 1920, p. 5

46 'Four Men Killed in County Clare', *Irish Times*, 18 November 1920, p. 3.

47 'Four men Shot Dead', *Larne Times*, 20 November 1920, p. 2.

48 Kautt. (1999), p. 106.

49 *The American Commission on Conditions in Ireland* (New York, 1921), p. 22.

50 'The Terror in Ireland', *Mid Sussex Times*, 4 January 1921, p. 2.

51 'Escaping Prisoners (Shooting)', British House of Commons Debate 18 November 1920, http://hansard.millbanksystems.com/ commons/1920/nov/18/escaping-prisoners-shooting (accessed 27 March 2012).

52 *Ibid.*

53 Michael Brennan, BMH WS 1,068, p. 69; Brennan (1980), pp. 64–65.

54 MacLysaght (1954), p. 12.

55 William MacLysaght, 8 August 2019.

56 Graney, p. 106.

57 Grey (1920), p. 2.

58 NAUK, 'British Court of Inquiry, WO 35/153A.

59 Bolt, Usain, *The Fastest Man Alive: The True Story of Usain Bolt* (USA, 2012), p. 15.

60 NAUK, Court of Inquiry, WO 35/153A.

61 'The Terror in Ireland', *Mid Sussex Times*, 4 January 1921, p. 2.

62 McMahon Family Collection, papers of Johanna Scott

63 Grey (1920), p. 3.

64 Kathleen Mitchell, 6 July 2016.

65 Michael O'Gorman, 22 October 2012.

66 UCD, Ernie O'Malley Collection, interview with Patrick McDonnell, p 17 b/130, p. 30A.

67 Graney, pp. 111–12; publicly, it was claimed no inquest was held, see 'No Inquest on Clare Men', *Freeman's Journal*, 20 November 1920, p. 5.

68 Graney, p. 112.

69 'Scariff Barrack Attack', *Clare Champion*, 29 January 1921, p. 1.

70 *Ibid.*

71 Kierse, *The Killaloe Anthology*, p. 209.

72 Graney, p. 112.

73 Madden (1984), p. 43; Madden (2000), p. 178.

74 'Monument to be Erected', *Irish Independent*, 24 November 1920, p. 5.

75 'Killaloe Notes', *Nenagh Guardian*, 17 February 1923, p. 4.

76 John Fahey, 13 June 2019; the same claim was made by Pauline Collins, whose grandfather worked at the hotel, correspondence of Pauline Collins to me, 8 April 2011.

77 *Ibid.*

78 Fr James Russell became well-known for miraculous cures attributed to him. His grave in Kilcommon in Co. Tipperary is a site of devotion for many people.

79 NAUK, Irish Grants Committee (CO 762, 170/1), 'Claim by Rev. James Russell'.

80 Graney, p. 106.

81 Crozier (1992), p. 196. 8

82 'General Crozier', British House of Commons Debate, 9 June 1921; Crozier (1992), p. 196.

83 *Ibid.*

84 Crozier (1992), p. 195.

85 'Lt Col Richard John Andrews DSO, MC, QSA', http://theauxiliaries. com/men-alphabetical/men-a/andrews-rj/andrews.html (accessed 5 May 2018).

86 *Ibid.*

87 Leeson, *The Black and Tans* (2011), p. 115.

88 '2nd Lt Percy George Wiles M.M, QSA', http://theauxiliaries.com/men-alphabetical/men-w-x-y-z/wiles-pg/wiles.html (accessed January 2019).

89 Browne, Ger, *The Auxiliaries and Temporary Constables in and from Clare 1920 -22*, p. 2; www.findmypast.ie, (the Auxiliary Division - Register No. 1 Numbers 1-1516.,

90 Custance, *Shiner & Co*, p. 169

91 McNamara and Madden (1995), p. 114, 148.

92 Plunkett Dillon, G., *All in the Blood* (Dublin 2006), p. 303; *Connacht Tribune*, 27 November 1920, p. 4.

93 McCall, Ernest, *The Auxies: A Pictorial History of the Auxiliary Division Royal Irish Constabulary 1920–1922* (Belfast, 2013), p. 105; Mrs George Clancy, BMH WS 806, p. 13.

94 Custance, *Shiner & Co.*, p.171.

95 *Ibid.*, pp.171–172

96 *Ibid.*, p.178.

97 IE/MA/CP/5/2/22 (XXVII), HQ, East Clare Brigade, to IRA HQ, Dublin, 3 May 1921.

98 Thomas McNamara, BMH WS 1077, p. 13.

99 Patricia Donnellan, 12 September 2012.

100 Michael O'Gorman, 27 September 2011.

101 Tommy Bolton, 11 June 1989.

102 IE/MA/CP/5/2/22(i-LI), application for IRA Service Medal for Alphonsus E. Rodgers.

103 Grey (1920), p. 2.

104 RIC Service Records 1816–1922 (HO 184).

105 MAI, Collins Papers, IE/MA/CP/5/1/17 (XVIII).

106 *Ibid.* (XIX).

107 The names of the police who had been in Scariff barracks and who received awards after the Killaloe shootings are Constables William Griffin, John Brennan, Patrick Cunningham, John S. Dixon. William Lavelle, Daniel Sullivan, Edward Broderick and Sgt John McDonald.

108 Const. Peter Murphy died in Ennis Mental Hospital n tuberculosis of the lung, https://civilrecords.irishgenealogy.ie/churchrecords/images/deaths_returns/deaths_1923/05048/ 4381882.pdf, (accessed 12 October 2017).

109 Joseph Noonan, BMH, WS 1287, p. 14.

110 'Attack on Scariff Police Barracks', *Saturday Record*, 25 September 1920, p. 2.

111 'Clare Tragedy Mystery', *Irish Independent*, 20 November 1920, p. 5.

112 Tomás Mac Conmara, *The Time of The Tans, An Oral History of the War of Independence in County Clare* (Cork, 2019), pp. 78–82.

113 Crozier (1920), p. 195.

114 Pauline Collins claimed to have been told by Joe Clancy that a man called 'Horan' encouraged the men to run, thereby creating an excuse to shoot them. It was also claimed that Horan was later a member of An Garda Síochána and was shot dead as revenge. It has not been possible to verify this, Pauline Collins to me, 8 April 2011; John Conway and Mike Daly claimed that Crossley Tenders were placed at either side of the bridge with their lights on. While this may relate to the collection of the bodies, it is also possible they were in place as the men were brought across the bridge.

Conclusion

1 Brian Ó Dálaigh, (ed.), *The Strangers Gaze, Travels in County Clare, 1534–1950* (Ennis, 1998), pp. 291–4.

2 Jessie Craigen, Report on a visit to Ireland in the Summer of 1881 (Dublin 1882), pp. 54–5, see https://digital.ucd.ie/get/ivrla:3439/content (accessed 12 May 2018).

3 *Ibid.*, p. 56.

4 *Ibid.*, p. 58.

5 'Brutal Outrage at Bodyke', *Clonmel Chronicle*, 13 June 1894, p. 3.

6 Although not always openly hostile, there was a marked division between

many in the community and the RIC, particularly after the evictions. During that episode, people seen talking to the police were publicly denounced and considered 'a foe to the country'. The uncles of Jack Quigley were involved in the resistance at Bodyke. When one of their sisters later married an RIC man, she was ostracised from the family and ended up living estranged in Cork, Jack Quigley, 14 March 2012.

7 'Register of Birth for John Dillon', 21 January 1894; https://civil records. irishgenealogy.ie/churchrecords/images/birth_returns/ births_1894/ 02268/1852416.pdf (accessed 1 June 2019).

8 Census of Ireland 1911, Residents of House 21 in Caherhurley; http://www. census.nationalarchives.ie/reels/nai001796004/ (accessed 12 May 2014).

9 John Brennan, Glenamaddy, Co. Galway, Register of Death https:// civilrecords.irishgenealogy.ie/churchrecords/images/ deaths_returns/ deaths_1953/04466/4170519.pdf (accessed 28 May 2019).

10 At the request of the correspondent, identification has been withheld.

11 Correspondence, Alison Smith to me, 23 December 2020.

12 'Colonel's Accidental Death', *Evening Telegraph*, 24 January 1923, p. 5.

13 'Real Reason for Transfer of Palestine Police Officer', *Jewish Telegraphic Agency*, 20 February 1934; https://www.jta.org/1934/02/20/archive/ real-reason-fo-transfer-of-palestine-police-officer (accessed 12 May 2018).

14 McCall, *The Auxies*, p. 162.

15 Lt John Alexander Mulloy Faraday MC, KPM; https://www.theauxiliaries. com/men-alphabetical/men-f/faraday-jam/faraday.html (accessed, 19 October 2018).

16 'Victor Stuart Gwynne', http://theauxiliaries.com/INCIDENTS/ killaloe-bridge-1920/gwynne/vs-gwynne.html (accessed 23 April 2017).

17 'Capt. Patrick Benignus Cullinan MC, Leinster Regt', http://theauxiliaries. com/men-alphabetical/men-c/cullinan-pb/cullinan.html (accessed 3 November 2018).

18 'Father Daniel Flannery', http://homepage.eircom.net/~oflannery/bio/ bioDF18431920.htm (accessed 2 November 2019). Flannery died in June 1921 and is buried in Killaloe church grounds.

19 RC, Kathleen Rodgers, 16 December 1920.

20 Correspondence, Arthur O'Donnell, Cahir to me, 21 November 2020.

21 Field Notes, John Martin O'Brien, Ballyvannon, Tuamgraney, 15, December 2020.

22 'Whitegate Tragedy', *Saturday Record*, 28 November 1925, p. 5.

23 *Ibid.*

24 John Minogue, 16 November 2019.

25 Maeve Hayes died in Killaloe on 9 March 2020; John Minogue died on 19 May 2021.

BIBLIOGRAPHY

Irish Jesuit Archive
Mungret College School Register, 1911-1914

Military Archives of Ireland
Bureau of Military History Witness Statements
IRA Brigade Activity Reports
Michael Collins Papers
Military Service Pensions Collection
Seán Clancy Collection
Uinseann Mac Eoin Collection

National Archives of Australia
Australian Imperial Force, Service Records, Series B884

National Archives of Ireland
Colonial Office Records of the Irish Government in Dublin Castle, 1872–1926
The British in Ireland, Colonial Office Records Police Reports, 1914–21
RIC County Inspectors' and Inspector General's Monthly Reports
Census of Ireland, 1901, 1911

National Archives of the United Kingdom
British House of Commons Parliamentary Papers
War Office (35): Army of Ireland: Administrative and Easter Rising Records
NAUK, Irish Distress Committee and Irish Grants Committee

Oral History Collections
Cuimhneamh an Chláir Archive
Fintan McMahon – Interview with Mary Kate O'Looney
John Joe Conwell – Interview with Anthony 'Sonny' Hackett
John S. Kelly – Interview with Tommy Bolton.
O'Meara Family Tuamgraney – Interview with Paddy O'Meara
Patricia Sheehan Collection – Interviews with Morgan O'Connell
Seán Kierse Collection – (transcripts)
Waterways Ireland Oral History Archive

University College Dublin
Richard Mulcahy Collection
Ernie O'Malley Collection
National Folklore Collection – Schools' Manuscript Collection

Note on Oral History Material
In most cases, I was the interviewer for each recording (denoted in endnotes without reference to an archive). Interviews I conducted for public archives are identified. Where material was recorded by another interviewer, this is specified in the endnotes.

Newspapers
Clare Champion
Clare Journal
Celtic Times
Clonmel Chronicle
Cork Examiner
Dublin Evening Telegraph
Galway Observer
Irish Bulletin
Irish Independent
Leeds Mercury
Limerick Chronicle
Limerick Leader
Mid Sussex Times
Nenagh Guardian
Pall Mall Gazette
Saturday Record
Sunderland Daily Echo
The Evening Post (NZ)
The Freeman's Journal
The Irish Times
Yorkshire Post
Young Ireland

Correspondence
Christy Moore, Dublin, 13 May 2020
Cyril O'Donoghue, Ennis, 6 July 2013
Fr Martin Bugler, New Zealand, 19 February 2014
Frieda Gleeson, Birdhill, 1 March 2020
Helen O'Shea, Australia, 4 June 2015
Jack Hogan, Killaloe, 29 January 2021
Joe Sammon, Galway, 4 October 2020
John Collins, Whitegate, 4 April 2020
John Fahey, Dublin, 13 June 2019

Kevin Ford, New Zealand, 10 December 2020
Liam Counihan, USA, 2013–2015
Mary McGrath, Tulla 19 June 2013
Michael McNamara, Ogonnelloe, 24 August 2019
Niall McMahon, Máire Lowe and Niamh O'Hanlon, 20–30 July 2019.
Pauleen Cass, New Zealand, 8 February 2021
Pauline Collins, Killaloe, 8 April 2011
Rosemary McCarthy O'Neill, 12 March 2020
Ruth Wheeler, England, 19 November 2011
Seán Kierse, Killaloe, 5 November 2010
Stiofán Ó Comhraí, Galway, 13 August 2019
Tony Cronin, Australia, 15 December 2017

Private collections in family ownership
James Foran Collection
Mac Mahon Family Collection
Mary Galvin Collection
Rodgers Family Collection

Secondary Sources
Abbot, Richard, *Police Casualties in Ireland, 1919–1922* (Mercier Press, Cork, 2019)
Bolt, Usain, *The Fastest Man Alive: The True Story of Usain Bolt* (Sports Publishing, USA, 2012)
Bonner, David, *Executive Measures, Terrorism and National Security: Have the Rules of the Game Changed?* (Routledge, Oxfordshire, 2007)
Brennan, Michael, *The War in Clare* (Four Courts Press, Dublin, 1980)
Buckland, Patrick, *Irish Unionism, Volume 1* (Gill & Macmillan, Dublin, 1973)
Carroll, Aideen, *Seán Moylan, Rebel Leader* (Mercier Press, Cork, 2010)
Connolly. Frank (ed.), *The Christy Moore Songbook* (Brandon, Kerry 1984)
Cottrell, Peter, *The Anglo-Irish War: The Troubles of 1913–1922* (Bloomsbury, Oxford, 2006)
Crowe, Seán, *A Peaceful Place, Poetry by Seán Crowe* (Clare, 2010)
Crozier, F. P., *Ireland Forever* (Jonathan Cape, London, 1932)
Custance, Mark, *Shiner & Co, From the Western Front to Bristol Millionaire* (SilverWood Books, Bristol, 2001)
Delany, William, *The Green and the Red: Revolutionary Republicanism and Socialism in Irish Socialism in Irish History: 1848–1923* (iUniverse, New York, 2001)
Dolan, Anne, *Commemorating the Irish Civil War, History and Memory, 1923–2000* (Cambridge University Press, Cambridge, 2003)
Duirnin, David, *The Irish Medical Profession and The First World War* (Palgrave, Dublin, 2019)

Fitzpatrick, David, *Politics and Irish Life, 1913–21: Provincial Experiences of War and Revolution* (Cork University Press, Cork, 1977)

Grey, Romer C., *The Auxiliary Police* (Peace with Ireland Council, London, 1920)

Griffin Kevin M., and Griffin, Kevin A., *The Renihan Diaries, c. 1882–1925* (Ballina Killaloe Print, Ballina, 2005)

Griffith, Kenneth and O'Grady, Timothy, *Curious Journey: An Oral History of Ireland's Unfinished Revolution* (Hutchinson, London, 1982)

O'Halpin, Eunan, *Kevin Barry: An Irish Rebel in Life and Death,* (Merrion Press, Dublin, 2020)

Hannigan, Dave, *Terence MacSwiney, The Hunger Strike that Rocked an Empire* (O'Brien Press, Dublin, 2012)

Heffernan, Brian, *Freedom and the Fifth Commandment: Catholic Priests and Political Violence in Ireland, 1919–21* (Manchester University Press, Manchester, 2016)

Hickey, Margaret, *Irish Days, Oral Histories of the twentieth century,* (Kyle Cathie, England, 2001)

Hogan, Seán, *The Black and Tans in North Tipperary* (Nenagh Guardian Ltd., Tipperary, 2013).

Hopkinson, Michael, *The Irish War of Independence* (Gill & Macmillan, Dublin, 2002)

Kautt, William, *The Anglo-Irish War, 1916–1921: A People's War* (Praeger Publishers, Connecticut, 1999)

Kierse, Seán, *The Killaloe Anthology* (Ború Books, Killaloe, 2001)

—— *History of Smith O'Briens GAA Club* (Ború Books, Killaloe, 1991).

Lee, J.J., Ireland, *1912–1985, Politics and Society* (Cambridge University Press, Cambridge, 1989)

Leeson, D. M., *The Black and Tans: British Police and Auxiliaries in the Irish War of Independence, 1920–1921* (Oxford University Press, Oxford, 2012)

Mac Conmara, Tomás, *Days of Hunger, The Clare Volunteers and the Mountjoy Hunger Strike of 1917* (Clare Library Services, Clare, 2017)

—— The Time of The Tans, An Oral History of the War of Independence in County Clare (Mercier Press, Cork, 2019)

Mac Eoin, Uinseann, *The IRA in the Twilight Years, 1923–1948* (Argenta Publications, Dublin, 1997)

MacLysaght, Edward, *Changing Times, Ireland Since 1898* (Colin Smythe Ltd., Dublin, 1978)

—— *East Clare 1916–1921* (*Clare Champion*, Ennis, 1954)

Mac Mathúna, Seosamh, *Kilfarboy, A History of a West Clare Parish* (Clare, 1978)

Madden Patrick (ed.), *History of Gaelic Games in Mountshannon and Whitegate, 1825–1984* (Clare, 1984)

Madden, Gerard, *A History of Tuamgraney and Scariff* (East Clare Heritage, Scariff, 2000)

Manning, Maurice, J*ames Dillon, A Biography* (Merlin Publication, Dublin, 1999)

McCabe, Ian, *A diplomatic history of Ireland, 1948–49: The Republic, the Commonwealth and NATO* (Dublin, 1991)

McCarthy, Daniel, *Ireland's Banner County, From the Fall of Parnell to the Great War* (Saipan Press, Clare, 2002)

McGillacuddy Tom (ed.), *The Crooked Ash, The History of Scariff GAA* (Scariff Hurling Club, Nenagh, 1987)

McKenna, Joseph, *Guerrilla Warfare in the Irish War of Independence, 1919–1921* (McFarland & Co., North Carolina, 2011)

McLaughlin, John, *One Green Hill, Journeys through Irish Songs* (Beyond the Pale Publications, Belfast, 2003)

McMahon, Paul, British Spies and Irish Rebels, British Intelligence and Ireland, 1916–1945 (The Boydell Press, London, 2007)

McNamara Máire and Madden, Maura (eds), *Beagh: A History* (Beagh History Project, Galway, 1995)

Moroney, Mary, *A Salute to the Heroes of East Clare* (Clare Champion, Ennis, 1976)

Nevinson, Henry W., *Changes and Chance* (Nisbet & Co., London, 1923)

Ní Dheirg, Iosold, *The Story of Michael Collins* (Mercier Press, Cork, 2011)

Niall, Brendan, *The Riddle of Father Hackett: A Life in Ireland and Australia* (National Library of Australia, Australia, 2009)

Noonan, Jack, *A Short Collection of Poems* (Limerick, 1984)

Noonan, Joe, *Songs and Recitations* (Ennis, 1990)

O'Brien, Paul, *Havoc: The Auxiliaries in Ireland's War of Independence* (Collins Press, Cork, 2017)

Ó Ceallaigh, Seán, *Éamonn Mac Giolla Iasachta, 1887–1986* (Coiscéim, Dublin, 2003)

Ó Comhraí, Cormac and Ó Comhraí, Stiofán, *Peadar Clancy: Easter Rising Hero, Bloody Sunday Martyr* (Cranny Publications, Galway, 2016)

Ó Dálaigh, Brian (ed.), *The Strangers Gaze, Travels in County Clare, 1534–1950* (Clasp Press, Ennis, 1998)

O'Donovan (Fr), Donal, *The Murder of Canon Magner and Tadgh O'Crowley* (Cork, 2005)

Ó Ruairc, Pádraig Óg, *Blood on the Banner, The Republican Struggle in Clare* (Mercier Press, Cork, 2009).

Parkinson, Alan *Belfast's Unholy War* (Four Courts Press, Dublin, 2004).

Rossing, Thomas D, Wheeler, Paul A. and Moore, F. Richard, *The Science of Sound* (Addison Wesley, San Francisco, 2002)

Ryan Michelle, 'The Sporting Lodge, Williamstown, Whitegate, County Clare: Architecture, Objects and History'. Unpublished Master's Thesis.

Ryan, Desmond, *Seán Treacy and The Third Tipperary Brigade* (Anvil Books, Tralee, 1945)

Ryan, Meda, *Tom Barry, IRA Freedom Fighter* (Mercier Press, Cork, 2003)

Sheedy, Kieran, *Feakle* (Saipan Press, Clare, 1990)
—— *The Clare Elections* (Bauroe Publications, Dublin, 1993)
Spellissy, Seán, *A History of County Clare* (Gill and Macmillan, Dublin, 2003)
Standford, Peter, *Judas: The Most Hated Name in History* (Counterpoint Press, London, 2015)
Toomey, Thomas, *The War of Independence in Limerick, 1912–1921* (self-published, Limerick, 2010)
The Spirit of the Nation (James Duffy & Co. Ltd, Dublin, 1928)
Vaughan, W. E. (ed.), *A New History of Ireland: Ireland Under the Union, 1870–1921* (Oxford University Press, Oxford, 2010)
Whelan, Bernadette, *United States Foreign Policy and Ireland* (Four Courts, Dublin, 2006)

Journal Articles and Documentaries

Lowe, W.J., 'Who were the Black-and-Tans?' *History Ireland*, Issue 3 (Autumn 2004), Volume 12.
The American Commission on Conditions in Ireland, Interim Report (New York, 1921)
Coughlan, Anthony, 'James Hogan, revolutionary, historian, political scientist (1898–1963)' *History Ireland*, Issue 1, Spring 1991, Volume 7
Mac Conmara, Tomás, 'Tomás Mac Curtain in Memory', *The Archive* (Volume 21, 2018)
Ó Ciosáin, Niall, 'Approaching a Folklore Archive: The Irish Folklore Commission and the Memory of the Great Famine', *Folklore* 115 (Dublin, 2004)
Ó Drisceoil, Donal, 'Moral Neutrality' censorship in Emergency Ireland', *History Ireland*, Volume 4, Issue 2 (Summer 1996)
Ó Longaigh, Seosamh, 'Emergency Law in Action, 1939–1945', in Dermot Keogh & Mervyn O'Driscoll (eds), *Ireland in World War II: Diplomacy and Survival* (Mercier Press, Cork, 2004).
Graney, Brian, 'East Clare's Calvary', *Vexilla Regis, Journal of Maynooth Laymen's Society* (Maynooth, 1953)
Ó Cómhraí, Cormac, 'The Murders of Pat and Harry Loughnane', *'Remembering the Scariff Martyrs, 90th Anniversary Commemoration Booklet* (November 2011)
Author Unknown, *Molua, Irisleabhar Cuallachta Gríogóir,* Organ of the Association of St. Gregory (Dublin, 1941)

Websites

Auxillares.com (The Auxiliary Division of the Royal Irish Constabulary)

O'Callaghan Collection, Patrick Dwyer Sworn Statement, March 1893,'Disturbances and Distress', http://www.clarelibrary.ie/ eolas/ coclare/history/bodyke_evictions/disturbances_distress.htm

Séamus Mac Mathúna, 'One Song Leads to Another', http://comhaltas. ie/music/treoir/detail/one_song_ leads_to_another/ (accessed 23 November 2011)

'Clare Men and Woman in the Great War, http://www.clarelibrary.ie/ eolas/coclare/history/clare_men_women _great_war_18.pdf

'John J Fitzgerald 1898–1920', http://www.bloodysunday.co.uk/ murdered-men/fitzgerald.html (accessed 28 September 2019)

'John Francis Eastwood', http://www.thepeerage.com/p22906.htm#i 229056 (accessed 7 August 2019)

INDEX